Chiquart's 'On Cookery'

American University Studies

Series IX
History
Vol. 22

PETER LANG
New York · Berne · Frankfurt am Main

Chiquart's 'On Cookery'

A Fifteenth-century Savoyard Culinary Treatise

Edited and Translated by
Terence Scully

PETER LANG
New York · Berne · Frankfurt am Main

Library of Congress Cataloging-in-Publication Data

Chiquart.
  Chiquart's On Cookery.

  (American University Studies. Series IX, History ; vol. 22)
  Translation of: Du fait de cuisine.
  Bibliography: p.
  Includes index.
  1. Cookery, French—Early works to 1800. I. Scully, Terence, 1935-
II. Title. III. Title: On cookery. IV. Series.
TX707.C4813   1986   641.5944   86-10531
ISBN 0-8204-0352-0
ISSN 0740-0462

CIP-Kurztitelaufnahme der Deutschen Bibliothek

Chiquart:
[On Cookery]
Chiquart's „On Cookery" : A Fifteenth-century Savoyard Culinary
Treatise / ed. and transl. by Terence Scully. - New York ; Berne ;
Frankfurt am Main : Lang, 1986.
  (American University Studies : Ser. 9, History ; Vol. 22)
  Einheitssacht.: Du fait de cuisine
  ISBN 0-8204-0352-0

NE: Scully, Terence [Hrsg.]; American University Studies / 09

© Peter Lang Publishing, Inc., New York 1986

All rights are reserved.
Reprint or reproduction, even partially, in all forms such as
microfilm, xerography, microfiche, microcard, offset strictly prohibited.

Printed by Weihert-Druck GmbH, Darmstadt (West Germany)

For Eleanor

... *Toutes foys vostre propre serviteur en grant affection et avecques grant desir.*
                              Chiquart, *Du fait de cuisine*

Table of Contents

Introduction
    The Circumstances ix
    Chiquart xii
    The Contribution of the *On Cookery* xvi
    Culinary Theory and Practice xviii
    Chiquart's Contribution xxv
    Editorial Principles xxxii

Select Bibliography xxxv

ON COOKERY (*Du fait de cuisine*)
    Preamble and Table 3
    Text 7

Index 127

The Circumstances

The manuscript in which the culinary treatise known as *Du fait de cuisine* survives has been owned for over twenty years now by the Archives for the Swiss canton of the Valais. It came into the Archives in 1962 with the conclusion of a purchase, initiated in 1930, of a number of particularly valuable works, most of which appear to have been assembled originally by the late-fifteenth-century Bishop, Walter Supersaxo and his son George. The works which comprised those bibliophiles' private collection included such eminent treatises as the *Travels* of Mandeville, *De proprietatis rerum* of Bartholomaeus Anglicus, and the *Speculum naturale* of Vincent of Beauvais, as well as several works of Justinian, Ovid, Seneca, Sallust and Quintillian. Because of the august nature of most of the works acquired for this library, one may wonder at the presence there of the volume of culinary advice compiled in 1420 by the chief cook of Duke Amadeus of Savoy, Master Chiquart Amiczo, and wonder whether it could ever have been accorded any great importance by its owners.

The appearance of the manuscript is not in itself impressive. In an age when vellum was still preferred by scriptoria in order to help ensure that really great works might survive as long as possible, the scribe who wrote out Chiquart's compendium, and under his immediate direction, used 12 leaves of the much cheaper substance, paper. These sheets, folded in gatherings of eight pages, were at some point in time bound within a single larger fold of parchment, but the book still looks as if Chiquart's patron, the Duke, was not willing to see more than a basic minimum of funds spent to preserve some record of the art and skill of his chief cook. Since the time of its production the volume has been so mistreated that most of the front cover has been ripped away—along with a title page, if there ever was one—and most of the first page of the Table of Contents. No illuminations embellish this codex; its text cannot boast of even a single ornamental capital.

The scribe whose labor helped produce this volume was not negligent in his professional work, however. His spacing is generous, his script always legible and his text almost wholly without errors. Such care in the transcription of written material is by no means usual in this period. There is no doubt that the author of the treatise worked very closely with his scribe, and probably over several months, passing to him lists of dishes and ingredients, and perhaps directing him in the layout of the text. He may even have dictated many passages directly. Certainly there is evidence that the scribe earned the author's respect for his conscientiousness: two stanzas of Chiquart's concluding poem are devoted to thanking Jehan de Dudens for his faithful collaboration.[1] All in all, while it was clearly not intended to be an expensive, elegant work of art, the book was carefully conceived and competently executed.

Why and how, then, did this work, *On Cookery*, come into being? Chiquart himself informs his reader. In the awkwardly formal, decorous language of the preamble he presents to his patron, and of course to his reader as well, a modest disclaimer for any imperfections his work may contain: Duke Amadeus had himself, Chiquart reports, requested, urged, and finally ordered his chief cook to produce this compendium of culinary science. While Chiquart had at first demured modestly, claiming that he was too aware of his own professional and intellectual shortcomings to comply readily and in good conscience with his master's wishes, he admits that he also realized he had an absolute obligation to obey his lord's command and to do his pleasure. And so at last the *On Cookery* was produced and took its place in the Duke's library, alongside such other works as a history of the Savoyard dynasty, which Amadeus had likewise ordered of Jean d'Orieville *alias* "Cabaret" in 1417, and

---

[1] See the nineth and tenth stanzas of the *Laux, graces et mercyz rendues par le compyleur de cest pitit livret* which begins on folio 107v. The scribe was further permitted the unusual tribute of inserting his own name into his copy; on folio 2r he tells us also that he is a clerk and a citizen of Annecy. The Annecy town rolls for 1428 and 1431 do indeed confirm that Johannes Doudens resided in that town, and that at those dates he exercised the function of notary.

which was completed in 1419, and an extensive juridical compilation, the *Statuta Sabaudiae*, which was compiled, again on the Duke's orders, by Pierre de Rostaing.

A good number of other treatises, political, legal and social, would be added to those shelves, all written for Duke Amadeus, and all intended more or less to be records of recent Savoyard life and times. One particular interest of the Duke, and one which was widespread at the time, was alchemy; the famous doctor Guillaume Fabri was to dedicate to Amadeus his treatise on the philosopher's stone and its medicinal powers, the *Book of the Two Words*. Recipe 65 in Chiquart's manual is undoubtedly inspired by this common belief in the pharmaceutical properties of precious stones.

Chiquart's work seems largely, therefore, a result of his master's scholarly desire to preserve knowledge—all that might be comprised under the universal term *science*, such as it existed within his domains. A further personal trait of Duke Amadeus of Savoy is also represented in the *On Cookery*, and that is the proclivity to ostentatious luxury for which several generations of his forebears had acquired, and fostered, the reputation. At fourteenth- and fifteenth-century princely courts the banquet table offered the most satisfactory means by which to impress visiting neighbors and potentates, and to gratify a taste for conspicuous opulence. Even before the marriage in 1393 of Amadeus (aged 9) with Mary of Burgundy (aged 7)[2], a daughter of Phillip, Duke of Burgundy, relations between the two houses had been quite close. Their lands adjoined. Burgundy, the wealthiest and most powerful state at that time in Europe, tried in various ways to assure that the politics pursued by little Savoy were always in harmony with its own. And the Savoyard counts for their part seemed often to strive to emulate, on their own considerably smaller scale, the munificent splendor they were invited on occasion to glimpse at the court of their neighbor.

In 1393 Phillip of Burgundy had offered a banquet in honor of

---

[2] Amadeus was born on September 4, 1383 in the castle at Chambéry, the seat of government for the County and the principal residence of its counts. Mary of Burgundy was born in 1385.

the young Amadeus and his even younger bride, Phillip's own daughter. Again in 1397 another banquet welcomed the Duke's thirteen-year-old Savoyard neighbor who had come to visit his bride, since this latter was still a minor and continued to dwell under the protection of her father's roof. To this festive celebration were invited the Dukes of Berry (Amadeus's grandfather) and of Bourbon (his great uncle). It appears to have been on the occasion of Mary of Burgundy's leaving home, her passage in the year 1403, at age 18, from the paternal authority of her childhood into the house of her twenty-year-old husband, that Amadeus, eighth Count of Savoy, had the first excuse to extend a similar offering of a banquet to his father-in-law. The joyous ceremonial event occurred on the 26th and 27th of October.

It so happened that in 1403 these were fast days, a Friday and Saturday. For this feast, therefore, Chiquart, as chief cook, was called upon to organize and prepare two days of lean dishes, that is, four meals or six servings of some forty-eight dishes in which there would be no meat or such meat products as milk or lard. Yet because the great Duke of Burgundy was the guest of honor, it was incumbent upon the chief cook of the House of Savoy that each of these lean dishes be of exceptional merit. We are fortunate to possess the menus of those two days, and it is Chiquart himself who, with a certain amount of pride, we suspect, transmits them to us at the end of the *On Cookery*. Between folios 109r an 114v, he lists each of the dishes which altogether composed as impressive a series of meals as could be served anywhere in Europe at this time. As it happens, whether by design or not, most of the prepared dishes presented before the Dukes of Burgundy and Savoy at this grand banquet are already described earlier among the recipes of the *On Cookery*.

Chiquart

Little is known about Master Chiquart. It is true that he names himself four times in the course of his culinary treatise, in every case in such a way as to suggest that, despite the modest protestations of only mediocre competence which he prudently places in his preamble, he was quite conscious of having attained a pre-eminent position in his profession and in his service to his master, the Duke.³ His tenure as chief cook in the Savoyard kitchens appears to have spanned rather a long period. By his own claim he had been responsible for the banquet offered to the Duke of Burgundy in 1403.⁴ In the year 1416 the name of *magister Chiquardus* appears in the household accounts as having requisitioned and received from the official court apothecary the spices needed for saucing a roast lamprey.⁵ The term *magister*, or *maître* in French, in the context of kitchen personnel designates exclusively the individual who is in charge of the activities there. By 1420 Chiquart had clearly arrived at a sort of apogee in his career, as his master, in urging him to write the *On Cookery*, seeks to ensure that the special knowledge and skill of one of his principal servants will be preserved for posterity. Finally, in 1428, in another fortunate piece of surviving documentary evidence, we again find the name "Mestre Chicart Amiczo", followed by a qualification of his status as *cuisinier*, in a list of kitchen staff who were to receive a new set of livery.⁶

The section of the 1428 list dealing with those whose labors were centered in the kitchen follows an enumeration of several other household retainers who were likewise to receive a new set of livery. Among them we find the names of three physicians and surgeons attached to the court, two "masters of the hall", who would supervise the serving of dishes on the dining tables, three pantlers, two butlers, two wine stewards, two spicers or apothecaries, and the Household Steward. At this time the person occupying this latter very important position was a certain Henri

---

³ At large courts at the time of Chiquart it was usual for the kitchen to provide for two distinct activities, cooking for the lord and his family and guests, and cooking for the mass of his retainers. By the time he wrote the *On Cookery* Chiquart was undoubtedly the chef responsible for the Duke's food. See Note 7 on folio 12v of the text.

⁴ See folios 111v–112r.

⁵ Chiquart included the recipe for this sauce as Recipe 27 in the *On Cookery*. See Note 125 to the text, below.

⁶ The list has been published by Henri Costa de Beauregard in *Souvenirs du règne d'Amédée VIII, premier duc de Savoie*, Chambéry (Puthod), 1859, p. 212.

de la Fleschiere; he is qualified in the list as being also *mestre de la cuisine*, and it is in this capacity that, as a sort of supreme kitchen clerk, he was in charge of all kitchen finances and expenses. It is to him that Chiquart was immediately responsible for the efficient running of the Duke's kitchen.

The kitchen personnel for whom Chiquart himself was responsible in 1428 appear below his name:

> Gillet de Rumillie, *cuisinier*, livrée de la duchesse
> Collet, *cuisinier*, livrée de la duchesse
> Mestre Chicart Amiczo, *cuisinier*, livrée de l'hôtel
> Mestre Pierre Sailler, *cuisinier*, livrée de l'hôtel
> Jehan Manget, *rotisseur*, livrée de la duchesse
> Jehan Roulet, *lardonnier*, livrée de l'hôtel
> Guichard, *pollalier*, livrée de l'hôtel
> Antoine et Gillet, *forniers*, livrée de l'hôtel
> Michelet, *carronnier*, livrée de l'hôtel
> Clavellet, *solliar*, livrée de l'hôtel
> Jehan du Pra, *solliar*, livrée de l'hôtel
> le fils de Clavellet, *solliar*, livrée de l'hôtel
> Guillaume Monet, *solliar*, livrée de l'hôtel
> Perro, *solliar*, livrée de l'hôtel
> Franczois Cotteau, *solliar*, livrée de l'hôtel
> Anthoyne, *solliar*, livrée de l'hôtel
> Jehan Magnin, *solliar*, livrée de l'hôtel
> Pierre Guillet, *solliar*, livrée de l'hôtel
> Vernet, *solliar*, livrée de l'hôtel
> Vincent Lambellin, *solliar*, livrée de l'hôtel

The first two cooks mentioned here, as well as the roaster whose name comes later, worked primarily within the private household of the Duchess, so that expenses for their maintenance, including the costs of any new clothing, would appear against the accounts of that establishment. That Chiquart is identified as the first of *two* chief cooks indicates a distinction between two general activities or functions of the kitchen, the preparation of food for the personal consumption of the Duke himself and his family and guests, and the everyday feeding of everyone else in the Ducal household, all of the many dozens of individuals who wore his livery from the Steward down to the least chambermaid. As the first of these two chief cooks, the *maistre queux de bouche*, Chiquart would have much the more demanding of the responsibilities.

Following the larder, the poulterer, the two bakers (of bread) and the butcher, the list of recipients of a new livery contains the names of eleven individuals all of whom are qualified as *solliar*, or scullion. The term designates literally a "mucker", someone who cleans away or cleans up. These eleven are the laborers of the kitchen, the humble troops without whom Chiquart's kitchen could not operate; before, during and after any meal they were busy disposing of refuse, gathering scraps for garbage or charity, hauling water, dumping water, and endlessly washing, scrubbing, scouring, wiping. Chiquart fully recognizes the vital importance of these scullions: in his book he insists continually upon the absolute necessity of cleanliness, that the foodstuffs be washed clean, that the pots, pans and utensils be cleaned thoroughly after each use, that the mortar—in constant service, it seems—be thoroughly rinsed out of anything which might contaminate a subsequent preparation, that the filter cloths be kept immaculate, and that the dishes returning from one service in the hall be washed spotless and ready for use two services later. There is perhaps no word which Chiquart uses more in the whole of the *On Cookery* than the word "clean".

Chiquart was in charge of this numerous kitchen personnel, but he had also to work closely with a number of other persons whose work contributed to the quality of the food produced at the court of Savoy. For Chiquart it was extremely important that all of his work be carried out in close consultation with what we might call the medical staff of the court. The physicians possessed all of the soundest of Greco-Arabic theory concerning the influence of humors within the human body and the necessity of maintaining a good balance of these humors. Such a balance was at the very basis of health and disease. Since every foodstuff ingested by a human being had its own peculiar temperament or complex mixture of humoral qualities, it was essential that a cook not put anyone's health at risk by creating an unhealthy combination of such foodstuffs—

by preparing, for instance, a "dry" sauce to accompany a "dry" meat—or by unwittingly contributing further to any sick person's temporary imbalance of humors, or to a natural proclivity, which might be present in his master, or in anyone eating in his master's house, towards one or another of the temperaments. At any rate, it is undoubtedly true that Chiquart had to cooperate with all of the physicians and surgeons in his efforts to see that only the best was done for the Duke and the Duke's table.

Chiquart was, therefore, in a very real sense responsible for his master's health. Moreover, it was an age in which food poisoning, which despite constant suspicion was the result much more frequently of accidental causes than of deliberate machination, was still quite a common occurence in all classes of society. For Chiquart to have earned the respect of Amadeus is evident in the Duke's request that his chief cook compile this treatise for him; that Chiquart remained the Duke's chief cook for over 25 years is sure evidence that Chiquart had earned from his master something about which he could be even more proud, his trust.

The Contribution of the *On Cookery*

Foods served on the tables of late medieval Europe differed in only a few respects from what we are familiar with today. Those foodstuffs peculiar to the New World, potatoes and turkeys, for instance, would remain unknown for several more generations. On the other hand all of the domestic meats, beef, pork, mutton, goat, poultry, were handled routinely by butchers and kitchen staffs. Garden vegetables, of both the leafy and the root varieties, were in normal use, although it is difficult to estimate to how great an extent they were eaten in a raw state because cookery manuals of the period are concerned primarily with those preparations in which a foodstuff undergoes some sort of cooking process. Similarly, agricultural treatises of the late middle ages always show a detailed and extensive knowledge of fruit-producing plants and trees; yet with the exception of apples, pears, peaches, plums, currants, cherries, grapes, figs and dates, and a variety of nuts, these fruits do not play a significant role in the recipe manuals. These and other fruits may too have appeared in a raw state on many dining tables at this time.

Meats constituted the basis for most dishes described in fourteenth- and fifteenth-century recipe books. Depending on the experience of the compiler of the particular collection, and on the availability of meat from game animals in the milieu in which his collection would be used, these recipes may make use of deer, stag and boar, and of the flesh of game birds such as pheasant, partridge and duck. Occasionally these meats are prepared very simply by either roasting or boiling, and are served with a side dish of coarse salt in which the carved chunks are dipped. More often, a more or less complex mixture of wine, vinegar or must with spices and herbs, thickeners (egg yolks, bread, toast, liver) and colorants (saffron, sandalwood, alkanet), forms both a cooking medium for the meat and a presentation sauce for the finished dish; this is the broth. Such a sauce could be served separately in a bowl into which the cooked meat was dipped.

Another sort of sauce was specifically to be eaten by allowing it to soak into elongated slices of bread or toast; this was known as a sop, or soup. Because eating utensils consisted primarily of a spoon and a knife, the consumption of such preparations was probably not very clean. A universally favored means of facilitating the relatively neat eating of minced meats and other foodstuffs which lacked any firm consistency was to encase them in a relatively firm sheath of pastry. This practice gave rise to the inclusion in cookery books of a large number of recipes for baked or deep-fried pasties and pies.

Salt is the almost universal preservative to which producers and merchants resorted throughout the Middle Ages. As a consequence, cooks had of necessity to be familiar with the most effective techniques for removing the excess salt from a meat or a fish before the first steps of any recipe could be undertaken. In any case the consumption of many foodstuffs, including meats, tended to be seasonal, depending upon their availability. Difficulties in transporting fresh fish live any great distance led to the establishment of fish-ponds on most noble estates. The relatively effective measures used to preserve raw sea-fish and the ready availability of fresh-water fish, in conjuction with strict Church regulations on fasting, account at least in part for a relatively high proportion of recipes involving fish in the cookery books compiled or copied for noble households.

Most recipes for prepared dishes seem to begin with the direction that the meat or vegetable or fruit be chopped or ground up. No medieval kitchen was complete unless furnished with a solid, serviceable mortar. Into this were dumped, for one recipe or another, virtually all of the foodstuffs which entered through the kitchen door. Spices, of course, are normally ground and then stored in usable quantities in leather pouches. Vegetables and herbs are regularly reduced to mash in the mortar. Meats and fish are dumped in and pounded to produce a ubiquitously used paste. Nuts, particularly almonds, are ground in the mortar to yield, when strained with water or white wine, a milk whose value to the medieval cook was even greater than cow's milk (perishable and unstable as it is) to a modern cook. Even cheese is reduced to a more viscous mass and mixed with other ingredients in a mortar. Glancing through such a recipe collection, a reader inevitably forms the impression that diners at this time lacked the teeth to tear and grind their own food. Such a generalized reliance upon the mortar did, though, allow the effective admixture of a number of ingredients, particularly spices, and it was in the chemistry of such combinations that the science of medieval cookery lay.

Culinary Theory and Practice

We are fortunate to possess a work from the beginning of the fourteenth century which indicates that culinary practice at this time must have been determined in large measure by contemporary medical theory. When, in about 1332, the physician and doctor Magninus Mediolanensis (Maino de' Maineri) composed his *Regimen sanitatis*, he devoted a series of ten chapters in its Part 3 to a systematic examination of the qualities of all foodstuffs generally in use in the households of his contemporaries.[7]

---

[7] A native of Milan, Magninus taught for a while in the medical faculty at the University of Paris before serving as personal doctor to Andrea of Florence, Bishop of Arras between 1331 and 1334; it is to this ecclesiastic that he dedicated his *Regimen sanitatis*. He died about 1364. See Ernest Wickersheimer, *Dictionnaire biographique des médecins en France au moyen âge*, 2 vols., Paris

Introduction   xix

For this analysis Magninus is clearly indebted to the Galenic tradition as this body of doctrine distinguishes the nutritive and humoral qualities of each species of grain, vegetable, fruit, animal, animal product, and so forth. While his work, in this respect, resembles a number of similar outlines compiled in this and the preceding century, it is remarkable for the detail and thoroughness of its examination of foodstuffs.

For anyone interested in late-medieval cookery, Part 3 of Magninus' *Regimen sanitatis* is especially precious because it contains as well a chapter entitled "De saporibus et condimentis" in which the physician defines the medical function of culinary sauces and, in view of this function, enumerates at great length the sauces appropriate to a wide variety of those meats and fishes analysed by him in other chapters of Part 3.[8] Because every noble household in Europe at this time had attached to it at least one doctor who necessarily was familiar with current medical doctrine, there can be little doubt that the cooks of these households were required to be guided directly or indirectly by this doctrine.[9]

Magninus states that all condiments functioned originally to make

---

(Droz), 1936; Vol. I, p. 533.

[8] The chapter "De saporibus et condimentis" is Chapter 20, folios 112r–115v in the edition published by Johannes de Westfalia, Louvain, 1482: *Regimen sanitatis Magnini Mediolanensis Medici famosissimi Attrebatensi Episcopo directum*. What appears to be a slightly modified version of the material in this Chapter 20 of the *Regimen* was copied also in a manuscript (Naples, Biblioteca Nazionale, VIII.D.35, folios 52r–53v) under the title "Opusculum de saporibus". This latter version was published by Lynn Thorndike in *Speculum* 9 (1934), pp. 183–190: "A Mediaeval Sauce-Book". This article contains biographical data on Magninus, as well as a transcription of that abbreviated part of the chapter "De saporibus et condimentis" (Part II, Chapter 24) that appears in the *Regimen sanitatis* which is attributed to Arnaldus de Villanova (*Hec sunt opera Arnaldi de Villanova*, ed. Thomas Murchius, Lyon (Fradin), 1504, folios 54v–79v).

[9] Several pieces of evidence testify to this direct, daily influence exercised by medical personnel upon the preparation of food consumed by a fourteenth-century lord. At the court of Burgundy at this time "six médecins veillent sur la santé de Monseigneur, en particulier sur son alimentation. Placés derrière

foods more delicious and therefore more digestible. However, in the regimen of a healthy man, according to Magninus, sauces now play a much more important role: they work to counteract any harmful superfluities in the foodstuffs which are to be consumed. They help render the digestion of various foods safe as well as easy. A fundamental premise for the use of condiments is expressed succinctly: *Diversificantur sapores ratione cibariorum pro quibus fiunt. Nam alia et alia cibaria indigent alio et alio sapore, sicut sciunt dominorum coci.*[10] Because the temperament of man is moderately warm and moderately moist, those dishes are to be preferred in which the net nature of all ingredients approximates this, or

---

lui pendant les repas, ils conseillent ou déconseillent les plats qui passent" (Charles Commeaux, *La vie quotidienne en Bourgogne au temps des ducs valois (1364–1477)*, Paris (Hachette), 1979). One of the most important early English cookery books, the *Forme of Cury* (c. 1390), states in its foreward that it was "compiled by assent and avyssement of Maisters of phisik and of philosophie" dwelling at the court of Richard II (*Curye on Inglysch*, ed. Constance B. Hieatt and Sharon Butler, London (Oxford University Press), 1985, p. 20). At the conclusion of this manual we read: "Explicit coquina que est optima medicina." "One of the duties of Edward IV's physician was to 'stond muche in the kynges presence at his meles, councellyng his grace whyche dyet is best'. Besides consulting with the steward and master cook as to the day's menu, the royal physician would also sit at the king's table to see that he ate nothing harmful to his health" (Colin Clair, *Kitchen and Table*, London (Abelard-Schuman), 1964, p. 63).

[10] "Sauces vary according to the foods for which they are made, for various foods require various sauces, as the cooks of noble lords know": Magninus, *Regimen sanitatis*, Part III, Ch. 20, ed. cit., folio 113v. The *Opusculum de saporibus* amplifies somewhat on this rule: *Quanto cibi sunt temperatiores et temperamento propiores, tanto minus ex saporibus est comedendum cum eis. Et similiter sapores eis competentiores sunt et esse debent temperamento propiores, et econverso quanto cibi sunt magis lapsi a temperamento tanto indigent saporibus magis lapsis ad oppositum lapsus ciborum. Unde si cibi declinant ad frigidum et humidum et viscosum, sapor debet esse calidus et siccus et subtiliativus; et econverso si cibi sunt calidi et sicci sapor debet esse frigidus et humidus* (ed. Thorndike, *loc. cit.*, pp. 186–187).

whose nature is at least temperate in relative temperature and humidity. The cooks of the great lords had therefore to be aware of the qualities of all of the foodstuffs which passed through their hands; they had to know what by its nature could safely be ingested, and to recognize what combinations of ingredients, of meats and sauces, were either requisite or permissible in view of the health and temperament of the lord and perhaps of his immediate family.

For this same reason the method employed to cook any meat or fish must be appropriate for that meat or fish, given that in the process of cooking, the exposure to moisture, whether this is water or oil, and to heat will tend to increase or decrease the natural relative moistness of the flesh, and to moderate or intensify its relative warmth. The principle to which medieval physicians subscribed in this respect is simply that dry meats should be boiled and moist meats should be roasted: "Elixatio ... obtemperat siccitatem," says Magninus, "et assatio humiditatem."[11] Depending upon the relative remoteness from temperateness of these natural qualities in the meats, it might be desirable to modify their temperature or their humidity; alternatively, an inappropriate modification of these could perilously disturb the healthy humoral balance within the person who is to consume the food.

It is not clear that Chiquart, any more than other compilers of recipes in the fourteenth and fifteenth centuries, subscribed entirely and without exception to the recommendations which Magninus makes in his chapter "De saporibus et condimentis" — either with regard to how each meat should be cooked or with regard to the most suitable sauces

---

[11] Magninus, *Regimen sanitatis*, Part 3, Ch. 17, ed. cit., folio 100v. See also J. Albini, *De sanitatis custodia* (1341–42), ed. G. Carbonelli, Pinerolo (Tip. Sociale), 1906, p. 81. Because wildfowl are for the most part considered to be of a warm and moist nature — that is, to be of the temperament of air — they are normally to be roasted, according to most recipes of this period. Chiquart, for example, begins his recipe for a Calunafree of Partridge (§47) by roasting the birds. Among the roasts presented as the second serving of his first day's dinner (and *cf.* the supper as well, folio 34r), there figure pheasants, partridge and herons. See the Latin dictum quoted by Chiquart on folio 15r.

to be used to dress each. Singular tastes and particular gastronomic traditions, to say nothing of economic considerations—that is, the cost and relative availability of certain foodstuffs—doubtless influenced the cook's work in any given household. What is usually reflected in the *On Cookery*, however, is a culinary practice which recognizes in a general way the doctrines propagated by contemporary medical schools concerning the most wholesome means of cooking particular meats, and the most salubrious condiments to be consumed in conjunction with them.[12]

Of the various cooking processes, roasting imparts the most heat to a meat, and at the same time dries it out the most: this process is most appropriate for a cold, moist meat, such as pork. Beef, being relatively warm and dry, should be boiled rather than roasted.[13] While boiling imparts a high degree of moisture to a meat, it does not warm it nearly as much as roasting does. That boiling was probably the usual treatment accorded beef by the cooks of the time, including Chiquart, seems evident by the ubiquitous requirement in the recipe books of a seemingly endless supply of beef broth.[14] Frying, a process intermediary between roasting

---

[12] For the particular choices made by Chiquart, either in cooking method or in saucing, as these are determined by the humoral qualities of the foodstuffs being prepared, see the commentary to the various recipes in the *On Cookery*, below.

[13] Pork is prominent in Chiquart's servings of roast meats (folio 26r). He roasts as well the meat of young animals (kid, piglet, veal) because the young of any species are by nature relatively more moist than older members of the same species, which generally dry out with age. The meat of wild animals, generically called venison, is on the other hand normally boiled. "Or devés savoir que totes chars c'on use, ou eles sont domesces ou ele sont sauvegines . . . . Et sachiés que totes sauvegines sont plus caudes et plus seches que les domesces . . . ." (*Le régime du corps de Maître Aldebrandin de Sienne. Texte français du XIIIe siècle*, ed. Louis Landouzy and Roger Pépin, Paris (Champion), 1911, p. 121). Chiquart's recipe for Chyvrolée of Stag (§13) requires not only that the deer meat undergo both a parboiling and a boiling, but that it be wrapped around with lard, a procedure intended to ensure that even more moisture be imparted to this dry meat.

[14] As a result of the attention paid to the natural temperament of food-

and boiling in its effects, warms moderately and, because of the oil or grease used in the pan, lends a moderate amount of moisture to a meat. Mature poultry has a meat whose relatively dry and cool properties make frying suitable at some point in its preparation.[15]

Sauces make use of a liquid base (water or broth, wine, vinegar or verjuice[16]) in which are infused spices and herbs, with occasionally the admixture of other agents for the purposes of binding, color or taste. In a noble household in the late Middle Ages spices were not merely the property of the culinary or gastronomic domains. They belonged under the management and control of the court apothecary, who dispensed

---

stuffs, a recipe involving roast beef is simply not found in the *On Cookery*. Chiquart's generous servings of roast meats on the first day, at the second serving of the Dinner and at the Supper, do not even include beef. Beef is considered to be the driest of all domestic meats and roasting to be the most drying of all cooking processes. Roasting such a meat would risk generating either cholera or melancholy in the person consuming it.

[15] *Inter carnes volatilium laudabilium in regimine sanitatis, quedam sunt temperatiores et temperamento propinquiores. Alie sunt minus temperamento propinque. Temperatores quedem sunt galline juvenes, galinarum, pulli et juvenes pingues capones que tamen ad aliqualem caliditatem et humiditatem declinant* (Magninus, *Regimen sanitatis* Chapter 17, "De carnibus"; ed. cit., folio 102r). Furthermore, according to Aldobrandino, chicks enjoy a moist nature common to most young creatures of any species—veal is more moist than beef, for example; with age hens become both drier and cooler in temperament (see *Le régime du corps*, ed. cit., p. 128). In Chiquart cockerels are fried in lard (in Recipe §63) because castration alters the warm, dry nature of male animals.

[16] The three grape products, wine, vinegar and verjuice, vary broadly in their temperatures. While all three are dry in the second, or moderately strong, degree, wine is warm in the second degree; vinegar is, on the other hand, moderately cool in the second degree; and verjuice is even more cool, in the third degree. Chiquart specifies that a relatively cool meat be cooked in water and wine in order to warm it (for instance, the mature wild boar of Recipe §54a). Similarly, ground liver (as in Chiquart's Recipe §11) is normally steeped in a wine mixture because animal viscera are generally considered to be both cool and moist.

spices in exactly the same way as he dispensed drugs — and for the same reasons.[17] Spices were held to be varieties of drug, which functioned by acting upon and altering the humoral state, the temper of the person or thing by which they are absorbed. For their sick patients, doctors prescribed medicines which were frequently composed in large measure of those very same spices used in the kitchen.

Spices are generally of a dry nature (an exception being ginger) and warm, varying in these respects merely between high (cinnamon and cloves) and extreme (mustard and pepper). Both of these latter spices came to be considered dangerous unless used specifically to moderate a cool and moist foodstuff which, by *its* nature, would effectively obviate any insalubrity in them.[18] Plain Camelin Sauce is basically a cinnamon and vinegar sauce whose ingredients make it moderately warming and very drying in its effects: it is therefore appropriate for use with such temperate meats as salmon and trout when these are baked (because they are normally somewhat moist in nature), or with veal when it is roasted (for the same reason).[19] Similarly, almonds are ubiquitously used in dressings and sauces because their qualities, warm and moist, closely approximate those of the human temperament.[20] For exactly the same reason, the warm and moist qualities of sugar are relied upon in many dishes prepared for sick persons.

Cold and moist fish such as pike and turbot require the special warming and drying treatment provided by Green Sauce, whose principal

---

[17] See the note, below, to Chiquart's Recipe 27.

[18] Chiquart makes very sparing use of both mustard and pepper. See Note 33 in Recipe 2, below.

[19] See folio 34r, and Recipes 44 and 47.

[20] See Magninus, *Regimen sanitatis*, Chapter 12, "De fructibus", ed. cit., folio 90v; and Aldobrandino, ed. cit., p. 154. Almond milk, made from a paste of ground almonds which is steeped in a liquid and then strained, served as a more durable alternative to animal milk whose use is very limited in the *On Cookery*. Almond butter is a common enough dish at this time, Chiquart providing a recipe for a version of it which would be suitable for serving to a sick person on lean days (Recipe 67).

ingredient, parsley, is considered to be very warm and very dry. Animal viscera, entrails such as liver, kidney or brains, are held to be cold and moist; for safe consumption they should be accompanied by condiments which are warm and dry. On the two occasions (in Recipes 12 and 50) in which Chiquart makes use of both chicken gizzards and livers, he is generous with his spices and "warm" sugar: on folios 75v–76r, he specifies "a lot of sugar" (and if one loaf isn't enough put more in, he directs). And on folios 34v–35r the sugar clearly is added not for purely gastronomic purposes, because Chiquart cautions that the dish is not to be made sweet: the sugar should not take away from the tart verjuice taste which is its essential quality.

Chiquart's Contribution

In his rather apologetic preamble, the author of the *On Cookery* claims that he was reluctant to undertake the requested cookery treatise in part because he had "never, through ignorance or negligence, turned my understanding to such knowledge or learning, nor have I any books or writings bearing on this subject, and I have told you that I have no capability or understanding in such things" (folio 11v). Making due allowance for Chiquart's hyperbolical modesty in this proemial disclaimer, we may accept as entirely possible that a cook at the beginning of the fifteenth century, even in as literate a household as that of Duke Amadeus of Savoy, may not have had a formal "book" of recipes or of culinary procedures at his disposal. What is abundantly clear, however, is that many of the recipes and procedures which he writes down for his own treatise are those which do appear in other cookery books of his day. It is likely that peripatetic courts, strong traditions, apprenticeship, efficent oral transmission and remarkably retentive memories normally eliminated the need for written guides in the kitchens of late-medieval Europe, even in the seigneurial ones. But similarities between foods customarily prepared in such widely separated places as Germany and Portugal did exist. To a large extent, with or without a "cookbook" to guide him, Chiquart himself in Savoy shared in this pan-European culinary practice.

The Savoy Broth (§3) itself was by no means unique to Savoy. It may in its distant origin have represented some sort of regional dish, with its reliance upon herbs, especially parsley, peculiar to the Savoyard hills, but it was by no means unknown in the rest of Europe. Near the end of the fourteenth century the bourgeois author of the *Menagier de Paris* copied a very similar recipe for the same dish.[21] Of even earlier date, more than a century before Chiquart, the work which was to become known as the *Viandier* of Taillevent contains a recipe for Sorengue of eels which is almost identical to the one which Chiquart transmits (§34).[22] And that dish which is represented in virtually every late-medieval cookery manual, the standard White-Dish, appears in Chiquart's collection too, in a version whose slight variations mark it as still admitting of particular local treatments.[23]

---

[21] The most recent edition of this work is that by Georgine E. Brereton and Janet M. Ferrier, Oxford (Clarendon), 1981. The Fifth Article of the Second Distinction contains an extensive series of culinary recipes, of which one for a Brouet de Savoye is found at §110 in the Brereton and Ferrier edition. This same dish is described as well in a recipe collection which was compiled in the center of France toward the middle of the fifteenth century: *Recueil de Recettes culinaires et d'un Réceptaire sur les greffes inédits du XVe siècle (Paris, B.N. Latin 6707)*, ed. Carole Lambert, unpubl. diss., Montréal, 1983; §8.

[22] Paul Aebischer, "Un manuscrit valaisan du *Viandier* attribué à Taillevent," *Vallesia*, 8 (1953), p. 94. This version of the book was copied about 1300. Later versions were published by Jérôme Pichon and Georges Vicaire in *Le Viandier de Guillaume Tirel, dit Taillevent*, Paris (Techener), 1892: the *Soringue d'anguilles* is found on pp. 21 and 97. See also the Sore Sengle in Thomas Austin, *Two Fifteenth-Century Cookery-Books*, London (Oxford), 1888, p. 25.

[23] The White-Dish is one of the most common European dishes of the period. In the early-fourteenth-century collection, the *Enseignements qui enseignent a apareillier toutes manieres de viandes* (ed. Grégoire Lozinski in his *Bataille de Caresme et de Charnage*, Appendice I, Paris (Champion), 1933), two recipes for Blanc Mangier are on ll. 119 and 161; in the *Viandier*, on pp. 25 and 101; in the *Menagier de Paris* (ed. Georgine E. Brereton and Janet M. Ferrier, Oxford (Clarendon), 1981), in §107. Across Europe the dish is known by similar names: in English collections the dish is Blamanger; in German,

Yet Chiquart is by no means merely an unimaginative user or adaptor of popular recipes. A good number of the dishes included in the *On Cookery* are found nowhere else. The preparation called a Tile-Colored Broth (§15), composed of bouillon, ground almonds, spices, sandalwood, white wine and verjuice, may well have been the invention of Chiquart himself. Likewise the dish elaborated out of chicken with beef marrow and cheese, the Jacobin Sops (§18), has a mark of inventiveness about it which points for its source to a cook who is much more inspired and technically competent than a person content with merely the traditional and routine.[24]

The presence of such unique dishes in Chiquart's manual is perhaps due to the unique nature of the work itself. Where other French recipe collections of the fourteenth and fifteenth centuries organize their material according to the type of dish (thin broth, thick broth, preservative, etc.), and according to the principal ingredient used in each dish (meat, venison, fowl, etc.), the *On Cookery* adopts as its format the presentation of a series of dishes appropriate for the two days of a formal banquet. Where the various authors who contributed to the *Enseignements*, the *Viandier*, and the *Menagier de Paris* clearly aim at comprehensiveness, Chiquart is content to offer to the apprentice cook a detailed exposé of a variety of the more or less complex recipes which that cook's master might expect him to be able to execute competently in fulfilling his normal service. Such an array of dishes will afford a good opportunity not only to review the best and gastronomically most satisfying preparations known in his day, but to review the major culinary techniques which the professional cook must master.

Incidental to the culinary instruction, Chiquart offers by his format an example of the composition of a menu for a noble banquet. And for Chiquart, what is important and what in the last analysis provides the rationale for all of the seigneurial cook's activities is just that, the

---

Blamenser; in Italian, Biancomangiare; in Spanish, Manjar Blanco; in Catalan, Menjar Blanc; in Portuguese, Mamjar Braquo; and in Latin Cibaria Alba.

[24] A generation or two after Chiquart, the *Recueil* copies a recipe for Souppe Jacopine (ed. cit., §6).

meal, the menu, the sum of everything that is set before the lord sitting at his high board. Chiquart's manual provides the neophyte with an illustration of a model of practical excellence to which he can reasonably aspire. Chiquart's sole concern is to help him be worthy of his master's reputation.

From his opening pages, Chiquart states that the production of an illustrious banquet is indeed the reason for his book. "To begin with, God having granted that a very honorable feast be given, at which there may be kings, queens, dukes, duchesses, counts, countesses, princes, princesses, marquesses, marchionesses, barons, baronesses and prelates of various classes, and nobles, too, in large number, the following things are necessary to cook both for the regular household and to do the feast honorably, and to the honor of the lord who gives it ... ." As a consequence of this conception of the cook's primary responsibility, the principal divisions of Chiquart's work are, in the first instance, the various meals the cook must prepare for a banquet and, within each of these meals, the sequence of servings properly composing them; and, in the second instance, possible additional dishes for those cases in which the banquet might be prolonged, or in which a sickly guest might require special foods to be prepared.

What the *On Cookery* lets us glimpse is an overall view of the chief cook's function, a view in which this cook is never considered to be a mere food technician. Rather, the chief cook must be a man of exceptional ability and understanding. As we have seen, his position required that he be able to coordinate efficiently the labors of a score of specialized workers in his kitchen, men whose duties and efforts had to mesh perfectly or else the work of the kitchen could result in disaster. Chiquart shows furthermore in the first section of his treatise that the chief cook had also to be something of a personnel manager, engaging all the help he required and ensuring that each person had adequate qualifications. The chief cook had an important role as quartermaster, too, setting up a temporary kitchen for a banquet, and securing a huge supply of foodstuffs and kitchen equipment long in advance. He had to be knowledgeable to some extent about the physical properties of the foodstuffs he handled, and conscientiously to bear in mind the full potential of their medical implications. He had to be enough of both an artist and an impresario to be able to help produce an impressive culinary *entremets*. And finally, it is clear from what Chiquart himself writes, and how he writes, that he expects his chief cook to be not only literate but literary.[25]

Because Amadeus of Savoy, the future Pope Felix V[26], was a devout Christian, his chief cook was surely expected to observe scrupulously all of the dietary restrictions associated with the Church's identification of meat days and lean days. Because, too, of the way in which Chiquart has arranged his work into various menus, we are very fortunate to be able to see in the *On Cookery* the rigorous parallelism between meat and lean dishes, which existed not just potentially and theoretically for a cook such as Chiquart but at quite a practical level. After setting out two full days of suggestions for a meat banquet, he repeats the same two-day outline, substituting in place of each of the meat dishes recipes for the preparation of equivalent lean dishes. The logic and clarity of the organization of such a parallel system of offerings is striking. While not too obvious in Chiquart's presentation, the parallelism can be appreciated in the following chart:

Meat (feast menu)	Fish (lean menu)
the first day: Dinner	
the first service	
great joints of meat: beef, mutton	great fish: (mujons), pike
salt meats: pork backs, chitter-	herrings (salted)

---

[25] See instances of Chiquart's erudition at folios 2r, 2v, 11r, 15r, 35r and 100r.

[26] Amadeus of Savoy was elected Pope, effectively anti-pope, by the Council of Basel in 1439, and abdicated this position ten years later. He had already, in 1434, retired in pious semi-seclusion to his estate at Ripaille, abandoning the duchy definitively in 1440 in favor of his son, Louis (1413–1465). Amadeus died in 1451; Marie de Bourgogne had died in childbirth in 1422, after bearing nine children.

lings, pork cutlets
mustard sauce   mustard sauce
(poree verde)   **pea puree** (§22)
White Broth of capons (§1)   **White Broth** (for fish) (§23)
German Broth of capons (§2)   **German Broth of fish** (§25)
Savoy Broth of poultry (§3)   **Savoy Broth of fish** (§26)
Lamprey Sauce of beef loin (§4)   **Tripes of large fish** (§24)

an *entremets*
Glazed Boars' Heads (§§5,6)

the second service

all sorts of roast: kid, piglet, veal   all sorts of sea-fish
& pork loin, mutton shoulders   fresh-water fish: pike, carp
poultry, goslings, capons, pheasants,   **Roast Lampreys** (§27)
partridge, rabbits, pigeons, herons
the proper sauces (26r)   the proper sauces (56v)
frumenty & venison   rice & **Fresh & Salted Dolphin** (§30)
pies   **Fish Pies** (§29)
talmoses and flans   **Almond Milk Flans** (§28)
Camelin Broth (§7)   **Camelin Broth of fish** (§31)
Civet of Hare
Pink Broth (§8)   **Pink Broth of fish** (§32)
Party White-Dish (beef bouillon) (§9) **Party White-Dish** (water) (§33)

a raised *entremets*
a Castle (§10)
sauce for the peacock (§11)

the first day: supper

all sorts of roast: kid, partridge,   roast pike, pollack
pheasant, veal
sauces: green verjuice, camelin (34r)   sauces: green sorrel verjuice,
     white almond sops (61r)
jelly   fish jelly
Partridge Tremollette (§12)   **Brown Sorengue of Eels** (§34)
Chyvolee of Stag (§13)   **Larded-Boiled Dish of Tench** (§35)
Rabbit in Saupiquet (§14)   **fried fish in Saupiquet** (§36)

the next day: dinner

great joints of meat; salt meats	large salt eel, trout, pollack, herring
Tile-Colored Broth (§15)	eggs on the coals
White Leek Sauce (§16)	white leeks
on mormotannes	
Hare Sops (§17)	pea puree sops
Jacobin Capon Sops (§18)	**Georgé Broth on fried fish** (§37)
Gravy of Small Birds & Poultry (§19)	**Gravy of Fish Tripe** (§38)
stewed greens: rape	stewed greens: rape

the next day: supper

all sorts of roast	white fish
Buchat of Rabbit (§20)	**Verjuice Broth on fried fish** (§39)
Parmesan Pies (§21)	**Parmesan Fish Pies** (§40)
dodine of water fowl	fried fish in saupiquet
boiled-larded dish	boiled-larded dish of big tench

One of the most valuable sections of the *On Cookery* is contained on folios 12r–18v. It is here that Chiquart has furnished the most extensive and detailed list that exists of culinary requirements for a medieval banquet. His supposition is that the chief cook must be able to arrange for such a banquet in one of his master's small castles, one which, as it happens, has totally inadequate kitchen facilities.[27] Of course Chiquart is still writing here of the cook's duties and responsibilities, but what we are able to construct is a remarkably real picture of some of the physical and organizational structures underlying such a festive event.

There are four general areas in which the chief cook must satisfy himself that all necessary preparations have been made: foodstuffs,

---

[27] The state banquet which Amadeus offered his father-in-law, the Duke of Burgundy, in 1403 was held in the small frontier castle of Tournus, on the border between Savoy and Burgundy. (See F. Cognasso, *Amedeo VIII*, 2 vols., Turin, 1930; Vol. I, pp. 38–40.) The kitchen at Tournus must have been of sufficient capacity to feed only the chatelain, his family and the normal garrison.

hardware, locale and personnel. Estimates of food requirements must be made far in advance of the banquet, and early arrangements must be made to ensure that the enormous quantities of foodstuffs needed for even the two days will be on hand. More is involved here than merely paying a visit to the local food merchant. The lord's huntsmen and falconers must be advised of the amount of game that will be required, and they must plan, two months beforehand, Chiquart says, to be able to deliver carcasses to be hung for three or four days. Domestic animals and fowl must be rounded up in quantities that must surely have depleted stocks in the neighborhood for many months afterward. Chiquart's precise enumeration of kitchen utensils, equipment and furniture is an archeologist's treasury. Again, the mention of firewood and coal — one thousand cartloads of the first and a "barnful" of the second — reminds us that the cook's concerns went beyond stirring the pot and tasting the stew. Locating the various work areas for the temporary kitchen was a task carried out in consultation with the Household Steward and the Kitchen Clerk. And finally the chief cook must be certain that there will be a sufficient number of *ouvriers* available, and he must assign them such specialized work as he will feel to be proper in the circumstances.

Cookery for Maistre Chiquart Amiczo was clearly both an art and a science. The modern reader is grateful to Duke Amadeus that he was enlightened enough to recognize the lasting cultural value of a treatise on cookery. And the modern reader is grateful, too, to the Duke's chief cook that he gave us, in the words of the preamble, *aucune science de l'art de cuysinerie et de cuysine*: "some understanding of cookery and cooking". As Chiquart says about the elaboration of a particularly complex dish in a tone, one imagines, which reflected the assurance he undoubtedly had in his own expertise: *chascun n'en est pas maistre*: "not everyone is a master of it."[28]

In this translation of the *Du fait de cuisine* I endeavor to retain

---

[28] Folio 55v.

as much of the stylistic "flavor" of Chiquart's original as possible. One of the major problems in this regard is to render the author's colloquially imprecise and rambling sentence structure faithfully (a good deal of this text was likely dictated orally to Jehan de Dudens), and yet at the same time to make Chiquart's meaning clearer to a modern reader than it might perhaps be with an entirely literal translation. To these occasionally incompatible ends I rely for the most part upon the use of punctuation which is not in the original, and frequently upon a suppression of the ubiquitous *et, et puis* and *encor plus*. The reader may still feel that such suppression was not carried out with sufficiently ruthless regularity.

A second difficulty arising from the peculiarity of Chiquart's style is less readily obviated in a translation: this is the repeated and disconcerting tendency he shows to shift from the third to the second persons in his discourse. Clearly he conceives of the *On Cookery* as a formal, impersonal manual which should be usable anywhere but mainly be helpful to the chief cook of a lordly household. As a result, he typically begins his recipes with a phrase such as, "Let him who would like to make this dish do such and such ... ." At the same time this author *is* a chief cook himself, of long experience and throroughly imbued with all of the craft he is describing. As he writes or dictates the details of a procedure he quite naturally imagines himself in *his* kitchen, directing his reader as if he were one of his own assistants. And so the third person in the discourse regularly gives way to the second person: the form "He should wash ... " becomes, almost imperceptibly, "You should get ... , take care that ... , you will find that ... ." The impersonal becomes personal. The translator who wishes to reproduce an author's style as faithfully as possible can only warn his reader of such an idiosyncracy.

Both Chiquart and Jehan de Dudens worked very conscientiously to produce a clear, legible, understandable book, as free as possible from textual errors. Despite these efforts, which are exceptionally successful in this work as a whole, an editor must for the sake of comprehensibility make a small number of emendations to what was written, and suggest for a number of other passages that in all probability the author's intention was something other than what we are able to read in the manuscript. All such cases are scrupulously noted in the French edition of the *Du fait de cuisine*[29]; a repetition of such observations, while relatively few in number, seems superfluous in this translation, and unnecessary for an appreciation of the value of this great culinary treatise.

I wish to extend sincere thanks here to the staff of the Archives du Valais, Switzerland, for their unfailing good will and help; to Messieurs Pierre Dubuis (Sion), Jean-Yves Mariotte (Archives de la Haute-Savoie, Annecy) and Fr. Robert Fritsch (Chambéry) for their interest and expert assistance; and most particularly to Messieurs Pierre Reichenbach, Editor of *Vallesia* and Maurice Casanova, of the *Glossaire des patois de la Suisse romande*, without whose invaluable help this edition would have been very much poorer.

---

[29] "*Du fait de cuisine* par Maistre Chiquart (1420), d'après le MS. S 103 des Archives du Valais," ed. Terence Scully, *Vallesia*, 40 (1985), pp. 101-231.

Select Bibliography

The following is a select bibliography of primary and secondary works on late-medieval cookery. Any siglum or abbreviation by which a particular work is normally referred to in the Introduction (above) or in the footnotes to the text of the *On Cookery* is indicated here at the head of the article.

Dictionaries and Glossaries

Alibert: Louis Alibert, *Dictionnaire occitan-français d'après les parlers langdociens*, 1965.

Alphita it ou Synonima herbarum, ed. Salvatore de Renzi, "Sopra un vocabolario di voci tecniche del medio evo," *Collectio Salernitana*, III, Naples, 1854, pp. 271–322 (A medico-botanic glossary, mss. from the 13th c.)

Bloch-Wartburg: Oscar Bloch et Walther von Wartburg, *Dictionnaire étymologique de la langue française*, 5th edn., Paris, 1968.

Bridel: Philippe Bridel, *Glossaire du patois de la Suisse romande*, Lausanne (Georges Bridel), 1866.

Constantin-Désormaux: Aimé Constantin et Joseph Désormaux, *Dictionnaire savoyard*, Paris and Annecy, 1902.

Cotgrave: Randle Cotgrave, *A Dictionarie of the French and English Tongues*, London, 1611.

DEAF: Kurt Baldinger, Jean-Denis Gendron and Georges Straka, *Dictionnaire étymologique de l'ancien français*, Québec-Tubingen-Paris, 1974– (G–).

DuCange: Charles DuFresne, Sieur DuCange, *Glossarium mediae et infimae latinitatis*, suppl. D.P. Charpentier, new ed. Léopold Favre, Niort, 1883–1887; repr. Paris, 1937–38.

FEW: Walter von Wartburg, *Französisches etymologisches Wörterbuch*, Bonn, 1928- .

Godefroy: Frédéric Godefroy, *Dictionnaire de l'ancienne langue française*, Paris, 1881–1902.

GPSR: L. Gauchat, et al., *Glossaire des patois de la Suisse Romande*, Zurich and Lausanne, 1903-

Livre des mestiers: Jean Gessler, ed., *Le livre des mestiers de Bruges et ses dérivés; quatre anciens manuels de conversation*, 6 vols., Bruges, 1931 (The original work dates from c. 1340.)

NG: *Novum glossarium mediae latinitatis ab anno DCCC usque ad annum MCC*, publ. under the direction of Franz Blatt Copenhagen, 1957- (letters L-O).

Niermeyer: J.F. Niermeyer, *Mediae latinitatis lexicon minus*, Leyden, 1976.

REW: W. Meyer-Lübke, *Romanisches etymologisches Wörterbuch*, Heidelberg, 1911.

Schüle: "Les comptes de l'Hospice du Grand Saint-Bernard (1397–1477)," glossary by Ernest Schüle, *Vallesia*, 30 (1975), pp. 341–384.

Tilander: Gunnar Tilander, *Glanures lexicographiques*, Lund, 1932.

TLF: *Trésor de la langue française*, Paris (CNRS), 1971- .

Tobler: Adolph Tobler et Erhard Lommatzsch, *Altfranzösisches Wörterbuch*, Berlin, 1915 (repr. and currently, Weisbaden, 1955-).

Works on foods and cookery

in Latin

Anthimus, *De observatione ciborum ad Theodoricum regem Francorum epistula*, ed. Shirley Howard, Leyden, 1924; ed. also E. Liechtenhan (*Corpus Medicorum Latinorum*, 8), Leipzig (Teubner), 1877; Leipzig and Berlin, 1928; new edn., Leipzig, 1963.

Constantinus Africanus, *Liber de gradibus*, MS Paris, BN lat. 6891, ff. 88ra–89ra. (This work is almost identical to Isaac, *De gradibus simplicium*.)

Platearius, Matthaeus, *Liber de simplici medicina, dictus Circa instans* (c. 1100); a fifteenth-century French translation, *Le livre de simples medecines*, ed. Paul Dorveaux, Paris, 1913.

Regimen Sanitatis Salernitanum: Flos Medicinae Scholae Salerni, ed. Salvador de Renzi, et al., *Collectio Salernitana*, 5 vols., Naples (Filiatre-Sebezio), 1852-59; repr. Bologna (Forni), 1967 (See the *Régime tresutile et tresproufitable* ... , below.)

Tacuinum sanitatis in medicina, ed. Luisa Cogliati Arano, Milan (Electra), n.d.; tr. by Oscar Ratti and Adele Westbrook as *The Medieval Health Handbook Tacuinum Sanitatis*, New York (Braziller), 1976.

Musandinus, Petrus, *Summula Musandini*, ed. Salvador de Renzi, et al., *Collectio Salernitana*, 5 vols., Naples (Filiatre-Sebezio), 1852-1859; repr. Bologna (Forni), 1967; Vol. 5, pp. 254-268: "*Incipit summula de preparatione ciborum et potuum infirmorum, secundum Musandinum.*"

Crescentius, Petrus (Pietro de' Crescenzi), *Commodorum ruralium* (c. 1285 -1309), Augsburg, 1471; Mayence, 1493.

Matthaeus Silvaticus (of Mantua), *Pandectae medicinae* (c. 1336), Bologna, and Naples, 1474; Venice, 1478; etc.

Liber de coquina, ed. Marianne Mulon, "Deux traités inédits d'art culinaire," *Bulletin philologique et historique*, Paris (Comité des Travaux Historiques et Scientifiques), 1968 (publ. 1971), pp. 369 435.

Tractatus de modo preparandi et condiendi omnis cibaria, ed. Marianne Mulon, *ibid.*

Magninus Mediolanensis (Maino de' Maineri), *Opusculum de saporibus*, ed. Lynn Thorndike, "A Medieval Sauce-Book," *Speculum*, 9 (1934), pp. 183 190.

Magninus Mediolanensis, *Regimen sanitatis*, MS. Vatican, Palatin 1331, ff. 228r-302v; Louvain (Johannes de Westfalia), 1482; publ. also under the name of Arnaldus de Villanova, in *Hec sunt opera Arnaldi de Villanova*, ed. Thomas Murchius, Lyon (Françoys Fradin), 1504.

Sanitatis conservator: Eine Diätethik aus Montpellier dem Ende des 14. Jahrhunderts und "Tractatus medicus de Comestione et Digestione vel Regimen Sanitatis" benannt, ed. Hugo Faber, Leipzig, 1924.

Platina di Cremona, Baptista (pseudonym of Bartolomeo Sacchi), *De honesta voluptate et valitudine*, n.p., 1474 ; Rome (Uldericus Gallus), 1475; Venise (Petro Mocenico). 1475.

Hortus sanitatis, Strasbourg (Russ), *c.* 1507; in French as the *Jardin de santé*, 2 vols., Mayence (Jean Meydenbach), 1491; and Paris (A. Verard), *c.* 1499; publ. also in Latin under the title of *Herbarius*, Mayence, 1484; Padua, 1485, 1486; etc.

Durante da Gualdo, Castor, *De bonitate et vitio alimentorum centuria*, Pesaro, 1565 (Translated into Italian by the author as *Il tesoro della sanità*: see below).

—in French

Enseignements, ed. Grégoire Lozinski in his *Bataille de Caresme et de Charnage*, Paris (Champion), 1933; Appendix I, pp. 181–190; ed. also by L. Douet-D'Arcq as *Petit traité de cuisine* (Bibliothèque de l'Ecole des Chartes, 21st year, Series 5, Vol. 1), Paris (Dumoulin), 1860; and by Jérome Pichon and Georges Vicaire in their *Viandier de Guillaume Tirel*, pp. 211–226 under the title *Traité de cuisine écrit vers 1300*.

Le Viandier de Guillaume Tirel, dit Taillevent, ed. Jérôme Pichon and Georges Vicaire, Paris (Leclerc & Cormuau), 1892; new ed. Sylvie Martinet, Paris, 1892; repr. Geneva (Slatkine) 1967. The Valais MS of the *Viandier* was ed. by Paul Aebischer in *Vallesia*, 8 (1953), pp. 73–100.

Le Mesnagier de Paris, traité de morale et d'économie domestique composé vers 1393 par un bourgeois parisien, ed. Jérôme Pichon, 2 vols., Paris (Crapelet & Lahure), 1847; repr. Paris, 1896; repr. Geneva (Slatkine) 1970: ed. also by Georgine E. Brereton et Janet M. Ferrier, *Le Menagier de Paris*, Oxford (Oxford University Press), 1981. (In the present work, references to the *Menagier* are to this latter edition.)

Meyer, Paul, "Notice sur le ms. Old Roy. 12. C. XII du Musée britannique (Pièces diverses. — Recettes culinaires)," *Bulletin de la Société des anciens textes français*, 19 (1893), pp. 38–56. (A miscellany of 32 recipes.)

Chiquart: "*Du fait de cuisine* par Maistre Chiquart (1420)," ed. Terence Scully, *Vallesia*, 40 (1985), pp. 101–231.

Recueil: Edition d'un Recueil de recettes culinaires et d'un réceptaire sur les greffes inédits du XVe siècle (Paris, B. N. latin 6707), ed. Carole Lambert, mémoire de maîtrise, Université de Montréal, 1983.

Le grant herbier en françois, contenant les qualitez, vertuz et proprietez des Herbes, Arbres, Gommes et Semences. Extraict de plusieurs traictez de medecine, Paris (Pierre le Caron), c. 1498.

Jardin de santé: see the *Hortus sanitatis*, above.

Le régime tresutile et tresproufitable pour conserver et garder la santé du corps humain, ed. Patricia W. Cummins, Chapel Hill (University of North Carolina), 1976. (A fifteenth-century French translation of the commentaries attributed to Arnaud de Villeneuve on the *Flos Medicinae Scholae Salerni*.

Arnaut de Villeneuve, *Regimen sanitatis en françois*, Lyons (Claude Nourry), 1501 (See Magninus Mediolanensis, *Regimen sanitatis*, above.)

Livre fort excellent de Cuysine tres-utille & proffitable ... , Lyon (Olivier Arnoullet), 1542; publ. also under the following titles: *Le Grand Cuisinier de toute cuisine*, Paris (Jehan Bonfons), n.d.; *La Fleur de toute cuysine*, Paris (Alain Lotrian), 1543; *Livre de cuysine tres utille & prouffitable*, Paris, c. 1540; and *Le Livre de honneste volupté*, Lyon (Benoist Rigaud), 1588. (This last work is not to be confused with the treatise of Platina).

The printed *Viandier: Ci apres s'ensuyt le Viandier pour appareiller toutes manieres de viandes que Taillevent queulx du roy nostre sire fist* ... , n.p., n.d. (c. 1490 ?); ed. Pichon and Vicaire in their *Viandier de Guillaume Tirel*, pp. 143–199: frequently garbled versions of the *Viandier*'s recipes are followed by additions made by Pierre Gaudoul (1532–1537), themselves copied from Book 7 of the *Platine en françoys*, pp. 201–209.

Platine en françoys tresutile & necessaire pour le corps humain, qui traicte de honneste volupté et de toutes viandes et choses que l'omme menge ... , Lyon (Françoys Fradin), 1505; tr. of Platina di Cremona,

De honesta voluptate (see above).

Le Bastiment de receptes, Lyon (A l'escu de Coloigne), 1541 (A French translation of the Italian *Opera nuova intitolata Edificio di Ricetti*; see below.).

—in English

Forme of Cury, ed. Samuel Pegge, London (J. Nichols), 1780; ed. also by Richard Warner in *Antiquitates Culinariae: Curious Tracts on Culinary Affairs of the Old English*, London (R. Blamire), 1791; and in a recent new edition by Hieatt and Butler (Part IV), below.

Hieatt and Butler: Constance B. Hieatt and Sharon Butler, eds., *Curye on Inglysch. English Culinary Manuscripts of the Fourteenth Century* (Early English Text Society, S.S. 8), London (Oxford University Press), 1985. (An edition of five recipe collections.)

Liber cure cocorum, ed. Richard Morris, Berlin and London (Asher, for the Philological Society), 1862.

Austin, Thomas, *Two Fifteenth-Century Cookery-Books* (Early English Text Society, O.S. 91), London (Oxford University Press), 1888; repr. 1964.

Noble Boke of Cookry ffor a Prynce Houssolde or eny other Estately Houssolde, ed. Robina Napier, London (Elliot Stock), 1882.

Furnivall, Frederick James, *Early English Meals and Manners* (Early English Text Society, O.S. 32), London (Oxford University Press), 1868; repr. 1931.

in Italian

Libro della cocina por un anonimo toscano, ed. Emilio Faccioli, *Arte della cucina. Libri di ricetti, testi sopra lo scalco, il trinciante e i vini dal XIV al XIX secolo*, 2 vols., Milan (Il Polifilo), 1966; I, pp. 19–57; ed. also by Francesco Zambrini, *Il Libro della cucina* del Secolo XIV, Bologna (Pressogaetano Romagnoli), 1863.

Libro per cuoco, ed. Emilio Faccioli, in *Arte della cucina*, I, pp. 59–105; ed. also by Alberto Consiglio, *Libro di cucina del secolo XIV*, Rome (Canesi), 1969; and by Ludovico Frati, Leghorn, 1899, repr. Bologna (Forni), 1970.

Martino, Maestro, *Libro de arte coquinaria*, ed. Emilio Faccioli, in *Arte della cucina*, I, pp. 115-204.

LVII Ricette d'un libro di cucina del buon secolo della lingua, ed. Salomone Morpurgo, Domenico and Giacomo Zanichelli, Bologna (Nicola Zanichelli), 1890.

Durante da Gualdo, Castor (d. c. 1590), *Il tesoro della sanità*, Rome, 1586 (See this author's *De bonitate et vitio alimentorum centuria*, above.)

Opera nuova intitolata Edificio di Ricetti ... , Venice, 1541 (Translated into French as the *Bastiment de receptes*; see above.)

—in Catalan, Portuguese, Arabic

Libre de sent soví (Receptari de cuina), ed. Rudolf Grewe, Barcelona (Barcino), 1979; ed. also by J. Osset Merle, "Un libro de cocina del siglo XIV," *Boletín de la Sociedad Castellonense de Cultura*, 17 (1935), pp. 156-177.

Mestre Robert, *Libre del coch. Tractat de cuina medieval*, ed. Veronika Leimgruber, Barcelona (Curial Edicions Catalanes), 1977 (2nd edn., 1982) (A fifteenth-century work: see the editor's n. 1, p. 123.)

Newman, Elizabeth, *A Critical Edition of an Early Portuguese Cook Book*, Ph. D. thesis, University of North Carolina, Chapel Hill, 1964.

Huici Miranda, Ambrosio, *Traducción espanola de un manuscrito anónimo del siglo XIII sobre la cocina hispano-magrabi*, Madrid (Ayuntamiento de Valencia), 1966. (In Arabic, the *Kitab al-tabij*.)

Perry, Charles, "*Kitab al-tibakhah*: A Fifteenth-Century Cookbook," *Petits Propos Culinaires*, 21 (1985), pp. 17-22.

Nola: Ruperto de Nola, *Libro de guisados manjares y potages intitulado libro de cozina*, Logrono (Miguel de Guia), 1529; reprod., Bilbao, 1971; ed. Dionisio Pérez (Los clasicos olvidados, 9), Madrid, 1929.

—in German

Eberhard, *Das Kochbuch Meister Eberhards*, ed. Anita Feyl, diss. Albert-Ludwigs-Universität, Freiburg im Breisgau, 1963; text publ. also by the same editor in "Das Kochbuch des Eberhard von Landshut (erste

Hälfe des 15.Jhs.", *Ostbairischen Grenzmarken*, 5 (1961), pp. 352–366 (The numbering of the recipes in the two editions is identical.)

Guter Spise: *Das bouch von gouter spize. Aus der Würzburg-Münchener Handschrift*, ed. Hans Hajek (Texte des späten Mittelalters, 8), Berlin (Erich Schmidt), 1958.

Wiswe, Hans, ed., "Ein mittelniederdeutsches Kochbuch des 15 Jahrhunderts," *Braunschweigisches Jahrbuch*, 37 (1956), pp. 19–55; see also Wiswe's "Nachlese zum ältesten mittelniederdeutschen Kochbuch," *ibid.*, 39 (1958), pp. 103–121.

Birlinger, Anton, "Kalender und Kochbüchlein aus Tegernsee," *Germania. Vierteljahresschrift für deutsche Alterthumskunde*, 9 (1864), pp. 132–207.

Various related works

Balbi: Joannes Balbus, *Catholicon* (1460); repr. Farnborough, 1971.

Beck, P., "L'approvisionnement en Bourgogne ducale aux XIVe et XVe siècles," *Manger et boire*, I, pp. 171–181.

Benoist, J.O., "Le gibier dans l'alimentation seigneuriale (XIe-XVe siècles," *Manger et boire*, I, pp. 75–87.

Bolens, Lucie, "L'art culinaire médiéval andalou est baroque: les ruses de la science au service du goût (XIe-XIIIe siècle," *Manger et boire*, II, pp. 141–148.

Bruchet, Max Pierre Marie, *Le Château de Ripaille*, Chambéry, 1904; Paris, 1907.

Carbonelli, C.G., *Come vissero i primi conti di Savoia da Umberto Blancamano ad Amedeo VIII*, Casale Monferrato, 1931.

Castorina, *Farmaci*: Mara Castorina Battaglia, "Notizie sui farmaci usati alla corte di Savoia dal 1300 al 1440," *Minerva Medica*, 69 (1978), pp. 501–525.

Castorina, *Medici*: Mara Castorina Battaglia, "Medici e chirurghi alla corte di Savoia (1300–1440)," *Minerva Medica*, 70 (1979), pp. 1305–33 and 1369–95.

Chapperon, T., *Chambéry à la fin du XIVe siècle*, Paris, 1863.

Clair, Colin, *Of Herbs and Spices*, London and New York (Abelard-Schuman), 1961.

Cognasso, Francesco, *Amedeo VIII*, 2 vols., Turin, 1930.

Depping, G.B., *Règlements sur les arts et métiers de Paris rédigés au XIIIe siècle et connus sous le nom du Livre des Métiers*, Paris, 1837.

Edmunds, Sheila, "New Light on Bapteur and Lamy," *Atti della Accademia delle Scinze di Torino*, Vol. 102 (1967–68), pp. 501–554.

Flandrin, Jean-Louis, "Brouets, potages et bouillons," *Médiévales*, 5 (1983) "Nourritures", pp. 5–14.

Frescura Nepoti, S, "Macellazione e consumo della carne a Bologna ... per gli inizi del secolo XV," *Archeologia Medievale*, 8 (1981), pp. 281–297.

Freeman, Margaret B., *Herbs for the Mediaeval Household for Cooking, Healing and Divers Uses*, New York (Metropolitan Museum of Art), 1943.

Gay, Victor D., *Glossaire archéologique du moyen âge et de la Renaissance*, 2 vols., Paris, 1887–1928.

Gislain, G. de, "Le rôle des étangs dans l'alimentation médiévale," *Manger et boire*, I, pp. 89–101.

Gonon: Marguerite Gonon, *La vie quotidienne en Lyonnais d'après des testaments des XIVe-XVIe siècles*. Paris (Belles Lettres), 1968.

Gonon, *Foréziens*: Marguerite Gonon, *La langue vulgaire écrite des testaments foréziens*, Paris (Belles Lettres), 1973.

Gottschalk, Alfred, *Histoire de l'alimentation et de la gastronomie*, 2 vols., Paris (Hippocrate), 1948.

Gual Camarena, Miguel, *Vocabulario del comercio medioeval*, 2nd edn., Barcelona (Albir), 1976.

Guégan, Bertrand, *Le cuisinier français*, Paris (Emile-Paule), 1934.

Hauréau, Barthélemy, *Initia operum scriptorum latinorum medii potissimum aevi*, 8 vols., MS. n.p., n.d.; reprod. Turnhout (Brepols), 1974.

Heyd, Wilhelm, *Histoire du commerce du Levant au moyen-âge*, 2 vols., Leipzig, 1885–1886; repr. Amsterdam (Hakkert), 1967.

Joret, Charles, *La Rose dans l'antiquité et au moyen âge*, Paris, 1892; repr. Geneva (Slatkine), 1970.

Lafortune-Martel, Agathe, *Fête noble en Bourgogne au XVe siècle*, Montréal (Bellarmin) and Paris (Vrin), 1984.

Landry, Robert, *The Gentle Art of Flavoring*, London and New York (Abelard-Schuman), 1970; a transl. by Bruce H. Axler of *Les soleils de la cuisine*, Paris (Laffont), 1967.

Laurioux, Bruno, "De l'usage des épices dans l'alimentation médiévale," *Médiévales*, 5 (1983) "Nourritures," pp. 15–31.

Lebault, Armand, *La table et le repas à travers les âges*, Paris (Laveur), 1910. See also "Spices in the Medieval Diet: A New Approach," *Food and Foodways*, 1 (1985), pp. 43–76.

Lecoq, Raymond, *Les objets de la vie domestique. Ustensiles en fer de la cuisine et du foyer des origines au XIXe siècle*, Paris (Berger-Levrault), 1979.

Manger et boire au moyen âge, ed. Denis Menjot, 2 vols., Nice (Faculté des lettres et sciences humaines de Nice), 1984.

Marie-José, Reine, *La Maison de Savoie*, 3 vols., Paris (Albin-Michel), 1956 and 1962: Vols. II and III: "Amédée VIII".

Montanari, Massimo, *L'alimentazione contadina nell'alto Medioevo*, Naples (Liguori), 1979.

Nada Patrone, Anna Maria, *Il cibo del ricco ed il cibo del povero. Contributo alla storia qualitativa dell'alimentazione. L'area pedemontana negli ultimi secoli del Medio Evo*, Turin (Centro Studi Piemontesi), 1981.

Neckam, Alexandre, *De utensilibus*, ed. Thomas Wright in *A Volume of Vocabularies*, 2nd edn. London (privately printed), 1882, p. 96 f.

Pegolotti, Francesco Balducci, *La pratica della mercatura*, ed. Allan Evans, Cambridge (Massachusetts, Medieval Academy), 1936; repr. New York (Kraus), 1970.

Platine (pseud.), "Les sauces 'légères' du Moyen Age," *L'Histoire*, 35 (June, 1981), pp. 87–89.

Plouvier, Liliane, "Cuisine: et le potage fut ... ," *L'Histoire*, 64 (Feb.,

1984), pp. 79–81.

Redon, Odile, "Les usages de la viande en Toscane au XIVe siècle," *Manger et boire*, II, pp. 121–130.

Sabban, Françoise, "Le savoir-cuire ou l'art des potages dans le *Menagier de Paris* et le *Viandier* de Taillevent," *Manger et boire*, II, pp. 161–172.

Scully, Terence, "The *Opusculum de saporibus* of Magninus Mediolanensis," *Medium Aevum*, 54 (1985), pp. 178-207.

Stouff, Louis, *Ravitaillement et alimentation en Provence aux XIVe et XVe siècles*, Paris and The Hague (Mouton), 1970.

Weiss-Amer, Melitta, *Zur Entstehung, Tradierung und Lexik deutscher Kochbücher und Rezepte des Spätmittelalters*, Thesis, University of Waterloo (Canada), 1983.

Wilson, C. Anne, "The Saracen Connection: Arab cuisine and the mediaeval west," *Petits Propos Culinaires*: Part 1, 7 (1981), pp. 13–22; Part 2, 8 (1981), pp. 19–27.

Wiswe, Hans, *Kulturgeschichte der Kochkunst*, Munich (Heinz Moos), 1970.

Zängger, Kurt, *Contribution à la terminologie des tissus en ancien français*, Bienne, 1945.

ON COOKERY
(*Du fait de cuisine*)
by Maistre Chiquart

Lubrica gencium memoria, frequenter que clara sunt reducit dubia, propter que fides veterum provida decrevit rerum seriem scripture testimonio perhempnari, ut ea que mentis humane fragilitas non recolit scripturis appareant auctenticis, stabilita noscant igitur, tam modernorum presencia quam futurorum posteritas, hec infrascripta.[1]

Here follows the repertory of what is contained in this little compendium and booklet which has been compiled *On the Matter of Cookery* by Master Chiquart, cook of our most respected lord, the Duke of Savoy, in the course of the year of the nativity of Our Savior Jesus Christ thousand four hundred and twenty, and written down by me, John of Dudens, clerk, burgess of the town of Annecy. To begin with, the introit or preamble /2v/ contains the four principal causes which ought to be found in every good composition, to wit, the efficient, material, formal and final causes; and the divine invocation, in response to the wise precept which holds that, "Where Jesus Christ is not the foundation, the entire structure will collapse."[2]

The provision of meats .... *folio xii*
The provision of spices .... *xiii*
How cooks should be recruited .... *xiiii*
The provision of cauldrons and other things necessary for cooking *xiiii*
The provision of fish, both sea-fish and fresh-water fish .... *xvi*

---

[1] "Man's unretentive memory often reduces clear things to doubt; as a consequence, the noble foresight of the ancients decreed that ephemeral things should be rendered immortal by being written down, so that those things which the feebleness of the human mind cannot retain might survive through faithful writings; and so, therefore, that those of the current age as well as of future generations may know something with certainty, there is what follows."

[2] Cf. Luke 6:49

The provision of cheeses, cloths, knives and other necessary things ..... *xvii*
/*3r*/ The matter of pastry³ .... *xviii*
The disposition of the various workers .... *xviii*
The first service: A white broth (§1) .... *xviiii*
A German Broth (§2) .... *xx*
A Savoy Broth (§3) .... *xxi*
A Lamprey Sauce for loin of beef (§4) .... *xxii*
Fat Beef Pasty .... *xxii*
Entremets of Boars' Heads, glazed and emblazoned (§§5 & 6) ..... *xxiii*
For the second service .... *xxv*
Camelin Broth (§7.) of a castle (§§10 & 11) .... *xxx*

/*3v*/ For the supper .... *xxxiiii*
A Tremollette (§12) .... *xxxiiii*
Chyvrolee of Stag (§13) .... *xxxv*
Saupiquet to put on rabbits (§14) .... *xxxvi*
The menu for the second day's dinner: and firstly,
    a Tile-Colored Broth (§15) .... *xxxvi*
White Leek Sauce (§16) .... *xxxvii*
Hare Sops (§17) .... *xxxviii*
Jacobin Sops (§18) .... *xxxviii*
A Gravy of small birds and poultry (§19) .... *xl*
The menu for the second day's supper .... *xli*
A Buchat of Rabbit (§20) .... *xli*
Parmesan Pies (§21) .... *xliii*
Tractatus de piscibus cum salsis incombentibus .... *xlviii*
A White Broth of fish (§23) .... *xlviiii*
An Arbaleste of fish (§24) .... *l*
/*4r*/ A German Broth of fish (§25) .... *li*
A Savoy Broth (§26) .... *lii*

---

³ Most of folio 3 has been torn away. All that remains is a bit of a tab on which, recto and verso, only a few letters or numbers can be read.

What will comprise the second service[4] .... *liii*
Almond-Milk Flans (§28) .... *liiii*
Fish Pies (§29) .... *lv*
The exposition of the sauces appropriate for both sea-fish
    and fresh-water fish .... *lvi*
How fresh dolphin and salted dolphin should be prepared (§30) ..... *lvi*
A Camelin Broth (§31) .... *lvii*
A Pink Broth (§32) .... *lviii*
A Party White-Dish in four colors all together (§33) .... *lix*
How roast lampreys should be prepared (§27) .... *lix*
The second[5] day's supper, /4v/ for a lean meal, and its exposition:
    A Brown Sorengue of eels (§34) .... *lxi*
A good Larded-Boiled Dish of tench (§35) .... *lxii*
A Saupiquet on both sea-fish and fresh-water fish (§36) .... *lxii*
The menu of the second day's lean dinner .... *lxiii*
A Georgé Broth on fried fish (§37) .... *lxiii*
A Gravy of Fish Tripe (§38) .... *lxiiii*
The exposition of the supper following .... *lxv*
A Verjuice Broth on fried fish (§39) .... *lxv*
Parmesan Fish Pies (§40) .... *lxv*
The exposition of additional dishes and *entremets*, should anyone wish,
    /5r/ for the service of the previous two days .... *lxvii*
Firstly: The Coquart Pasty (§41) .... *lxvii*
Specification of the sauces with which it is to be eaten(§§42.43 & 44)*lxviii*
Pilgrim Capons (§§45 & 46) .... *lxx*
A Calunafree of Partridge (§47) .... *lxxii*
A Calaminee and Cold Sage (§§48 & 49) .... *lxiii*
Norse Pasties (§50) .... *lxxv*
Rissoles (§51) .... *lxxvi*
A Hot-Dish (§52) .... *lxxvii*

---

[4] Whoever compiled this table of contents overlooked the recipe (§27) for lamprey, which begins on folio 53r. He does insert it a little later in this copy, but with the wrong folio number.

[5] The text reads *Le soupper du second jour*; this menu is still for the first day, however.

Shoulder of Mutton eaten its blood (§53) .... *lxxviii*
Breast of Boar, both young and fully grown (§54) .... *lxxviii*
The sauce in which it is eaten (§55) .... *iiii^{xx}*
Mortoexes (§56) .... *iiii^{xx}*
A Vinaigrette (§57) .... *iiii^{xx}ii*
/5v/ A Jance (§58) .... *iiii^{xx}iii*
A Gruel Broth of Capons (§59) .... *iiii^{xx}iii*
Glazed Kid Heads (§60) .... *iiii^{xx}iiii*
Crow (§61) .... *iiii^{xx}v*
A Chicken Gratunee (§62) .... *iiii^{xx}vi*
A Spanish Gratunee (§63) .... *iiii^{xx}ix*
Shoulder of Mutton, stuffed and glazed (§64) .... *iiii^{xx}x*
A section of dishes for the sick† .... *iiii^{xx}xiii*
Firstly: A Restorative (§65) .... *iiii^{xx}xiii*
A Precipitate (§66) .... *iiii^{xx}xvi*
An Almond Butter (§67) .... *iiii^{xx}xviii*
Stuffed Crayfish (§68) .... *iiii^{xx}xviii*
A Green Puree for the sick (§69) .... *iiii^{xx}xix*
Another Puree made of almond milk (§69a) .... *c*
Quince in a Pasty for lords (§70) .... *c*
A Cullis (§71) .... *cii*
/6r/ Pears cooked without coals or water (§72) .... *cii*
An Applesauce (§73) .... *ciii*
A White-Dish of Capons (§74) .... *ciiii*
A White-Dish of Partridge (§74a) .... *ciiii*
Furthermore, Oatmeal (§75) .... *cv*
A Pea Dish (§76) .... *cv*
A Semolina Dish (§77) .... *cvi*
A Barley Dish (§78) .... *cvi*
And lastly, the praise and thanks rendered by the compiler
    of this little book .... *cvii*

---

† In the margin is the notation: *Vide vide pro infirmis.*

/11r/ *Assit principio sancta Maria meo. Jhesus Christus.*

To you, exalted, renowned and mighty Prince and Lord, Amadeus, First Duke of Savoy, be all honor and reverence, together with ready willingness, proffered with humble and devoted commendation, to obey all your commands. In the past, most respected Lord, on many occasions you have requested and ordered me, Chiquart, even though the last of your humble subjects, yet nevertheless your devoted servant in great affection and desire, that, the memory of man being insecure and faulty and there being no record of things were it not for writing—*Quoniam memoria hominis est labilis et sepe memorie injuriatur oblivio nisi scripture suffragio innaretur, idcirco ad infrascripta per scripture memoriam decernanda*[6]—and you being occasionally desirous of and inclined to making feasts and solemn banquets, I should set in writing some knowledge of the art of cooking and of cookery, /11v/ particularly, so you state and affirm, as I am learned in this science and art, for your consideration and pleasure; yet, as you know, I have several times refused and even contradicted you, for in knowledge as well as in life I sit in the lowest places—*in ymis locis*—and have never, through ignorance or negligence, turned my mind to such knowledge or learning, nor have I any books or writings bearing on this subject; and I have told you that I have no capability or understanding in such things. But you, most respected Lord, responding constantly and firmly, told me that, no matter what excuses I might allege before you, I am not to be excused, and that if only I were to set the hand of my will to this task God would grant

---

[6] This is a variant of a common maxim in the Middle Ages. Chiquart has himself already expressed much the same idea in the opening passage of his book, and even provides his reader with a summary of its sense here before writing the Latin. For instances of passages with the same idea and similar terminology, see Hauréau, IV, 1v; V, 85v; and V. 139v.

me the will-power and the strength for it; and that whatever tends to the use, profit and pleasure of many, and particularly of yourself among all others, great merit, /12r/ commendation and honor would accrue to me. And so, most respected Lord, finally won and overcome by these and many other arguments of yours, yet nevertheless fearful and trembling, though with the help of God, and your good will and pleasure, bending to your desire and command, I very humbly tender my assent. And, animated and encouraged by these things, not without great pain and great labor, I have undertaken to accomplish this work by my own strength in the manner which follows.

To begin with, God having granted that a very honorable feast be given, at which there may be kings, queens, dukes, duchesses, counts, countesses, princes, princesses, marquesses, marchionesses, barons, baronesses and prelates of various classes, and nobles, /12v/ too, in large number, the following things are necessary both to cook for the regular household[7] and to do the feast honorably and to the honor of the lord who gives it.

And firstly, one hundred fat oxen, some one hundred and thirty sheep[8], also fat, six score of pigs; and, for each day during the feast, one hundred small piglets, both for roasting and for other uses, and sixty

---

[7] In the original, *pour le ordinayre de la cuisine*: Chiquart has always to distinguish between what food will be required merely to sustain the large body of retainers accompanying and serving the noble lord and his guests, and what food will be dedicated to the special banquet meals to be "honorably" presented to those constituting the noble party itself. See also *pour le commun*, "for the regular meals" on folio 23v.) At the beginning of the seventeenth century, Martínez Montino still assumes the existence of two distinct kitchens, the *cocina de boca* and the *cocina de estado*: in the first of these the lord's meals are prepared, and in the second are cooked the meals of the palace personnel. See Ruperto de Nola, *Libro de Guisados*, ed. Dionisio Pérez, Madrid (Ibero-Americana), 1929, p. xxix and p. 239, nn. 356 and 357.

[8] Chiquart has *cent trentaines de moustons*. Such an impossibly large quantity, 3000, may be the result of an oral transmission of this section of the text, and of Jehan de Dudens inadvertently adding an *s* to *trentaine*.

large fat pigs, salted, for larding and cooking.

To this end, the butcher would be well advised to have a good provision of meats so that, should it happen that /*13r*/ the feast lasts longer than is intended, all that is needed will be immediately available. Even if there should be any surplus meat, that will not matter because nothing will be wasted.

For each day of the aforesaid feast you need two hundred kids and lambs, one hundred calves and two thousand head of poultry.

And your purveyors of game[9] should be able, diligent and foresighted enough to have forty horses to get to various places for deer, hares, rabbits, partridge, pheasants, small birds (whatever they can find of these without number), doves, cranes, herons, any wild fowl— whatever sort of game they can get.[10] They should set about this two months or six weeks /*13v*/ before the feast; and all of them should bring or send whatever they have been able to get at least three or four days before the feast so that this game can be hung and properly prepared in each case.

And for each day of the feast they should be provided with six thousand eggs.

Furthermore, for the aforesaid feast they must have two charges of

---

[9] Etienne Boileau's *Livre des métiers* (Paris, 1837, p. 178) contains the statutes of the company of *poulailliers*, or purveyors, in Paris. For the function of the courtly counterpart of these purveyors of game, and the *venatores*, see Montanari, Parte seconda, B, II "La caccia," pp. 254–276.

[10] Concerning the taste which the House of Savoy had developed for the meat of game-birds and game-animals, fresh or salted according to the season, see Nada Patrone, *Il cibo del ricco*, pp. 297–316 in general and pp. 309–10 in particular.

gross spices[11], that is, white ginger, Mecca ginger[12], cinnamon, grains of paradise[13] and pepper.

---

[11] The terms *grosses espices* and, below, *menues espices* distinguished essentially between the spices which were more or less commonly used. As to the category in which any particular spice would be understood to belong, this would depend upon the relative popularity of its use in any given period and region, and perhaps even upon the frequency of its use by any given cook. For example, the *Viandier* lists grains of paradise among the minor spices, whereas for Chiquart they had become a common condiment to be listed among the gross spices. See the contents of each category, *spezierie grosse* and *spezierie minute*, according to Balducci Pegolotti, p. 431.

For an enumeration of the spices which were considered important in cookery at the late-fourteenth-century French court, see the *Viandier*, pp. 109–110; and in Parisian cookery of the same period, the *Menagier*, p. 186, ll. 6–25. See also B. Laurioux, "De l'usage des épices dans l'alimentation médiévale," *Médiévales*, 5 (1983), pp. 15–31.

[12] "Note that there are three differences between Mecca ginger and Colomban ginger: Mecca ginger has a darker bark, it is softer to cut with a knife, and is whiter inside that the other. It is also better and always more expensive" (*Menagier*, §272). In the fourteenth century, Italian merchants regularly distinguished between three types of ginger: *baladi*, the Arabic name for common ginger; *colombino*, ginger shipped from Columbum, or Kolam, a port in Travancore state in India (Madras); and *micchino*, which name indicated that the ginger was arriving on the European markets after passing through Mecca. See Colin Clair, *Of Herbs and Spices*, p. 61; Pegolotti, pp. 360 and 419; and the *Libre de conexenses de spicies*, ed. Miquel Gual Camarena, in the *Anuario de Estudios Medievales*, 1 (1964), p. 439.

[13] Grains of paradise is the name designating the spice which becomes one of the most commonly used in French cookery in the latter half of the fourteenth century. This is malagueta pepper, not a true pepper but the seeds of the plant *Amomum melegueta*, which belongs to the *Zingiberacea*, or ginger, family. Balducci Pegolotti writes of *meleghette* for grains of paradise (p. 422). While quite common in commerce in the fourteenth and fifteenth centuries, grains of paradise remained always very costly; only cloves, and occasionally mace, were more expensive a common commodity.

Of minor spices, that is, nutmeg (6 lbs), cloves (6 lbs), mace (6 lbs), galingale[14] (6 lbs); /14r/ thirty loaves of sugar[15], 25 lbs of saffron, six charges of almonds, one charge of rice, 30 lbs of starch[16], twelve *cabas* of candied[17] raisins, twelve *cabas* of good candied figs, twelve *cabas* of candied prunes, a *quintal* of dates 40 lbs of pinenuts, 18 lbs of Orchil lichen[18], 18 lbs of alkanet[19], 18 lbs of goldleaf and, yet furthermore, one

---

[14] "Galingale is a root, growing underground, rather heavy, its stem set within, its outer and inner color a dark russet, and tending to be odiferous and sharp to the tongue" (Pegolotti, p. 374).

[15] Sugar was normally sold in the solid loaves in which it was poured from the refining process and left to crystallize: see Pegolotti, pp. 362–365. On the making of sugar in the Middle Ages, see R.J. Forbes, *Historia de la técnica*, Mexico, 1958, p. 109; and Noel Deerr, *The History of Sugar*, 2 vols., London, 1949.

[16] The process used in the fifteenth century for the production of starch from wheat flour is described in an English recipe published by Austin, p. 112, in the *Liber cure cocorum*, p. 7, and in the *Noble Boke of Cookry*, p. 101. Much the same procedure was already well established in antiquity according to Pliny's *Natural History*, Vol. XVIII, Ch. xvii, p. 76 f.

[17] The use of sugar in the Middle Ages as a preservative for fruits and vegetables was a common practice. It had given rise to a whole industry, active particularly in the Iberian peninsula, specialized in such confectionery and in the art of preserving foods by this means. See, for example, the *Libre de totes maneres de confits*, ed. Luis Faraudo de Saint-Germain, "Un tratado manual cuatrocentista de arte de dulcería," in the *Boletín de la Academia de Buenas Letras de Barcelona*, 19 (1946), pp. 97–134.

[18] Orchil lichen (*tornesautz* in Chiquart) is used widely at this time as a source of a colorant for both foods and fabrics. The dye which this lichen yields (and which is used in modern litmus compounds) possesses the peculiar feature of varying its color according to the acidy or alkalinity of any substance with which it is mixed: the first will produce a red color, the second a blue.

[19] The nature of alkanet (*organites* in Chiquart) is described in the *Menagier de Paris*: "You should know that *arquenet* is a spice which gives a red color, just like galingale, and it should be soaked in wine and the meat bouillon, and then ground up" (§290).

lb of camphor[20], one hundred *aunes* [130 yds] of good, fine bolting-cloth: these things are solely for cooking purposes. Moreover, for the feast you need two hundred boxes of all sorts and colors of dragees[21] to garnish the dishes. And if the feast should last longer, additional materials should be available.

For the profit of the lord who is offering the feast, and to expedite its preparation as much as possible, /*14v*/ the abovementioned spices, in whatever generous amount is necessary for the feast, should be ground into powder, and each should be set aside in good big leather bags.

In order to do this feast as well as possible and without blame or fault, the Household Stewards, the Kitchen Squires, and the Chief Cook should meet to locate, inspect and organize good, adequate places to carry out the cooking activities. This space should be large enough that great double work-tables can be set up in such a way that the Kitchen Squires can move comfortably between the serving-tables and the work-tables, in order to pass the dishes on and to receive them back again.

There should be a provision of good big cauldrons to boil large cuts of meat, and a great number of moderate-sized ones for making pottages /*15r*/ and for other cooking operations, and great suspended

---

[20] For a description of the best camphor available in fifteenth-century commerce, see Pegolotti, p. 375.

[21] The term *dragiee* may designate a powdered mixture of sugar and spices, as in the *Menagier* (p. 183, l. 15 and n.). The word may also refer to this mixture in a candied form. Since Chiquart uses the word in the plural (folios 50r and 58v), it may be supposed that he is thinking of the piece of candy, a sort of lozenge. See Pegolotti, p. 414, and Victor D. Gay, *Glossaire archéologique du moyen âge et de la Renaissance*, s.v. *dragée*. Dragees were held to be good digestives by medieval physicians because sugar, being warm and moist by nature, complemented the human temperament and facilitated the stomach's task of assimilating food. See Magninus Mediolanensis, *Regimen sanitatis*, Part 2, Ch. 3, §26: "De confectionibus et earum usu"; and Castorina, *Farmaci*, §56.

The boxes which Chiquart mentions in this passage are probably *drageoires*, containers ceremonially used for the presentation of dragees. See this term in Cotgrave and Pegolotti.

pans for cooking fish and other things, and a great number of large and ordinary-sized boilers for pottages and other things, and a dozen good big mortars. Decide on the place where sauces will be prepared. And you will need some twenty large frying pans, a dozen great kettles, fifty pots, sixty two-handled pots, a hundred hampers, a dozen grills, six large graters, a hundred wooden spoons, twenty-five holed spoons, both large and small, six pot-hooks, twenty oven-shovels, twenty roasters, both those with turnable spits and those with spits mounted on andirons. You should not put your trust in wooden skewers or spits, because you could spoil all your meat, or even lose it; rather, you should have six score iron spits which are strong and thirteen feet long; and you need three dozen other spits which are just as long but not as thick, in order to roast poultry, piglets and water birds: *Si volucris verrat, qui torret eam procul errat; volucrem a torre procul de flumine torre.*[22] And besides this, /15v/ four dozen slender skewers for doing glazing and for fastening things.

You need two *boces* of vinegar, one white and the other claret[23], each of eight *sommes*; one good twenty-*some boce* of good verjuice; and a ten-*somme boce* of oil.[24]

---

[22] A somewhat less garbled version of this culinary dictum is found in Hans Walther, *Proverbia sententiaeque latinitatis medii aevi*, Göttingen, 1963–69; vol. 4, §29436:

Si volucris verrat, qui torret eam, procul errat;
Sed procul ab igne volucrem de flumine torre.

(If the bird is at home on the land, he who roasts it will go far; but if it is a water-bird, it should be roasted far from the fire.) The rule, a logical corollary of greco-arabic humoral theory, is broadly accepted at this time: "*Notandum quod grues, faszani, perdices atque columbe, meliori modo semper sunt preparandi, assandi et a remotis primo, et non in aqua, dequoquendi*" (*Tractatus*, Pt. II, §10).

[23] Chiquart does not seem to distinguish between these two types of vinegar in any of his recipes.

[24] This oil is likely to be olive oil. "*Oleum: quando simpliciter ponitur, de oleo olivae intelligitur*" (*Alphita*, p. 303).

You need one thousand cart-loads of good dry firewood, and a large barnful of coal; and you should always know where to get more so as not to run out.

So that the workers not be idle or lack anything, ample money should be assigned to the Kitchen Squires to get salt, ingredients and any other things which might be necessary for cooking—of which I shall make no mention at present. /*16r*/

For the sake of decency and cleanliness, and to speed the service as much as possible, you must have a great supply of dishes, of gold, silver, pewter and wood, that is to say, four thousand or more of them, in such quantity that when you have presented the first serving you will have enough for the second serving and still some left over; and in the meantime you can wash and clean the dishes used in that first serving.

Since at such a feast there may be very high, mighty, noble, venerable and honorable lords and ladies who will not eat meat, it is necessary to have similar amounts of sea-fish[25] and fresh-water fish[26], both fresh and salted, and these in as varied preparations as can be.

And because the dolphin /*16v*/ is king of all the other sea-fish, it will be put first, then congers, grey mullet, hake, sole, red mullet, John Dory, plaice, turbot, lobsters, tuna, sturgeon, salmon, sprats, sardines, sea-urchins, mussels, eels, bogues, ray, calamary, weever and anchovies;

---

[25] The Red Count, Amadeus VII, father of Chiquart's master, had bought the County of Nice in 1388 and had thereby incidentally assured his court of a broad variety of relatively fresh sea-fish.

[26] "Vers (1340) on avait établi au château (of Chambéry) un vivier dans lequel on avait eu soin de placer des carpes, des tanches et des brochets. ... Le comte (Amadeus VI) possédait encore un autre vivier, près de la route de Chambéry à Montmélian" (T. Chapperon, *Chambéry à la fin du XIVe siècle*, Paris (Dumoulin), 1863, p. 98). During the times between 1381 and 1430 when the court of Savoy was located at Ripaille, the account books show that the costs of fish for the table outstrip those for all other sorts of food. See specifically Bruchet, pp. 316-17; and, concerning the great role of fish in diets in general at this time, Massimo Montanari, *L'alimentazione contadina nell'alto Medioevo*, Naples (Liguori), 1979, pp. 277-95: "La pesca".

the eels, both fresh and salted.[27]

Of fresh-water fish: large trout, large eels, lampreys, filets of char, great pike filets, great carp filets, great perch, dace, pollacks, greylings, burbots, crayfish, and all other fish.[28]

Because there are at this feast a few great lords or ladies, as was mentioned before, who will have with them their Chief Cook whom they will order to arrange and cook particular /17r/ things for them, that Chief Cook should have supplied and dispensed to him, quickly, fully, generously and cheerfully, anything he may ask for or that may be necessary for his lord or lady, or for the both of them, so that he may serve them as he should.

In addition, you must have six score *quintals* [3600 lbs] of fine cheese;

six hundred *aunes* [750 yds] of good, fine white cloth to cover the serving tables and the fish, meat and roasts; sixty *aunes* [75 yds] of linen to make the strainers for jellies; and enough fine white sheeting to make a dozen strainers similar in nature to a hippocras strainer.

You need two large two-handed knives to cut up the oxen, /17v/ a dozen dressing knives for dressing, and two dozen knives for cutting up ingredients for pottages and for stuffings, and to prepare poultry and fish;

and, as well, a half-dozen rasps to clean the work-tables and the chopping blocks, a hundred baskets for carrying meat to the pots and vats — both raw meat and cooked meat that is being borne to or from

---

[27] The phrase *tant freis que salés* which concludes the paragraph may well be intended to qualify the entire list of sea-fish: such fish, when they could not be transported live in large tanks of sea-water, often reached inland kitchens in salted condition. If this is what is intended here, either Chiquart or Jehan de Dudens has repeated the mention of "eels", and has omitted herrings from this list of sea-fish.

[28] This list curiously omits any explicit mention of the tench, which will prove to be one of the most useful fishes specified by Chiquart's recipes. See the study of G. de Gislain, "Le rôle des étangs dans l'alimentation médiévale," *Manger et boire au moyen âge*, Vol. 2, pp. 89–101.

the work-tables; and also to carry coal for roasts and for whatever other purpose; and also to carry and to gather the dishes.

If it should happen that the feast is held in winter, each night for cooking you will need sixty torches, twenty lbs of tallow candle, and sixty lbs of suet tapers to inspect the butchery, the pastry kitchen, the fish kitchen, and all of the activities of the kitchen. /18r/

And, as for the pastry kitchen you must have a good big room as close as possible to the kitchen to hold two good big ovens for baking meat- and fish-pies, tarts, flans, custards and *ratons*[29], and all other things that are necessary in cooking.

And for this the workers should be supplied with thirty *sommes* [3600 lbs] of fine flour for the abovementioned purposes, and they should be sure of being able to get more if the feast should last longer.

Since by the pleasure of the blessed Hóly Trinity, which unfailingly grants us freely of everything, we shall have good, fine, great provisions to do our feast in grand fashion, we must get /18v/ Chief Cooks and workers who will make the dishes and *entremets* for that feast; and if it should turn out that these cooks and workers are not available, send someone to look for some in places where they can be found, so that the feast can be done in a grand and honorable fashion.

Now that we have the chief workers that we need for the feast, it remains to organize them, which ones will be handling meats and which fish. And let them be well instructed on how to make fish dishes of colors similar to those of the meat dishes for each serving, as will be explained.

And let us take as the first serving the gross meats, that is to say, beef and mutton; and those who cut up the oxen should make good, /19r/ big, royal pieces, and those who cut up the sheep should slice the length of the sheep without removing anything but a little of the neck.

---

[29] All of these last items are varieties of pies or pasties. The *ratons* appear in a censure of gluttony by Nicole de la Chesnaye, *Condamnation de Banquet*, in which they typify a decadently luxurious desert. English recipes for *rastons* are found in Austin, pp. 52 and 98. Cotgrave describes them as "a fashion of round, and high Tart, made of butter, egges, and cheese".

To serve those pieces of beef and mutton, they should be put on a great gold plate without anything else.

And on another great plate should be served, alongside, the salt dish depending on the season of the year: that is, in winter, loin of pork, sausages, and salt pork ribs. And for this first serving, the puree of greens; and no other sauce is needed but Mustard.[30]

With this should be served a White Broth of Capons, together with the meat with which is eaten. /19v/

1. For this, to instruct you on the elaboration of that White Broth, as it should be made[31], you take good capons, and clean that meat well which is to be eaten—whether it is pork or kid or veal, or whatever meat is suitable—and cook it thoroughly in cauldrons big enough for whatever amount you need of it; and add in a little parboiled lean pork, which has

---

[30] According to Chapperon (p. 367, n. 1), Chambéry mustard was well known in the Middle Ages.

[31] The Blanc brouet de chappons outlined in the *Viandier* is somewhat different from what Chiquart's recipe makes. Taillevent relies to a greater extent upon spices, adding in cinnamon, cloves, galingale and long pepper, along with the ginger and grains of paradise to which Chiquart restricts himself. Furthermore, the earlier version is thicker, specifying the admixture of both chicken liver and egg yolks, two of the standard thickeners, where normally in such broths only one of several possible thickeners is considered adequate; and less sweet, since there is no mention of the sugar which Chiquart includes. It may be noted in passing that sugar is called for in many of Chiquart's dishes, dishes for which the oldest recipes in the *Viandier* rarely list sugar among the ingredients. Only in the recipes for their sickdishes do the fourteenth-century French collections make significant use of sugar, this being done because the warm and moist properties of sugar made it eminently appropriate to restore a healthy balance to body humors.

Concerning the genre of dish known as a *brouet*, or "broth", and the distinction made between this and a *potaige*, or "pottage", see Jean-Louis Flandrin, "Brouets, potages et bouillons," in *Médiévales*, 5 (1983), pp. 5–14; and Liliane Plouvier, "Cuisine: et le potage fut ... ," in *L'Histoire*, 64 (Feb., 1984), pp. 79–81.

previously been thoroughly cleaned. According to the quantity of the pottage you want to make, take a large quantity of almonds, peel, wash and grind them; for this grinding, use the bouillon from the capons to moisten them. When your capons are cooked, as well as the meat which is with them, set the capons off to one side and the meat to another; and, according to how much meat there is, strain some of the bouillon into a properly sized clean pot, then take good white wine and verjuice and add this in, to the amount of the bouillon you have, /*20r*/ with white ginger and grains of paradise in proportionate amounts, and these should be strained through the filter used for the almonds. According to the amount of the broth, take the vessel—that is, the good clean cauldron or boiler—to boil it and, according to the quantity of the broth, add in sugar to boil with it. Check that it is salted neither too much nor too little. Then take your meat and set it out in your dishes, with your broth over top.

2. Next, a German Broth[32]: to instruct the person who is to make it, depending on the quantity he is to make of it let him take his capons, prepare them cleanly and cut them into quarters; then, according to the quantity of that pottage he has been charged to make, he should take the meat in an amount proportionate to the poultry, just as in the other pottage, either pork, lamb, kid or veal, /*20v*/ and this meat should be cut up to the size of the quartered poultry. And for this take a quantity of onions according to the amount of meat you will be making, and cut them up very small; and take the fat of bacon and melt it fully, and put the amount of meat you have in either good, clean cauldrons or boilers, and then put your onions and the fat around your meat and fry all of it together. Depending on the amount of your meat, get a quantity of almonds and clean them so that there are no bits of shell left, and

---

[32] The *Brouet d'Allemagne* is one of the most commonly known dishes in late-medieval French and English cookery. See very similar recipes for it in the *Viandier*, p. 83; the *Menagier*, §108; the *Recueil*, §1; Meyer, §15; the *Forme of Cury*, §47; the *Liber cure cocorum*, p. 11; and Austin, p. 19. The character of the broth is determined by the combination of fried onions, pork fat, almonds and a variety of spices.

wash them in good hot water; then have them ground without peeling the skin off them, and moisten them with beef bouillon; then take a good two-handled pot and, with beef bouillon, strain the amount that you want to make of it; and check that it is not too salty. Then take good white wine and verjuice in an amount suitable for the quantity of the broth /21r/ and add them in, together with white ginger, grains of paradise, pepper—and not too much of it[33], nutmegs, and all the lesser spices like cloves and mace, and some saffron to give it color; and use all of these spices judiciously. Once they have been ground, put them into your broth, and pour this broth over your fried meat, together with a large amount of sugar appropriate for the quantity of the broth. When everything is together, taste it to see whether there is too much or too little of anything so that you can correct this, and taste it too for saltiness. And be careful about the meat that it does not cook too much, because kid and veal are more tender than poultry. When your meat is cooked just right and it is time to serve it up, put it to one side and set it out in dishes, and then pour the broth over top of it.

3. Next, /21v/ another pottage, that is, a Savoy Broth[34]: to instruct the

---

[33] Chiquart is always very careful in his use of pepper; cf. similar *caveats* at folios 27r, 28r, 34v, 36r and 37r. It may be surmised that for Chiquart, the more delicate-flavored grains of paradise, for which he appears to show some predilection, had effectively replaced the strong taste of pepper which had perhaps become considered to be rather vulgar. In this regard it is interesting also to observe that Chiquart never specifies white, black or long pepper, varieties which are distinguished quite clearly in other cookery manuals of the period. By "pepper" Chiquart implies black pepper alone.

[34] A recipe for a *Brouet de Savoye* is included in the *Menagier de Paris* (§110), but the dish is not mentioned in the *Viandier*. According to both the *Menagier* and the *Recueil* (§8), both chicken liver and bread should be used to ensure that the liquids in this broth bind. The sixteenth-century recipe book, the *Fleur de toute cuisine* (edited by Pierre Pidoux, Paris, 1548), continues to reproduce much the same recipe for Savoy Broth as had been followed in the earlier period. For the *Recueil* the meat to be served under this broth, apart from the chicken, is either veal or pork.

person who will be charged with making this broth, he should take his poultry and meat in the quantity which he will be ordered to make; and he should prepare his poultry and set it to cook cleanly, and the meat in the quantity he is ordered to make of the pottage, and set it to boil with his poultry; then he should get a good piece of lean bacon, a good cut of it, clean it well and properly, and set it to cook with the poultry and the meat. Then get sage, parsley, hyssop and marjoram; they should be thoroughly washed and cleaned, and a *bouquet garni* should be made of them without chopping them up, and put them in to boil with the pottage and with the meat; and, depending on the amount of the broth, take a large amount of cleaned and washed parsley and grind it well and properly in the mortar[35]; and when /*22r*/ it is ground, check your meat to see that it is neither over- nor under-cooked and neither over- nor under-salted; then, depending on the quantity of the broth, get an amount of white ginger, grains of paradise and a little pepper, and set enough bread to soak in the broth that it will bind it; and when it has soaked properly, grind and crush the bread with the parsley and spices, and take it and strain it with the broth. Put in wine and verjuice in the necessary amount. And of all these things just mentioned use just the proper amount, so that there is neither too little nor too much. Then, when this is done, put it to boil in a great, good, clean boiler. Should it turn out that the pottage is too green, add in a little saffron and it will be on the light-green side.[36] And when it is time to serve, /*22v*/ set out your meat in dishes with that broth poured over the top.

4. Next, a Lamprey Sauce on loin of beef.[37] He who is charged with making this sauce should take his fat loins of beef and should wash them

---

[35] One of the distinguishing features of Savoy Broth is its green color.

[36] The color, in Chiquart and elsewhere in medieval French cookery, is *verd gay*. This leaf-green, or bright green, is most commonly produced by combining parsley (with or without sage) and saffron (with or without egg yolks). In English cookery of the period the color is known as "gawdy grene".

[37] This so-called *Saulce lampree de lomblos de beuf*, does not, as is obvious, contain any lampreys. (Cf. as well the *Arbaleste de poisson* (§24) which is the lean counterpart of this recipe.) The name comes not from an ingredient but from the principal use of this sauce, as is seen in Recipe 42 where the basic

carefully and mount them on good clean spits. Then he should take his bread and cut it in round slices and roast it on the grill until it is thoroughly toasted, and get a good big two-handled pot there in which to put the toasted bread. He should have a barrel of very good red wine—and if one is not enough he should get two—and put his bread into it. He should taste the beef bouillon to see that it is good and mild, and put the necessary amount of lean bouillon[38] into the bread, and add in red vinegar very carefully—and not too much, so that if necessary he could put in more. Then he should get his powdered cinnamon, /*23r*/ white vinger, grains of paradise, pepper, nutmeg, galingale, cloves, mace and all other spices, and mix them with that bread and strain everything very well. And see that you have enough good clean cauldrons and kettles to boil the quantity of the sauce you have made. And those loins of beef, when they have roasted as much as they should, take them and cut them up into decent small chunks[39] and put them to boil in the sauce. When everything has boiled together, set it all out in good dishes, that is, with two chunks to a dish and with that sauce over top.

Next, after that, well made pasties of fat beef: the pastry chefs should be careful to get fat loins of beef and to tell the person who will be cutting up the ox to set aside all of the beef marrow /*23v*/ to put it with the loins of beef which are to be served to the lord.

---

recipe which we find here in a meat dish is repeated for use on lampreys.

[38] According to the *Viandier*, a *brouet maigre* is obtained by skimming the greasy scum off the surface of a bouillon. See the recipe for *Toumeaux de beuf* in the version of the *Viandier* which is now in the Bibliothèque Mazarine and was published by Pichon and Vicaire at p. 40 of their edition.

[39] The cook had always to keep in mind that the person eating this meat would want to be able to put each piece into his mouth with his fingers, as a single bite, without having to cut it or to tear at it gracelessly with his teeth. The *Forme of Cury* refers to such decent-sized chunks of meat by the descriptive French term "gobbets". The French books of table manners (for example the *Contenances de Table* ed. by S. Glixelli, *Romania*, 47 (1921), pp. 1-40) inveigh at length against the unpardonable social sin of stuffing one's mouth too full. (See also the English *Stans Puer ad Mensem*, ed. by Edith Rickert in Frederick J. Furnivall, *The Babees' Book*, London, 1868, pp. 26-31.

For serving the household[40], use legs of beef in such great quantity that there is enough for everyone. And the pastry chefs should be canny and careful enough to season their salt with spices, so that it is not too salty.

5. Next, as an *entremets*, Boars' Heads, glazed and emblazoned and breathing fire[41], and for this it is necessary to instruct the person or persons who are charged with working on this thing, and I shall tell them how to do it. When they have their boars' heads prepared, singed and thoroughly washed and cleaned, they should open the animals' jaws and set a piece of stick in each one to keep it open, and then /24r/ put them into big, good clean cauldrons to cook in water and wine with a good amount of salt. And take the two forelegs of the boar and clean them properly and put them to cook with those heads—and do not let them cook too much.

6. To begin the glazing, you need a great quantity of eggs, depending on the number of boars' heads there are; and to instruct the person who will be making these things, he should have a great quantity of wheat flour, and a lot of parsley which is clean and ready to be ground up; and you need to separate the eggs, putting the whites off to one side and

---

[40] In the original text, the phrase is *pour le commun*. The meals served to the mass of servitors at a court benefit to some extent from what is planned for the their masters, but lose out on the more dainty and tasty ingredients such as the beef marrow of the previous paragraph.

[41] *Hures de sengliers dorees et armees et embanderees et gictans feu.* The name of this impressive preparation can be compared with the English Bores hedys enarmyd which appears in the Menus 3, 5, 7 and 9 published by Hieatt and Butler (pp. 40-41). A flaming dish has constituted a *pièce de résistance* in gastronomic circles for a long time, it seems. Chiquart will resort to a multiple of the same device in his second *entremets*, which follows the second serving at this same meal and affords a delightful punctuation for it. For its part the boar's head, fire-breathing or not, enjoyed a choice position among several standard *entremets* at this time. Chiquart's use of it may have something to do with this animal's ubiquity in the wild hills of Savoy, and to the respect it had undoubtedly earned from noble hunters.

the yolks to another, and they should be raw. To make a green color, take a great amount of parsley which has been cleaned well, washed and drained, and it should be firmly ground and then mixed together with the egg whites and wheat flour; when all this has been mixed thoroughly together, strain it neatly /*24v*/ and properly into a good big bucket. For the gold color, that wheat flour is mixed with the egg yolks, also with whole eggs to thin out the mixture; and saffron powder is added in, but carefully so that it is not too much on the russet side. Mix and strain this well, as is said above for the other color, into a good clean bucket. When the boars' heads are cooked—but not so well done that the meat is falling off the bones—and the feet as well, remove them from the cauldrons and set them to drain on good wooden work-tables. When this is done, take your heads and put them properly on spits, then take the two forelegs of the boar and set out and glaze each head, placing the feet closely and properly on each side of those heads, down below the ears; they should be placed and fixed adroitly with good /*25r*/ skewers; and, when this is done, they should be set to roast until the skin is slightly on the crisp side. After that, take your green and yellow colors and put the green color on one part of each head and on the other part put the yellow color, then put them to drain properly by themselves until they are as drained and dry as they should be; and care should be taken that they are not given too much heat, so that the glazing does not darken. Then they are taken down and removed from the spits and set on good, immaculately clean work-tables to dry, and afterwards seek out painters in order to gild those heads with gold leaf.[42]

To instruct the master cook who will have the charge of those heads, to make them give out and breathe fire by their mouths, take /*25v*/ a double-wicked wax candle and wrap it around with cotton which

---

[42] At Amadeus's court, it appears to have been a reserved privilege for painters to apply the gold or silver coloring used to decorate any dishes prepared in the kitchen. When the *Viandier* directs the cook on how to dress his stuffed chicken with sheets of beaten gold, he says: "You must take the sheet of gold or silver and wrap them around the fowl, and you need a little egg white to moisten them so that the sheet will adhere better" (p. 121; cf. pp. 122 and 128).

has been moistened in alcohol in which a little camphor has been dissolved.[43]

And because things should be done so honorably as to be to the honor of the lord and the chief workers, the Master Cook should ask the heralds to inquire of their lord who will be at that feast to find out what arms each of them has, so that those arms can be put on banners, in order to set on each Boar's Head the banner of the lord in front of whom it will be placed.[44]

For the second serving, roasts of all sorts for serving honorably at a royal table such persons as kings, queens, dukes, duchesses, and similar powerful, noble and venerable lords as were mentioned above. /26r/

For the most honorable service, great roasts must be served by themselves: to wit, a whole goat-kid, a whole piglet, a great loin of veal, a great loin of pork, and shoulders of mutton set on a great golden platter.

Afterwards, poultry set on a great golden platter: to wit, fat goslings, grain-fed capons, pheasants, partridge, rabbits, doves and herons; of these, some of each should be set out in such great quantity that the platter should be quite full and heaped high. And make sure of the saucing for this roast service, which will be: for the goslings and grain-fed capons, Jance; for the pheasants, partridge, piglets and rabbits, Camelin[45]; for the roast kids, Green Verjuice Sauce; for the fat

---

[43] Among the recipes added in the fifteenth century to the end of the *Viandier* there is one for an *entremets* consisting of a papier maché lion which will breathe fire. Its tongue and maw are to be of white metal, and the author writes, "Insert camphor and a little cotton in there and, when it is time to serve this in front of the lords, set fire to it" (p. 136). The candle's wick supplied by Chiquart amounts to a slight refinement over the *Viandier*'s procedure.

[44] We find the same care, and means, to flatter the noble guests' vanity at the point of serving Recipe 21, the Parmesan Pies, folio 48r.

[45] The ingredients of Cameline sauce (see Recipe 44, below) make it a temperately warm and dry sauce appropriate for such temperate meats as those of pheasant, partridge, suckling pig and rabbit. Later we shall see Cameline sauce used on veal—the most desirable of meats according to many Greek and

pork, Saupiquet; and for the doves, fine salt. /*26v*/

Moreover, frumenty[46], venison[47], pies, talmouses[48], cream flans[49], Camelin Broth, a Hare Civet[50], a Pink Broth, a party White-Dish in four colors all together; and, as *entremets*, a raised castle in the middle

---

medieval physicians, because of its moderate warmth and moisture; and upon salmon and trout — these fish being likewise highly esteemed because of their relatively temperate natural qualities.

[46] Frumenty or furmety, *fromentee* in French, is a relatively simple porridge made from the cream of wheat, combined with milk, egg yolks and ginger. Both the *Viandier* (at pp. 15 and 92) and the *Menagier de Paris* (at §234) provide detailed recipes for its preparation. So common was this dish in the cookery of the time that it served as a standard when cooks wished to describe a particular shade of yellow or a particular consistency, both of which were quickly recognizable in frumenty. See the *Viandier*, pp. 178 and 186.

[47] These two dishes, frumenty and venison, normally form a pair on dining tables: see, for example, Austin, pp. 14 and 91, "Venysoun with Furment". In the *Viandier*'s recipe for *Fromentee* the bouillon in which the venison has been cooked enters expressly into the making of the frumenty (pp. 16 and 92), while the *Menagier* specifies that on lean days this bouillon should be replaced with almond milk. Cf. also the *Recueil*, §11.

[48] A Talmouse is defined by Cotgrave as "A Cheese-cake; a Tart, or cake made of egges, and cheese". In the fifteenth-century printed edition of the *Viandier* a recipe for a Talmouse reads: "Made from fine cheese cut up into squares the size of beans, mixed thoroughly with a generous quantity of eggs; the crust is (flour) moistened in eggs and butter" (ed. Pichon and Vicaire, p. 173).

[49] Cf. the recipe for Almond-Milk Flans (§28), below. In the *Libre de sent soví* (§156: *Let molt bona al fforn*) there is a preparation which its Catalan author calls "similar to flans" and which consists of milk, eggs, butter, spices and saffron. There is some similarity also between Chiquart's dish and the *Torta di latte* found in the *LVII Ricette*, §6. For the author of the *Menagier*, cream flans constitute part of the *issue* or dessert of a meal (p. 179, l. 36).

[50] One of the most common medieval dishes is Hare Stew. For very similar examples of its preparation in France, see the *Viandier*, p. 29, the *Menagier*, §116, and the *Recueil*, §10.

of which is the Fountain of Love.

7. To instruct him who is to make the Camelin Broth[51], he should take his poultry and the meat—whether it is pork or kid or veal or lamb—in the quantity he is ordered to prepare, and set it to cook well and properly in good clean bright cauldrons or kettles, together with a good big piece of fat salt pork which has been previously cleaned, washed and singed.[52] Then arrange to have a large quantity of almonds, a quantity adequate for the amount of the broth you are ordered to make, and clean them thoroughly of any bits of shells and /*27r*/ of anything else that might be among them, and wash them energetically in good hot water, as was said above for the German broth[53], and grind them up properly without removing their skins, and moisten them with the

---

[51] A similar recipe for Camelin Broth was already copied in both the *Viandier* (p. 81) and the *Menagier* (§102); in these versions there are fewer spices and no sugar. In both of these earlier collections, the name of the dish, Cinnamon Broth (*Brouet de canelle*), recognizes the importance of the principal ingredient, whereas Chiquart adopts a name, here as elsewhere in his work, which identifies the dish by its color. The adjective *camelin* is a derivative of the word camel: camel-colored, dun or light-brown. (See note 132, below.) The scribe responsible for the copy which we possess of the *Recueil* wrote *Brouet hamelin* (Recipe §3).

Camelin Broth is clearly related to Camelin Sauce (see Recipe 44, below), but is different in its culinary and gastronomic functions. A broth is a liquid concoction of a relatively thin consistency; it is primarily a cooking medium which imparts its flavor to the meat which is broken or cut up into it. A sauce, however, is normally prepared apart from the meat it will dress, and may be either boiled or unboiled, either hot or cold; it is relatively thick and is served either separately—in a bowl into which the meat is dipped—or poured over the meat as a garnish.

[52] The recipe for *Menus oysiaux* in the *Viandier* (p. 12) reads, "(The small birds are) plucked dry, singed and mounted on the spit." The singeing removes any fine down which still remains after the fowl are plucked.

[53] *Broet d'Alamany*, Recipe §2; the reference is to an instruction on folio 20v, above.

bouillon of that meat. Then you should watch carefully that your meat be neither under- nor over-cooked. Then take your spices, that is to say, a great deal of cinnamon, and white ginger, grains of paradise, not so much pepper that it comes through, galingale, mace, cloves and nutmeg. And when your meat is cooked, take it out and put it in good clean two-handled pots; then take your bouillon and strain it carefully into the good clean two-handled pots. Then draw out your almonds and spices and, when this has been done, put enough wine and verjuice into your broth to give it /27v/ a good taste; and always take care that there is never too much nor too little salt, or anything else. Then set it to boil in good clean cauldrons or kettles in which it has room to boil, and add in a large amount of sugar proportionate to the amount of the broth you have. When this is done, to dish it up take your meat and set it in good dishes with the broth over top.

8. To make the Pink Broth[54], the person who is charged with making it should make sure he has enough meat for the quantity that is wanted of the dish; he should take his meat and set it to cook neatly. According to the amount of the meat he should have a quantity of almonds which are well skinned and cleaned, and grind them up strongly; /28r/ and when the meat is cooked, put it in good two-handled pots and strain the bouillon carefully into other good two-handled pots. Then get good white ginger, grains of paradise and a little pepper, and strain your almonds and spices with the bouillon, and add in whatever wine and verjuice is needed; then set this broth to boil in a clean cauldron or kettle large enough to hold it, and be very careful that of all these things there is neither too little nor too much. When your broth has boiled, take a good big frying pan which is very clean, and put very good clear oil into it and heat it up hot; when it is very hot and boiling, throw in

---

[54] Both the *Viandier* and the *Menagier* contain recipes for a Pink Broth (at p. 82 and §104, respectively); but the version of the *Viandier* which was copied in the fifteenth century and which is now in the Vatican Library also contains, in a section of recipes added close to the time of its copying, a *Rozé a chair* (Pink Dish for Meat Days, at p. 117) which is almost identical to that of Chiquart's recipe. See also the *Rosee* in Meyer, §12.

some good alkanet[55] which has been cleaned well, and cook it and take it out at the right time, then strain it neatly /*28v*/ through a layer of bolting cloth into good dishes, and put it into your broth in just the right amount so that the color of the broth is more pinkish than reddish. And when it is to be served, set out your meat in good dishes and then put that broth over the top.

9. Furthermore, for a Party White-Dish[56] in four colors all together, that is to say, of gold, blue, red and silver[57]; and to explain this preparation to

---

[55] In the *Viandier*'s *Rozé a chair*, *orcanet* is an alternative option for *tornesoc* (see Chiquart's *tornesaut*, "orchil lichen", in the next recipe). According to the *Viandier*, either of these additives will yield a pink color, and alkanet is just as usable as the orchil lichen, "if you can get it," but the color which alkanet produces is not so bright. It is interesting that neither of these colorants is mentioned in the *Menagier*, nor in those parts of the *Viandier* which antedate the Vatican Library version.

[56] The White-Dish, its name translated into a variety of equivalent forms across Europe, remains one of the oldest and most common preparations on the medieval table. Recipes for it are found in virtually every collection: for instance, in the *Enseignements*, l. 119; the *Libro della cocina*, p. 38; the *Libro per cuoco*, p. 64; and the *Libre de sent soví*, pp. 49 and 50. Based on almonds, which are considered by physicians to possess natural characteristics of warmth and moisture closely approximating those of humans (see Aldobrandino, p. 154), the White-Dish is universally employed as a food which can be consumed safely and beneficially by a sick person. As a sickdish it is frequently reinforced with the addition of chicken, a meat which shares in the same temperately warm and moist qualities (see, for example, the *Viandier*, p. 101).

At the origin of the *Blanc mangier*, the epithet *blanc* may well have been the word *blant*, designating a dish whose blandness made it readily digestible. With such regular ingredients as the dark meat from chickens and grains of paradise, it is a little difficult to understand otherwise how such a name as *Blanc mengier* could have been coined and retained by the earliest cooks.

[57] As well as for its *Blanc mengier pour malades* (pp. 25 and 101), the *Viandier* offers a recipe for a *Blanc mengier parti*, or Party White Dish among those additions made to it in the fifteenth century (p. 122). The colors pre-

the person who is to make it, he should take a great quantity of almonds and have them skinned neatly and have them ground and moistened with beef or mutton bouillon. Then take beef and mutton bouillon, equal quantities of each, being careful about the salt, and strain it /29r/ into a two-handled pot or ordinary pot, depending on the amount of that broth you want to divide into colors, and put white ginger powder into that bouillon; then draw out your almonds with that bouillon and make milk of them, and split this milk among four good clean, bright kettles, so that there is the same amount in each, then set them to warm on glowing coals.[58]

After that, take a large amount of starch, wash it well and properly, then put it in a dish as a binding for the kettles, and into it add some of the broth from the kettle you wish to bind, and strain it through a good cloth; then put it liberally into that kettle until you see that it is bound good and thick, so that when one mixture is set out alongside another in a dish the one will not run into the other at all; and you do the same with all four of the kettles. /29v/

To make the gold white-dish, soak saffron in a little bouillon, then mix it gently into your pot, beating and stirring it firmly; and be careful not to have too much, and that it be bound good and stiff.

To make the red white-dish, take a good clean frying pan and put good clean oil into it and heat it up and clarify it; then put quite a

---

pared here are red, blue, green and yellow.

[58] At this point in his directions Chiquart says that each of the four containers of almond milk is to be set on *gractons de feu de charbons* in order to warm up (or, perhaps, to keep warm). The sense of the word *gractons* poses a problem, but the term seems to indicate some sort of metal basket in which live coals could be placed and upon which a dish or pot could be set in order to be warmed gently. Such kitchen articles did exist: see Victor Gay, *Glossaire archéologique*, Vol. 1, p. 349b; and Raymond Lecoq, *Les Objets de la vie domestique*, p. 62. Marguerite Gonon reproduces a list of kitchen utensils in Latin which includes, *conchiam, gratuneum, de doliis* (*La Vie quotidienne en Lyonnais d'après des testaments des XIVe-XVIe siècles*, p. 164. The Old High German *cretto* (modern German *grette*), "basket", is suggestive here and may be at the origin of Chiquart's word.

large amount of alkanet into it, and check that it is good and clean, and boil it, though not too much. When this done, pass that oil through a corner of the bolting cloth and then put some of the oil into the kettle you wish to make red, and put it in very carefully, beating thoroughly and strongly; and watch that there is not too much of it. /30r/

To make the blue preparation, take a large amount of orchil lichen[59] and put it to soak in the milk of the pot in which the blue is to be made, then strain it finely through a good cloth; then put it into the kettle that has that broth. And take your starch and strain it thoroughly with that broth and stir the starch into the broth so that it binds good and thick.

And for the fourth white-dish, the one with the silver color, take your starch and soak it in the broth of the right kettle, and it should be well strained and put with the broth in the right kettle; and this should be beaten well and strongly, and it should be bound in the same way as was said for the others above.

10. For a raised *entremets* /30v/, that is, a castle[60], you need for its base a good big four-man litter, and in that litter you need four towers set at

---

[59] The lichen which is called Orchil, *Gozophora tinctoria* is naturally blue in color, but turns red under the influence of acids and blue under the influence of alkalis. This variable nature made *tornesaut*, as Chiquart calls it, particularly valuable to medieval cooks as a colorant, though obviously a user had to be aware of the likely effect of its addition to any given preparation. Here in the White-Dish, the ingredients into which the Orchil is mixed are sufficiently alkaline to ensure that that color produced will be blue. The *Viandier* likewise uses Orchil to make the blue White-Dish, but specifies Orchil to give the color to its Pink Dish which contains wine and verjuice.

[60] This sort of elaborate *entremets* is not unknown in the fourteenth century. Indeed this very subject, in a rather simpler version, was treated in the English *Forme of Cury* (about 1390): under the title "Chastletes", the text of Recipe 189 of that collection (IV, §197 in the Hieatt and Butler edition) describes a castle with five towers made of pastry and packed with various stuffings. At the beginning of the fifteenth century the *Viandier* (Vatican Library version) presents an *entremets de paintrerie*, that is, a "painted", artificial construction, consisting of a tower whose wooden frame is covered with

each corner of it, each and every tower to be fortified with breteches and machicolations. In every tower there must be archers and crossbowmen to defend that fortress, and furthermore in every tower there will be a candle or torch to give light. They will support branches bearing flowers and fruits of every sort of tree, and upon those branches will be birds of every variety. In the courtyard at the foot of each tower there will be: in one of the towers, a boar's head, armed and glazed, breathing fire; in another one, a large pike, and this pike will be cooked in three ways[61] — the one-third at the tail, fried, the one-third in the middle, boiled, and the one-third at the head, roasted /*31r*/ on the grill; and this pike will be set up at the foot of the second tower looking out on the fire-breathing animal.[62] (Now you must consider the saucing with which that pike

---

fabric painted to resemble masonry (p. 133).

    Chiquart's contribution to the genre remains one of the most complex and impressive of all the creations of which we have any record. Amadeus seems to have loved dramatic spectacles of various sorts (see Cognasso, Vol. I, pp. 123-4). Of the various *entremets* which his kitchen staff were called upon to help produce, we possess two further pieces of historical evidence: in February of 1433 the arrival in Chambéry of Anne of Cyprus, wife of Prince Louis of Savoy, was feted with a banquet which featured an *entremets*; and from August of 1442 there date two very precious documents detailing the expenses involved in a *mumrie* and *entremets* arranged to welcome the visit of Charles I, Duke of Bourbon. (For the first, see Bruchet, *Le Château de Ripaille*, pp. 164-5; for the second, see Edmunds, *New Light on Bapteur and Lamy*, §§54 and 55, at pp. 529-34. In this latter work the documentation of the expenses involved in a Savoyard *entremets* is extensively detailed.) A general survey of the function and nature of the noble *entremets* at this time is included in the study of Agathe Lafortune-Martel, *Fête noble en Bourgogne*.

[61] See Eberhard, §17: "*Dreyerlej essens an einem visch*". It is the same fish, a pike (*ein hecht*), which is dealt with in the *Kochbuch*, in exactly the same ways as Chiquart proposes.

[62] Each of the four towers of the castle contains a preparation — a boar, a pike, a piglet and a swan — which would normally constitute an adequate *entremets* by itself alone. On folios 109r-112r, which contain the menu of the

should be eaten, and that is, the fried with oranges[63], the boiled with a good Green Sauce sharpened with a little vinegar[64], and the roasted pike should be eaten with Green Verjuice Sauce which is made with sorrel[65].) At the foot of the next tower, a glazed piglet looking out and breathing fire; and at the foot of the last tower a skinned and redressed swan[66], likewise breathing fire. In the centre of the courtyard among the four

---

lean banquet offered to the Duke of Burgundy, this Pike Cooked in Three Ways is the *entremets* which concludes the first serving of the dinner.

[63] This garnish is used again on folios 109v and 113r. Later, on folio 56v, another fish, sole, will be served with orange verjuice (*verjust de orenges*): this latter sauce, if not simply plain orange juice, would be a mixture based upon orange juice.

[64] Green Sauce (which appears again on folios 56v and 109v) is one of the most common in medieval kitchens.

[65] Magninus Mediolanensis uses *succum acedule viridis* only on capons and on pheasants in his *Opusculum de saporibus* (ed. cit., p. 189).

[66] The procedure seems to be quite well known among court cooks by the fifteenth century: Chiquart does not feel obliged to provide detailed, step-by-step instructions for the operation. The skin of the bird, with its feathers and with or without its appendages, is carefully removed before the bird is roasted, by inserting a hollow straw between the flesh and the skin and, by inflating this, separating the skin from the fowl's body; then when the carcass is cooked and ready for eating, it can be "redressed" and the whole bird served in all its original glory. (See the *Viandier* for the directions for the operation, pp. 19, 75, 94, 130 and 131.) At this point in Chiquart's *entremets* it is a swan which undergoes this treatment; a little later it will also be a peacock.

In other recipe collections other animals and fish are subjected to much the same skinning and redressing treatment, though often the original skin is merely stuffed with a meat or fish paste: see, for example, the stuffed eel (*Anguilla rinvestita*) described in the *LVII Ricette*, §50, for which a carefully removed eel's skin is stuffed with a mixture of minced eel, tench and herbs.

towers a Fountain of Love[67], from which fountain rosewater[68] and mulled wine[69] should gush through a spout; over that fountain should be set

---

[67] The fountain which has the capacity of instilling love in the heart of the person who drinks from it is a perennial motif in courtly literature of the Middle Ages. Only two or three generations before Chiquart, the eminent poet Guillaume de Machaut had elaborated an entire narrative poem, the *Dit de la fontaine amoureuse* (c. 1361), on this theme. Amadeus himself had had one of his private chambers decorated with tapestries, bed-hangings and carpets which worked variations on the same theme; the room became known as "*la chambre aux fonteines du Dieu d'Amour*" (see Cognasso, Vol. 1, p. 79). Perpetually flowing drinking-fountains, which could be fed with any beverage, were in use from the thirteenth century on and their mechanisms had become relatively refined by the fifteenth (see Lebault, p. 409).

[68] Rosewater had initially a medical and cosmetic function, and only more recently a culinary use and gastronomic value. Generally by the fifteenth century "rose water" is understood to be a distillate of an infusion of roses and water: "*Alembicum, id est vas distillatorium, ut in quo fit aqua rosata et aqua ardens et coetera*" (*Alphita*, p. 273). In the *Menagier de Paris*, however, the recipes for rosewater (§§326–9) make no mention of distilling the liquid. See also Charles Joret, *La Rose dans l'antiquité et au moyen âge*, pp. 461–77; and Wilson, Vol. II, pp. 21–3.

[69] The drink known as *claret* is usually a spiced wine in the Middle Ages. "*Claret est faict de bonnes especes*," says the *Vocabulaire pour aprendre Romain et Flameng* (published in the *Livre des mestiers*, Vol. IV, p. 21). "*Ypocras et clarey sont fait de vin et bonnes espices*," says the *Tres bonne doctrine pour aprendre briefment françoys et engloys* (*ibid.*, Vol. III, p. 17). "*Claretum - Vino detto Clareto. Vino profumato e drogato. Si usava come eccitante e sostenitore delle forze; i suoi componenti erano il cubebe, garofani, noci moscate, cannella, zenzero, grana di paradiso, ambra grigia e muschio, cotti con miele o zucchero in vino bianco addizionato di uva passa di Grecia*" (Castorina, *Farmaci*, p. 511, §34; the author quotes Carbonelli, p. 64). A similar recipe for *claret* can be read in the *Tractatus*, Pt. I, §18, p. 383: "*Claretum hoc modo fit aliter: recipe sextarium vini boni, cinamomi electi uncias .III. et dimidium, zynziberi uncias .3., .II. galange, gariofili ana .3. et dimidium folii, squernanti, ana uncias .II. macis, spice nardi, cubebe, ana unciam, mellis despumati dimidium*

cages furnished with doves and every sort of flying bird.[70] At the highest points of the castle there should be standards, banners and pennants. Alongside the fountain /*31v*/ there should be a peacock which has been skinned and redressed.[71] And for that, I, Chiquart, already named, will instruct the master doing it in the artifice of that peacock, and that is done in order to do the courtesy and honor of his lord and master; which is that he should take a big fat goose and mount it properly on a spit and roast it well, neatly and heartily, and redress it in the raiment[72] of the

---

quarterium si vis, vel amplius potes apponere." See also the exact same recipe, with ingredient quantities, in the *Libro de Guisados* of Ruperto de Nola, p. 46. The *Enseignements* concludes with a notation that it (or a preceding recipe collection, the *Tractatus*, has taught the reader how "to prepare all beverages, such as wine, claret, mulberry wine, and all others": claret is clearly a standard preparation.

[70] Such bird cages seem not to have been exclusive to the Savoyard *entremets*. The Italian *Libro della cucina* contains a *Pastello di uccelli vivi* in which live birds are placed in a baked pastry cage, and this is hung from a tree, made similarly of pastry, in which there are (as in Chiquart) artifical (moulded) birds (pp. 43, 50). See Odile Redon, "Les usages de la viande en Toscane au XIVe siècle," *Manger et boire au moyen âge*, vol. II, p. 125.

[71] Cf. the previous Note 66 concerning the "skinned and redressed swan". For Redressed Peacocks, the *Viandier* indicates that "it is proper to blow and inflate (peacocks) like swans, and to roast them and glaze them in the same way; and they should be served as the last serving [*i.e.*, as the *entremets*]" (p. 130).

[72] Chiquart used the word *armes*, in the sense of "harness" or "vestment", referring to the peacock's splendid plumage. While the peacock had been adopted as a symbol of courtly honor and glory, its role at grand banquets was somewhat restricted by the remarkably tough and insipid quality of its flesh. "The flesh of the crane, the peacock, the bustard and the larger birds is of gross nourishment, and of difficult digestion, and is scarcely suitable as nutrition and food for the human body" (*Regime de vivre et conservation du corps humain*, Paris, 1561, folio 43r). Chiquart's solution to this, a typically culinary dilemma, is simply to combine the beauty of the peacock's appearance with the delectability of the goose's roast flesh. With this "larceny", as he

peacock and place it in the spot where the peacock should be set, beside the fountain of Love, with its wings stretched out; and make it spread open its tail, and hold its neck up high as if it were alive, fixed on a wooden stick which is in that neck holding it upright.[73] For that reason the cook should not skin the peacock but should remove the pinions in order to dress the goose with them, and remove the skin and rump of the peacock with their feathers all together; and when he sets out the goose, he should use good skewers to make /*32r*/ the goose spread its tail in exactly the same way as the peacock would do if it were alive.

At the crenels of that courtyard there should be hens, skinned, redressed and glazed, and glazed hedgehogs[74], and glazed meat balls, and Spanish pots made of meat and all glazed[75]; the moulded work of paste, that is to say, hares, brachet hounds, stags, wild boars, the huntsmen with their horns, partridge, lobsters, dolphins, all this moulded work

---

calls his substitution of the redressed "peacock", he thus contrives to retain a symbol of his master's magnificence while providing his master with an unexpectedly succulent treat.

[73] "One should have little skewers of wood and put them into the neck (of the swan) in order to hold it up as if it were alive" (the *Viandier*, p. 130).

[74] "Hedgehogs (*heriçons*) are made from the rennet stomach of sheep, and they are costly and a great deal of work and little honor and hardly worthwhile. Therefore, of them *nichil hic*" (*Menagier de Paris*, §366). In the fifteenth-century printed edition of the *Viandier* (p. 166), there is a recipe for *Irson d'amandes* which is undoubtedly the preparation which Chiquart and the *Menagier* had in mind: a membrane is stuffed into the shape of a small animal with spiced meat paste and pricked with slivered, roasted almonds in order to resemble a hedgehog's quills. This same realistic touch is prescribed in an English version of the Hedgehogs, called "Yrchouns" in English (Austin, p. 38).

[75] All four of these "dishes", glazed hens, glazed hedgehogs, glazed meat balls and glazed Spanish pots, are culinary fabrications which are found at the end of the *Viandier* (Vatican Library version, at pp. 119, 128, 120 and 128 respectively). All of them are made of meat paste. For the *Viandier* the last item here is either Spanish Pots (*pots*) or Spanish Farts (*pets*); the *Menagier* writes only *Pes d'Espaigne* and *Petz d'Espaigne* (p. 178, l. 21 and p. 182, l. 30).

of pea- and bean-paste[76]; make of moulded meat paste all the castle's curtain walls which will go all around the castle, and they should be long enough down to the ground that the bearers of the castle cannot be seen.[77] Those curtain walls, up to a height of two feet off the ground, should be painted with waves and great tossing billows; in those waves should be painted all sorts of fish, and on /*32v*/ the billows and waves should be painted galleys and ships full of all sorts of armed men in such a way that it should seem that the ships are coming to assail that fortress and castle of Love, looking as if it were on a great rock in the sea; of those men some should be archers and crossbowmen, others armed with lances, and yet others with ladders to lean against the fortress, some scaling up them, others descending and others tumbling down, some of them hit and so forth, one man face down, the next on his back, some of them killed by arrows and others by stones.

Inside the curtain walls there should be three or four young men playing very well on a rebec, a lute, a psaltery and a harp; and they should also have good voices and be singing melodious, /*33r*/ sweet and pleasant songs in such a way that they will really seem to be sea sirens for the clarity of their singing.[78]

And the peacock of which mention was made above, which on the direction of me, Chiquart, has cunningly been left over, take it and clean it carefully and dry it well and thoroughly, and put it on a spit and roast it; when it is almost done, stick it with good whole cloves in the proper way. And if the roasting is spoiled, set it on the spit over again. Then let your lord know about your fraud with the peacock and let him order

---

[76] To reproduce partridges, crayfish and dolphins, eaten during lean meals, Chiquart seems to specify the use of a lean foodstuff, paste made of peas and beans: this is no longer moulded work of meat-paste.

[77] At the end of the *Viandier* an *entremets* depicting the Knight of the Swan uses a great wheeled, lead-lined box containing water on which the Knight's boat, drawn by the Swan, floats. The "recipe" calls for this box to be hung with "fabric painted with waves to look like water, and nailed to the top of the cart in such a way that the men beneath are not seen" (p. 133).

[78] On the important place enjoyed by music at the court of Amadeus VIII, see Bruchet, pp. 158–9.

whatever it is his pleasure to do about it.

11. To teach him who is to make the proper sauce for the peacock /*33v*/ what it is made of and how it is made[79]: he should take the liver of the peacock and of capons and wash and clean them thoroughly; them put them on a spit and set them to roast over coals. Then he should take bread and toast it properly on the grill until it is nicely brown, then put it to soak in the best claret wine[80] that he can find and a little vinegar; and take those livers and grind them up in the mortar, then take your bread and grind it in together. Then take your spices, that is to say, white ginger, cinnamon, grains of paradise, a little cloves and nutmeg, strain it all together and draw it out with wine and a little vinegar; and watch out that not too much is put in. Then set it to boil in a good pot, and add in a reasonable amount of sugar; and taste it that there is not too much of anything, /*34r*/ whether salt, spices, vinegar or sugar, so that it has a bitter-sweet taste.[81] Then serve it wherever the peacock is to be eaten.

For supper: roasts of all sorts, jelly[82], a Tresmollete of Partridge, a Chyvrolee, and a side-dish of Rabbits in Saupiquet.

The saucing for those roasts[83]: for the kid, Green Verjuice; for the partridge, pheasants and veal, Camelin Sauce.

---

[79] This sauce recipe is almost identical to the one for *Ssalsa de pago cens let de amelles* which is found in the *Libre de sent soví* (§45). The preparation seems similar as well to the *Savore a capponi* in the *LVII Riceete*, §52.

[80] This claret wine may be the rich spiced wine mentioned on folio 31r. See also the "claret" of folio 64r.

[81] Concerning this *aigre-doux* taste, see C. Anne Wilson, "The Saracen Connection," Part 2, p. 14.

[82] "*Galatina est piscium sive carnium quaedam mucilago coagulata, quae nascitur de illis, quando post alixationem servantur infrigidata in aceto*" (*Alphita*, p. 293). See the "Sanitatis conservator", ed. Hugo Faber in *Eine Di'atethik aus Montpellier*, Leipzig, 1921, p. 21. Jellies appear later in Chiquart's work in Recipe 79, and in Recipes 80 and 81 which may not have been written by Chiquart himself.

[83] Knowing what sauces were appropriate for what meats and dishes consti-

12. In order to explain the Tremollete[84] to the person who will be making it, take a great quantity of poultry gizzards and livers, prepare them very cleanly and put them in a pot, with beef and mutton bouillon to plump them; then put them on slender wooden spits and roast them over /*34v*/ glowing coals. Then take enough bread for the quantity of the sauce which you are to make, and cut it into good slices and set these to toast on the grill; when your bread is toasted, get the amount of beef or mutton bouillon you need, and check that it is not too salty; then take good wine and verjuice and put it into the bouillon along with the soaked bread, in a good two-handled pot or bucket. Take your gizzards and livers, put them into a mortar and grind them thoroughly, moistening them with the bouillon in which your bread is soaking; then take your gizzards and livers out of the mortar and put them into the bouillon in which your bread is soaking. Take spices: white ginger, cinnamon, grains of paradise, a little pepper—but don't let it be too pronounced—nutmegs, mace and cloves; and of each of these spices watch that you put in only a moderate amount. Set it all to boil in good clean kettle, and then add in sugar, but not so much that it /*35r*/ takes away the verjuice taste because it should not be sweetish. After this, take all of the roast partridge you have to the dressing table and the Household Stewards will come to decide how many of them are to be put on each dish to serve kings, dukes, counts—for example, six partridge on one dish, five on another, four on another, and three on another. And, over top, the

---

tuted much of the "science" of court cookery in the late Middle Ages. "*Diversificantur sapores ratione cibariorum pro quibus fiunt. Nam alia et alia cibaria indigent alio et alio spaore, sicut sciunt dominorum coci*" (Magninus Mediolanensis, *Regimen sanitatis*, Pt. III, Ch. 20 "*De saporibus et condimentis*", fifteenth-century edition, n.p., n.d.).

[84] A *Trimolette de perdrix* is another of the "modern" dishes which were appended to the *Viandier* in its Vatican Library copy (p. 118). The author of this recipe specifies only the liver of the fowl but, with Chiquart, strives to create a bitter taste by adding vinegar at the moment the sauce is removed from the fire. The dish can be compared with the Calunafree of Partridge which Chiquart will present later (Recipe §47). Cf. as well the *Trimolete de perdris* in the *Recueil*, §14.

tremollete. And there should be an ample provision of two hundred cockerels and young poultry ready for serving in case the partridge runs out.

13. The Chyvrolee of Stag[85]: to instruct the person who is to make this, he should take his deer and cut it up into good pieces and wash them thoroughly and set them to plump in a good cauldron full of clear water; when it is boiling, skim it neatly and, as soon as you have skimmed it, take the meat out and put it into good fresh water in a pot and immediately wash it thoroughly again, and put it to drain /*35v*/ on good work-tables or in good pots. Next, take a great amount of good lard and with it lard all your pieces of meat well and properly, and, when this is done, put it all back again to cook in a good clean great cauldron or kettle depending on the amount of meat you have; then get beef or mutton bouillon and fill that cauldron or kettle up to half with

---

[85] This is the recipe for wild goat (*Chèvre sauvage*) in the *Viandier* (p. 88) and in the *Menagier* (§88). The name of Chiquart's dish does not seem to appear in the other French recipe collections of the period or in the English ones. It does turn up, however, in two Italian collections of the fourteenth century as *Civiro a carne de cavriolo o de livore* (in the *Libro per cuoco*, p. 68), and as *Civeri di lepore e altre carne* (in the *Libro della cocina*, p. 37). Faccioli, the editor of the Italian collections, has supposed that the generic name of those dishes was related to the French *civet*: "*civero: sorta di salmi (del francese* civet)" (p. 393), but neither scallions (*ciboulles*), nor chives (*civettes*), nor even onions (Latin *cepa*), which are at the origin of the French *civet*, appear in the *Chyvrolee* of Chiquart or in the versions of it contained in the *Viandier* or the *Menagier*. The name of the dish seems rather to derive from the name of its principal ingredient, the deer or roe-deer, in French *chevreuil*.

In the *Recueil*, the recipe for *Venoison de serf au soupper* (§17) would produce a dish similar to Chiquart's.

Deer meat was highly valued in the regions in which this game animal could be hunted. The Arab physician Avicenna declared that deer meat was the healthiest and most nutritious of all wild meats: "*Inter venationes gloria est caprea*" (*Canon medicinae*, ed. Fortunato Plempio, Louvain, 1658, Bk. II, p. 186b).

it, and then add into it some very good wine. Then take your spices, white ginger, grains of paradise, cinnamon, pepper, nutmeg, mace and cloves, and put them into your broth, and all in proper amounts. Then get sage, parsley, hyssop and marjoram, clean them thoroughly, make a good *bouquet garni* of them and set them to cook with your broth, if[86] the verjuice[87] and spices in it taste right. Then /*36r*/ carry it over to your dresser.

14. For making the Saupiquet to be put on the rabbit[88], depending on the quantity to be made, take two onions and slice them finely, and take good pork lard, melt it and sautee your onions; to prevent them from burning as they fry, put in a little bouillon. Then put in a lot of white wine to the amount of the saupiquet you want to make for the rabbits. And take your spices, good ginger, grains of paradise, a little pepper, which should not predominate, and saffron to give it color; and add vinegar to taste so carefully that it is neither too sharp nor too little; and the same with salt.

For the second day, the dinner[89]: gross meat and salt meat, in

---

[86] What Jehan de Dudens wrote seems to suggest that the cook should taste the broth before adding the bouquet of herbs to it. It appears likely that either he or Chiquart has skipped a phrase here, such as " ... and check to see *whether* ... "; this particular phrase is so common elsewhere toward the end of recipes that it amounts almost to an habitual formula.

[87] No verjuice has been mentioned previously in the list of ingredients.

[88] Only the version of the *Viandier* which is found in the Vatican Library offers the cook an option of dressing " ... Roast hares ... in Saupiquet, that is to say in the grease which drips into the pan, and add in finely chopped onions, wine, verjuice and a little vinegar ... " (p. 88). The *Menagier de Paris* copied the same recipe, adding certain unspecified spices: " ... and let the spices dominate" (§284). As its name indicates, a piquant savor lent by the vinegar, both here and in the Saupiquet on Fish (Recipe 36), is the essential quality of this sauce.

[89] It should be noted that there is only one serving, and no *entremets*, at this supper meal, whereas for the dinner of the First Day Chiquart has provided for the preparation of dishes for two servings and for two *entremets*.

a different dish a Tile-Colored Broth, White Leek Sauce— *hoc est, porros albos*—on Mormotannes[90] and salt geese, together with Hare Sops, /*36v*/ Jacobin Capon Sops, a Gravy of small birds and poultry; and, for pottage, turnips.

15. To instruct the person who is to make the Tile-Colored Broth[91], he should take the quantity of meat that the Kitchen Squire orders him to prepare, the quantity of poultry which you receive to put into that pottage, and other meat, whether pork, goat, veal or lamb. Depending on the quantity which is delivered to you, take your almonds, cull through them and clean out the bits of shell and anything else, and wash them well in hot water. Set the meat you have been given to cook in good clean cauldrons or kettles, and then grind your almonds well and moisten them with the meat bouillon. Then, when your meat is cooked, remove it into good two-handled pots, with your poultry separate from the meat; then strain and filter your bouillon into good two-handled pots /*37r*/ and your ground almonds as well in that bouillon. Get your spices, that is, good ginger, grains of paradise, a reasonable amount of pepper, nutmegs, mace and cloves, and put them into the bouillon with

---

[90] The dish which Chiquart calls *Mormotannes* has not been identified. It is likely that it is a variety of "molded" dish of meat-paste, shaped like a marmot and similar in fabrication to the factitious Hedgehogs of Recipe 10 (folio 32r).

[91] There are versions of a dish called *Tuillé* for both meat days and lean days in the fifteenth-century Vatican copy of the *Viandier* (p. 126); the *Menagier* distinguishes between these two in its recipes for *Tuille de char* (§118; and see also the variant *Ung tieule de char* at p. 176, l. 21) and for *Tuille d'escrevisses* (§77), which should probably be read as *Tuillé* and *Tieulé*. The name of this preparation may derive from its color, as I translate it, or perhaps from its method of preparation in an earthware baking dish. This latter explanation seems to be suggested in the case of a Portuguese dish called a *Tigellada de perdiz* (ed. Gomes Filho, p. 141; ed. Newman, p. 2): it is baked in the oven in a *tegella de fogo*, an earthenware baking dish shaped like a roofing tile. The Portuguese term *tigellada* appears to be generic for anything baked in such a dish.

the almonds, and put in only an amount appropriate for the amount of broth you are making; and get enough sandalwood powder[92] for the amount of bouillon, to give it color, and put in enough for it to have the color it should have, and strain it with your almonds and spices; and get white wine and verjuice with it and strain your almonds and spices into it. When that is strained, set it to boil in a large good clean kettle and add in sugar to the amount of the broth you have; and check carefully that it tastes as it should with all things and verjuice and salt. And when it is time to serve, set out your meat skilfully on good dishes with the broth over top.

16. To make the White Leek Sauce[93], /*37v*/ have him who is charged with them get his leeks and chop them up small, wash them well and put them to boil. Then have him get a good chunk of salt pork back, clean

---

[92] Sandalwood was used in some European kitchens as an alternate colorant for alkanet or animal blood. In Chiquart the word is *poudre sandre*; in English recipes it is sawnder (*Liber cure cocorum*, p. 13), sandres (*Forme of Cury*, §170) and saunderys (in Austin, *passim*; in Italian, *sanavro* (*Libro per cuoco*, p. 76) and *sandoli* (Martino, p. 132). Concerning the use of this colorant, Maestro Martino tells the cook: "*Metti con esse assai de sandoli occió che.l sapore sia rosso*" (p. 132). Though he does not use it, the *Menagier* does mention sandalwood as a culinary ingredient: "Red cedar is a wood which is sold at the spice merchants'" (§84). For its importance as an article of trade, see Pegolotti, p. 377 and *s.v. sandali rossi*, p. 429.

[93] This White Sauce made from leeks forms something of a pair with the Green Sauce of parsley and was fairly well known across Europe. Chiquart's recipe for it is found, in a simpler version under the names Blawnche perrye and Blanche porrey in Austin (pp. 14 and 91) and Blaunchyd porray in the *Liber cure cocorum* (p. 44). For the *Menagier de Paris*, "White *poree* is called that because it is made from the white of leeks (*poreaulx*). ... And you should know that no other fat but pork is proper for it" (§50). An interesting feature of the *Porrata bianca* of the *LVII Ricette* (§33) is its use of 1 oz of ginger to the 2 lbs of almonds and 4 bunches of leeks; when served, this sauce is garnished with powdered spices. The recipe which the *Sent soví* offers for *Porada ab let* (§95) allows the option of adding beaten eggs to the mixture.

it very well and put it with them to boil; and when they have boiled at length, take them out and put them on good clean wooden tables, and keep the bouillon in which they have boiled. There should be a good mortarful of white almonds; take the bouillon in which the leeks have boiled and draw out your almonds in it, and if there is not enough of that bouillon, get beef or mutton bouillon, and watch that it is not too salty.[94] After that set your broth to boil in a good clean kettle. Then take two good clean knives and chop up your leeks, then take and grind them in the mortar; once they are ground, put them into your broth, made of equal quantities of almonds and water[95], half boiled. After they have boiled, when they get to the dressing table, place your meat in good dishes and then pour some of that leek broth over top. /38r/

17. To begin the Hare Sops[96], the hares must be neatly skinned, and sear them over a good bright fire[97], then split them open skilfully and clean them out; and check on those that are whole whether the bowels are burst, and that the liver is taken out and the bitter part [the gall] is removed; and they should be washed in very good claret wine. The ones which were broken by the dogs[98] should be singed and cleaned and

---

[94] Chiquart repeats this warning throughout the work probably because much of the bouillon kept on hand in medieval kitchens originated in the boiling of meats preserved by salting. Boiling was invariably the first step in removing the salt from such meat in order to render it edible.

[95] By stating specifically that the broth should consist of equal parts of almonds and water Chiquart indicates that the base of the sauce is to be quite thick. In the English recipe for Blanche Porrey in the Harleian ms. 4016 we find the same insistance upon thickness: "Drawe hem (the almonds) thorgh a streynour into a good stuff (*i.e.* stiff) mylke" (ed. Austin, pp. 90–1).

[96] This is not a common dish in medieval recipe collections.

[97] The searing of raw flesh over an open flame is good culinary practice, having the effect of sealing in the meat's natural moisture. The procedure is followed in the treatment of hares in both the *Viandier* (p. 83) and the *Menagier* (§83). Later, in the recipe for Shoulder of Mutton (on folio 78r), Chiquart speaks of this searing as drying up the surface moisture of the meat.

[98] That is, during the hunt or the final kill.

washed in good pots in good fresh water, and the ones which are not broken should be cut up into good pieces and put in a good clean kettle. Then get good beef stock, and also some of the wine in which the hares were washed, and strain it through a good bolting cloth, then pour it all around the hare meat filling your kettle with equal amounts of bouillon and good claret wine. Then get a good piece of a good cut of bacon, clean it and wash it thoroughly and parboil it a little, then dump it in. Depending on the amount of broth, add in /*38v*/ some well washed whole sage, verjuice, a reasonable amount of salt, and the spices: cinnamon, ginger, grains of paradise, pepper, cloves. Let all of this boil until it is time to serve it; and, if it should cook too much, it should be pulled back off the fire and your meat put into good clean two-handled pots. And you should get a lot of table bread, and cut a hamper-full of it to make the hare sops.

18. To serve Jacobin Sops[99] you need your good capons—and, depending

---

[99] A century after Chiquart, the *Fleur de toute cuysine* (folio 13r) contains the same recipe for *Souppe jacobine*. In the *Recueil* the *Souppe jacopine* has "toasted bread; the best cheese that can be found, and put it on the toast, and soak it in beef bouillon and put good roast plovers or chickens on top" (Recipe §6). The two recipes for *Tartre jacopine* outlined in the *Viandier* which was printed at the end of the fifteenth century seem to have nothing to do with Chiquart's Jacobin Sops. As for the sense or implicit value of the qualification "jacobin", the word was used to refer to the Dominicans in Paris and appears to have come to suggest a certain gourmandism or gluttony:

> Boire à la capucine,
> C'est boire pauvrement;
> Boire à la célestine,
> C'est boire largement;
> Boire à la jacobine,
> C'est chopine à chopine;
> Mais boire en cordelier
> C'est vider le cellier.

(Quoted in Gottschalk, p. 344.) See also Marcel Schwob in *Romania*, Vol. XXX, p. 391, n. 1. Chiquart's Jacobin Sops are indeed a rather hearty dish.

on the size of the feast, that will be one or two hundred fat capons—and a large number of other poultry to serve if those capons run out; and they should be properly roasted. When fat oxen are being cut up, their marrow bones should be taken and carefully washed, and then set to boil in good clean cauldrons /*39r*/ with good mutton[100] among them. After that, arrange to get a *quintal* [120 lbs] of very good Crampone cheese and Brie cheese, the finest that can be made and found, and have this cheese properly pared and cleaned, then cut it up very small. The cook who is ordered to make these Jacobin Sops should take two or three hundred loaves of table bread and cut this bread into good slices and toast them very neatly without burning them, so that they are brownish, and then put them into good clean two-handled pots; and you should have two immaculately clean work-tables to slice that toasted bread for the Jacobin Sops. Then you should set out your gold, silver and pewter dishes in a row, and place your bread delicately on them with the cheese on top. Take your capons and dismember them, that is, remove the wings and legs, and remove /*39v*/ the rump; then take the white meat of each capon and cut it up very small and scatter this white meat from the capons over your Jacobin Sops. After that take the members of the capons, that is, the wings, legs and rump, and place them in orderly fashion on top of your Jacobin Sop. Check on your broth of beef and mutton marrow, that they are good and soft, and filter this broth into a large good clean kettle; get a good *bonnete*—*bouquet garni* of sage, parsley, marjoram and hyssop which should be thoroughly cleaned and washed, and put this into your broth. Over by the dressing table where you will be serving up the Jacobin Sops, arrange to have a good coal fire under the kettles containing your broth so that it will keep on boiling, and cover your Jacobin Sops with this broth. /*40r*/

19. Besides that, a Gravy of Small Birds and Poultry[101]: to instruct him who is to do this, he should take roughly a thousand small birds which

---

[100] *de beau mouston parmi*: Later, on folio 39v, Chiquart will write, *miolles de beufz et moustons*, that is, "beef *and* mutton marrow".

[101] This dish is represented in a number of cookery books: the *Viandier*, p. 82; the *Menagier*, §74; *Enseignements*, l. 115; Austin, "Smale Brydys y-stwyde", p. 9; and the *Recueil, Grane* (or *Grané, Gravé*) *d'alouestez*, §7. The

should be plucked and properly cleaned so that there is no trace left of any feathers or dirt; and take about a hundred head of large poultry which are good and clean, split them in two and break them apart so that in every quarter bird there are four pieces, and wash them good and cleanly with the small birds; when they are washed, set them to dry on immaculately clean work-tables. Get a large amount of lard and melt it in good great clean pans; get a good clean cauldron, put your small birds and poultry in it, and also pour neatly into it your melted lard /40v/ over those small birds and poultry. Take a great deal of bread, according to the amount of your meat, cut it into rounds and set it to toast on the grill until it is brownish; get beef or mutton bouillon, making sure it is not too salty, in a good clean pot, add a lot of claret wine, and when your bread has toasted set it to soak in that pot of bouillon and claret wine. Get your spices—cinnamon, ginger, grains of paradise and pepper, and minor spices—nutmegs, cloves, mace, galingale, and all spices: and the chef should watch that he doesn't put in too much of anything, but that he has a temperate and controlled hand to put in only what seems to him is wanting. While /41r/ he is straining his bread and spices, he should have his meat browned over a good hot fire; he should have a man always stirring it with a large holed spoon so that it doesn't stick on the bottom and burn. When he is straining his bread and spices, the chef should put a third or a half of it, or whatever[102], with his meat so that the meat will not be spoiled or burned, until he has strained it all and put it with the broth. When it has been strained and set to boil, the chef should taste it, checking to see whether spices, vinegar, salt or anything else is needed, or whether there is too much of anything. Don't wait so long that your meat is overcooked but draw it back over some

---

Viandier specifies which birds are comprised for this recipe: "Small birds, such as larks, quails, thrush, etc." (p. 89).

[102] Jehan de Dudens wrote " ... *en coulain son pain et ses espices si mecte en collent ou le tiers ou la moytié ou ce qu'il haura coulé avecques son grein ...* " The phrase *ou ce qu'il haura coulé*, which translates literally "or what he will have strained", could be understood as *ou qu'il aura à couler*: "or whatever he may have (there) to be strained".

warm coals[103], unless it is time to take it over to the dressing table; there, at the dresser, /41v/ it should be set out properly into dishes.

For the supper: roasts of all sorts, a Buchat of Rabbits, Parmesan Pies, Dodine of Water Fowl, and a Boiled-Larded Dish.

20. To instruct the chef who is to do that Buchat of Rabbits[104], he should take his rabbits and skin and clean them well, sear them and clean them out; he should take the rabbits' livers, set them aside, wash and clean them well, and put them to dry on good clean wooden tables; and he should be careful to remove the bitter part, that is, the gall and

---

[103] The sense of the word used here by Chiquart, *chilliens* or perhaps *chillieus*, is not absolutely clear. The context, here and where the term is again used on folio 107r, seems to call for a substance which would keep the contents of a pot warm for a certain length of time. The term *tselle* or *tsellen* (s.f.pl.) is attested, in nineteenth-century Swiss dialects, by Bridel (p. 392) who gives it the sense "la cendre, les cendres". See also the historical note to the word in the *GPSR*, Vol. IV, p. 595a, *s. v. krèsin*; and *FEW*, Vol. II, p. 91a. On the other hand, a variety of flat stone called *chilliou* or *chillon* is attested in the fifteenth century, the latter form of the word being associated with a quarry at Lausanne which produced building stone. See the *Dictionnaire historique et biographique de la Suisse*, Neuchâtel, 1924; Vol. II, p. 508. For the form *chilliou* (and *chillius*), see Bruchet, *Le Château de Ripaille*, p. 599.

[104] In the manuscripts of the *Viandier* the generic name of this dish is variously written as *Boussac, Bousac, Boussat* and *Bonsax*; in the *Menagier*, the dish is *Boussac* of hare or rabbit. In both of these fourteenth-century works the recipe is much simpler than in Chiquart, requiring neither herbs nor liver, nor such a broad variety of spices as is found in Chiquart's version. See as well the rather plain *Boussac de lievres* produced by the *Recueil*'s Recipe 35. Among the English recipes edited by Austin (p. 85) and in the *Forme of Cury* (§17), the dish called Bokenade, Bukkenade and Buknade bears some resemblance to the Buchat: herbs enter into both, but as a binder what is used rather than liver in the first English version is egg yolks, and in the second, rice. Hieatt and Butler relate the name of the dish to veal: *Curye on Inglysch*, p. 175.

anything else /42r/ that is not clean; and they should be washed in beef bouillon or in good boiling water. Also wash the rabbits, cut them up into good pieces and put them into a good clean cauldron. Then take pork backs, singe them well and cut them up into good little pieces, using a large quantity—in the amount you are ordered to make—and put them to be washed in good pots that are clean; then set them to dry on good wooden tables. When they have dried put them into the cauldron with your rabbit meat. Then get beef or mutton bouillon, pour it in and set it to cook. /42v/ Then make a good big *bouquet garni* of herbs, that is, of sage, parsley, hyssop and marjoram, all cleaned and washed, and throw it in to cook. Take the rabbits' livers, which have been properly cleaned, washed and drained, put them on slender spits and set them to roast over hot coals; when they have roasted through, take them off the spits, put them in the mortar and grind them up well; get your *bouquet garni* which you have had boiling with the rabbit meat, undo it and grind the herbs in the mortar, and then mix this with the ground rabbit livers. Then /43r/ check on your meat that it is not too cooked, but take it out while it is still slightly underdone; put the rabbits to one side and the pork to another, both in good clean two-handled pots, then put the bouillon from which you have taken the meat into other pots which are likewise good and clean. Then get a great amount of bread, depending on the quantity of the broth, and set it to toast on the grill. Then take your ground liver and herbs, put this into your broth with the toast and with spices: ginger, grains of paradise, pepper, cinnamon, nutmegs, mace and cloves—and be careful that you put in these minor spices very moderately; and add wine and verjuice, also in good measure; strain everything together into good clean two-handled pots. Then get your /43v/ good clean cauldron or good big bright clean kettle and put it to boil. Get a lot of good bacon lard, chop it very small and melt it in good big pans, then strain it well into big pans and put them on the fire; fry the rabbit meat by itself, and not too much, then the other meat similarly fry a little and keep it by itself. When it is time to dress the dish, take your meat and broth to the dressing table and set out your meat on good dishes of gold, silver, pewter, and so forth, and then pour your broth over the top.

21. Next, Parmesan Pies[105]: for these Parmesan Pies, should their preparation be ordered, /44r/ in order to instruct you how, get three or four large pigs and, if the feast should be larger than what I have in mind, get more[106], and cut the heads and hams off these pigs and set the fat aside to. be melted; cut up the rest into good slices or chunks, wash these well and put them to cook in good clean cauldrons, adding salt moderately. For the Parmesan Pies you need three hundred doves, two hundred chicks—and should the feast be held at a time of year when chicks are not available, get a hundred cockerels—and six hundred small fowl; these doves, poultry and small fowl should be plucked and thoroughly cleaned; take the doves and split them down the middle, likewise split the poultry and quarter it; then put the doves, poultry and

---

[105] Savoy was in a good position to know of these *Torte parmigiane*, a dish which, if not commonplace, was at least familiar to most northern Italian gourmets of the time: see Stanislao Cordero di Pamparato, *Documenti per la storia del Piemonte*, Turin, 1902 (cited by Carbonelli, p. 178, n. 312.) Indeed, and naturally enough, a recipe for this *Torta parmesana bona*, which is almost identical in its ingredients to what Chiquart specifies for his pie, is copied in the Italian *Libro per cuoco* (ed. Faccioli, p. 96). The Vatican copy of the *Viandier* has its *Tourtes parmeriennes* (p. 121); for this, mutton, veal and pork are allowed into the pie, while lard serves as a binding rather than the creamy cheese and eggs which Chiquart uses. It may be that Chiquart considered his Parmesan Pies to fulfil the role of an *entremets*, because he decorates them with the same banners and coats of arms as he used to present the Boars' Heads in Recipe 5.

A strange shift of geographic source seems to have taken place for some varieties of this dish. The *Menagier* writes of "*Tourtes pisaines, id est* from Pisa in Lombardy (and people say *Tourtes lombardes*, and there are small birds in the filling ...)" (p. 176, l. 5). In Austin's collection this dish is called *Crustade Lombarde*.

[106] Jehan de Dudens wrote *que on n'y mist plus*. It seems almost certain that the second *n*, making a negative, is in error and merely an echo of the first. I have guessed that Chiquart's intention here was that the amount of pork, the primary ingredient in the pie, should be increased if the size of the banquet warranted an increase in the number of pies to be made.

small fowl /*44v*/ into good pots, wash them very thoroughly in three or four changes of good clean water, then set them to boil in good clean cauldrons, adding salt moderately; and watch that they do not cook too much. When they are cooked perfectly, take your meat out into good clean two-handled pots, separating the small fowl from the other birds. Then take the pork fat and cut up a large amount of it; put it into good clean pans and melt it completely; when it is melted, strain it into other good clean pans. Then take your small fowl and brown them lightly, and not too much, in the lard, and afterwards do the same with the other meat. Get six lbs of figs, six lbs of dates, six lbs of pinenuts, six lbs of prunes, and eight lbs of raisins; then take the figs, prunes and dates /*45r*/ and chop them up small, as small as the raisins or smaller, and take out the seed from the raisins and clean them well. Then take your pinenuts in good dishes and rub them well, winnow them and remove the chaff from them; put them on a fine cloth and cull through and clean them carefully so that only the white seed is left. Then put your figs, prunes, raisins, dates and pinenuts into an immacultaely clean two-handled pot, and have it covered with a good clean white cloth so that nothing unclean can fall into it. Then get herbs. that is, sage, parsley, hyssop and marjoram, of which there is so much parsley that you have a big hamper full of it, drained, and just the leaves; and a moderate amount of sage, hyssop and marjoram; /*45v*/ put these into a good clean two-handled pot, and wash them thoroughly in three or four changes of fresh water, and then put them onto good clean work-tables and chop them up very small. Check whether your pork is cooked and put it onto good fine boards, and your work-tables should be good and big and very wide. You who will be making this fine Parmesan Pie, along with the helpers you put on it, should take care to remove the hide from the pigs in such a way that no bones are left, and chop up the meat very finely; and when you are chopping the meat, get herbs and put them among the meat; and get a good big clean and bright basin and put your meat in it—to explain the sort of basin I mean, it should be a good big pan of the sort used to cook /*46r*/ big large fish. Then get a *quintal* [120 lbs] of the very best Crampone cheese, or Brie cheese, or the very best cheese that can be had, and take that cheese and pare it, clean it well and thoroughly and cut it up small, then grind it very strongly in the mortar; then take six hundred eggs and moisten your cheese with them as you are grinding, and keep on moistening it with the eggs until they are throughly blended, and in the quantity required by the number of Parmesan Pies you have been ordered to make. Take the pan I described to you above and into it put some of the lard in which the meat has been browned, and which has been purified, and put in an amount proper for the amount of the ingredients you have, and set it over a good bright fire; you should have two good strong helpers to stir the mixture strongly and energetically with a big two-handed holed spoon, then take it down onto a good fire of hot coals. Wash your figs, prunes, dates, raisins and pinenuts, all cut up as was said above, /46v/ two or three times in good clean and clear water, and then wash them in good white wine and set them to drain and dry on good clean wooden tables; then when they have drained, throw them into your mixture, and this should be thoroughly stirred; and take your ground cheese which has been blended with the eggs as was said above, the amount you have made for the pie filling, and add it into your mixture working it in very strongly; then remove that pan from the fire. Take your spices: white ginger, fine spice powder[107], grains of paradise and saffron for its color, and add in

---

[107] Ordinarily in medieval cuisine the expression *poudre fine* (as it is here in Chiquart) designates a particular mixture of the most common spices, ground into powder. Chiquart uses the expression again on folios 56r and 56v. The *Menagier de Paris* includes a recipe for his own variety of spice powder: white ginger, cinnamon, cloves, grains of paradise and loaf sugar, all of this ground up (§314). Since *poudre fine* amounted to a sort of shorthand, or comprehensive designation of several of the individual spices which appear in this very same listing, we may wonder whether some sort of mistake has been made, by the author or scribe, in the list; when *poudre fine* and *poudre* appear on folios 56r and v, they are used alone and are quite understandable. Indeed in the *Viandier*'s recipe for *Tourtes parmeriennes* the manuscript reads, "... Then get fine powder and spice your meat with it sensibly" (p. 121). In any case the designation *poudre d'espices*, *poudre fine* and *fine poudre d'espices* is quite common in the *Viandier*: for this work, fine spice powder consists normally of ginger, cinnamon, cloves and grains of paradise (see pp. 83 and 98). For

a moderate amount of cloves, add these in and keep stirring. Have a lot of sugar crushed into powder and throw in a lot, depending on the amount of the filling, and keep stirring. Get enough good clean pans or, if you can find them, good clean earthenware shells, all you need for making the Parmesan pies, enough pans to have some /47r/ left over; then, when you have your good clean pans or earthenware shells, get twenty or thirty thousand sugared wafers[108]; take your pans or shells, get some of the lard in which you fried the small fowl and the poultry and put it on the inside of your pans or earthenware shells, then take your wafers and on the bottom and around the outside of each pan or earthenware shell put a layer of the wafers so that there are four or five of them on top of one another. On these wafers spread out a layer of the filling, then on the filling put the small fowl, setting them here and there and not all together; and between every two birds put a quarter of a dove, and elsewhere put a quarter of poultry between two birds, and do this in such a way that of the small birds, the quarters of doves and the quarters of poultry a good layer is made /47v/ on top of the layer of filling already spread out, and over this layer of small fowl, dove quarters and poultry quarters another layer should be made of the same filling, and on this layer of filling put a layer of wafers in exactly the

---

the *Libre de sent soví* (§219) in Catalonia, the *salsa fina* is a dry, carefully composed compound of ginger, cinnamon, pepper, cloves, mace, nutmeg and saffron. And finally we may consider the recipe for *Specie fine a tutte cosse* which is found in the Italian *Libro per cuoco*: "Take an ounce of pepper and an ounce of cinnamon and an ounce of ginger and an eighth of an ounce of cloves and a quarter ounce of saffron" (ed. Faccioli, §73, p. 86).

[108] The Savoyard form of the French word used by Chiquart is *neble* and still reflects some of the sense of its Latin etymon, *nebula*: this biscuit was as thin and as light as the biscuit bakers of the day could make it. According to the thirteenth-century *Règlements sur les arts et métiers de Paris* (ed. Depping, p. 350), a qualified *oublieur* or wafer-baker should be able to turn out 1000 of these *nieules* a day. Chiquart's Parmesan Pies would therefore probably "consume" about a month's output of some Chambéry wafer-baker. The author of the *Sent soví* indicates that *nelles* could constitute a proper dessert in and by themselves (§190, and n. 9).

same way as was said before for them to be set on the bottom of the pan or earthenware shell. When this is done, all of it should be covered over properly with those wafers. Take cold lard and spread it over the top; then put your pies into a temperate oven; and be very careful when they are baking that you have spinach and chard leaves, which are well cleaned and washed, so that if the wafers show any burning at all you can put the leaves over them. Then take your Paremsan pies out of the oven and carefully scrape off anything burnt on them, and set them out in good dishes. When they are in the dishes, get your gold leaf and lay it /48r/ on top of the Parmesan pies in the pattern of a checker board; sprinkle the tops with powdered sugar.[109] And when they are served, a banner should be set on each pie with the arms of each lord before whom these Parmesan Pies are served.[110]

Sequitur de salsis et de piscibus cum salsis incumbentibus.

Post carnes sequitur tractatus de piscibus cum salsis eisdem piscibus incombentibus. Et primo:[111]

Thanks to the grace /48v/ of the blessed Holy Spirit, we have just given, above, the specification for serving decently and generously the

---

[109] Concerning powdered (or granular) sugar see in particular Pegolotti, pp. 362-5: "There are many sorts of powdered sugar, that is of Cyprus and of Rhodes and of Soria and of Cranco di Monreale and of Alexandria, and all of them are made in whole sugar loaves, but because they are not cooked as much as the other sugars which hold together in their loaves ... the loaves fall apart" (p. 363).

[110] "And put in each pasty three or four quarters of poultry in order to set into them the banners of France and of the other lords who will be present. ... And you should have gold- or silver- or pewter-leaf to glaze them before setting the banners into them" (the *Viandier's* recipe for *Tourtes parmeriennes*, p. 122).

[111] "There follows (the section) on sauces and on fish with the appropriate sauces. After (the section) on meats there follows a treatise on fish, with the sauces appropriate for those fish. To begin with: ... " That this title appears in two versions suggests that Chiquart may not have struck out his first draft before passing the page to his copyist.

meats, the appropriate sauces and also the pottages for the two days of the aforementioned banquet.

Yet on each of those two days one must serve just as generously, decently and honorably with fish, both sea-fish and fresh-water fish, as the meats are served above, and to make a fish dish similar to every dish explained above for meat.

As the counterpart of the gross meats dealt with in the first serving, take large fish, salted mullets and big pieces of salted pike filets—those will be the counterpart /49r/ of the beef and mutton—and place them in a dish; then put herrings by themselves in another good dish, and on those all that is needed is mustard; also, in another dish, eggs cooked on the coals. For this the Kitchen Squires must be well furnished and provided with a large amount of white peas[112] in order to make the preparations connected with fish for each day of the feast.

22. The Chief Cook should be advised of the number of people they will have to serve and, depending on that number, they should take that quantity of peas, and cull through them, clean and wash them thoroughly, and set them to cook in good clean cauldrons or good big bright kettles, and cook them. When they are cooked, draw your puree into good kettles or two-handled pots, and draw out so much of it /49v/ that you can make the amount of the preparations you will be ordered to make.

---

[112] What follows in Recipe 22 is a White Pea Puree which will serve as the base for a great many of the lean dishes of this "treatise" on fish. It is significant that Chiquart places the recipe for Pea Puree at this point, almost as an essential preliminary: he ensures that the cook will have on hand a stock of a standard ingredient which will be drawn upon repeatedly throughout the whole of following section. The *Menagier* likewise contains a *Potage de pois vielz* (§29) and *nouveaux* (§136). Later on in the *On Cookery* Chiquart mentions *les pois colés*, "strained white peas", a preparation to which the *Menagier* also refers: "Of all these peas, whether they are old or fresh, you can strain them through sackcloth, a strainer or a filter ... " (§31). These strained peas are eaten as a separate dish: cf. the *Menagier*, p. 175, l. 7, and elsewhere.

23. To begin with, for your White Broth[113] get a quantity of almonds appropriate for the amount of pottage you have been ordered to make, have them skinned and cleaned and ground thoroughly, and moistened with white pea puree. When they are all ground up, draw them out with that same pea broth, putting in whatever is needed for the amount of the almonds. Add in good white wine, verjuice, white ginger and grains of paradise, all of these things in good measure; and salt; and check that there is not too much of anything; and put in an appropriate amount of sugar. Then get a good big clean kettle and set it to boil. When it is time /50r/ to serve it, set your fried fish on good dishes and pour this broth over top. And for any of the pottages you will be making of almonds in this section, when they are served up be sure not to forget the candies[114] which should be scattered on top.

And when you have ordered your pottages made in the quantity of those dishes, get that amount of fish, both sea-fish and fresh-water fish, and order your industrious kitchen help to fry them; they should be frying them at the same time as the pottages are being made.

24. As the counterpart of the Lamprey Sauce for meat[115], get the tripe of large fish and split them open, clean and wash them fully and put them to cook; when they are well cooked, take them out /50v/ onto good clean work-tables and cut them up small, as to make an arbaleste.[116]

---

[113] The White Broth for fish is the counterpart of the White Broth on chickens (Recipe 1) with which Chiquart's meat menus opened. The two recipes differ only in the substitution here in the lean version of pea puree for the earlier chicken broth.

[114] In the *On Cookery* the only occasion on which these droplets of spiced sugar (*dragiees*) are used is as a garnish on the almond-based sauces which are poured over fish (in Recipes 23, 25, 31, 32, 33 and 37). As an alternative garnish on fish sauces Chiquart has recourse to pomegranate seeds (in Recipe 26).

[115] This Lamprey Sauce for meat is the Lamprey Sauce for loin of beef seen previously (Recipe 4). The spices in this earlier dish include nutmeg as well. In the fifteenth-century printed version of the *Viandier* (ed. Pichon and Vicaire, p. 157) a recipe which is similar to Chiquart's §24 is titled *Arbaleste de poisson*.

[116] The *Arbolaste*, *Arboulaste* or *Arbolastre* copied in the *Menagier de Paris*

Get enough onions for the amount you will be making of that pottage and chop them up very finely. Get enough white bread for the amount of the pottage you have to make, and slice it into good rounds and set it to toast on the grill so that it is good and brown, then put it to soak in the pea puree in a good clean bucket according to the amount you have been ordered to make, with light red wine and some vinegar, too—and watch that you don't put too much of this in. Then get a lot of cinnamon, depending upon the amount of the broth, ginger, grains of paradise, pepper—and not too much—cloves, mace, galingale, and put in all of these spices in good proportionate amounts; and salt, though not excessively; put in all of this carefully, then set it to boil in good big clean kettles. Then get /*51r*/ good, well clarified oil, take your fish tripe and your onions and put them to fry, take them out when they are well done and put them into your broth to boil in proper fashion. When it is time to dress them, get your fried fish and set them out in good dishes with this tripe sauce over top.

25. For a German Fish Broth[117]: to make this, take your almonds in the amount of the pottage you are ordered to prepare, have them neatly culled so there are no bits of shell or dirt still among them, and wash them in good two-handled pots three or four times in good clean warm water; them have them well ground, moistening them with with white

---

is an herb omelette (§§ 225 and 231). The same is true of the preparations called in English Arbolettys in Austin (p. 20), Herbolace and Erbolates in the *Forme of Cury* (§§ 7 and 172); in Italian, *Erbolato* in the *Libro della cocina* (ed. Faccioli, p. 51), *Herbetella* in the *Libro per cuoco*, (*idem*, p. 74), and *Herbolata de maio* in the *Libro de arte coquinaria* of Maestro Martino, (*idem*, p. 159). However, the *Menagier* also contains an *Arboulaste* or *Arboulastre* of meat (§265) which begins with kid tripe, cooked, chopped and ground with herbs. As is the case with Chiquart's *Arbaleste*, there are no eggs in this dish. It seems clear that the name was used to designate two, and perhaps three, rather different types of preparation.

[117] Compare this with the meat version of the German Broth (Recipe 2). Apart from those ingredients listed in Recipe 25, the earlier dish contains pepper, nutmegs and mace (ground nutmeg husk).

pea puree; when they are thoroughly ground, take some puree and some white wine and verjuice, depending on the amount of the broth that is to be made, and your spices: /51v/ good ginger, grains of paradise, a few cloves and a little cinnamon—and do not put in too much of that; and, to give it color, a small amount of saffron. According to the amount you will have of all this, get onions, peel and wash them, then chop them very fine. When your almonds have been strained properly, set them to boil in a good big bright clean kettle, and put in a lot of sugar proportionate to the amount of the broth, and salt, too, being careful though that it is not too much. Then get good clean, well clarified oil and sautee your onions nicely in it, then put your onions to boil with your pottage. When the time comes to dress them, get your fried fish and set them out in good dishes with that broth over the top, and /52r/ be sure not to forget the candies that go on it.

26. To make the pottage corresponding to the Savoy Broth made above for the meat service:[118] to make a fish counterpart to that one, get white bread, remove the crusts and take enough of it for the quantity of the pottage you are to make and put it to soak in pea puree, white wine and verjuice, according to the quantity of that pottage you will be making. Get a lot of parsley, sage, hyssop and marjoram; have someone cull through a great quantity of that parsley, and of the other three herbs take only what is an appropriate amount because they are strong; put them together, then wash them thoroughly in three or four changes of water, /52v/ take and squeeze them out in your hands, drain and wring the water out of them, put them in the mortar and grind them up fully; when they are well ground, put them with your bread. Get your spices: ginger, grains of paradise and a little pepper—and not too much—and

---

[118] The reference is to Recipe 3 on folio 21v. The two versions of this sauce are identical except for the use of a presentation garnish in this second case. The dish bears some resemblance to a preparation found in the *LVII Ricette* which is called *Tinche a brodetto* (§26); in this, almond milk is used instead of pea puree, the latter being a favorite ingredient of Chiquart for lean dishes. The Italian recipe calls for mint as well as parsley and sage. The dominant qualities of each dish are their green color and their sharp verjuice taste.

strain them well into a good two-handled pot; then put them to boil in a good big clean kettle, its size depending on the amount you have, and only bring it to a boil so that the color of the greenery is not lost; to make it elegant[119], add in a little saffron so that it is a bright green. When it is ready to be dressed, get your fried fish and set them out on your dishes, and then put that pottage on top; and scatter pomegranate seeds over that.[120] /53r/

Fish pies.

At the second serving: first, sea-fish of all sorts on great gold platters separately; fresh-water fish, on another platter—big filets of pike, big filets of carp, with other fresh-water fish to fill out the platter; and, besides that, rice and salted dolphin in place of venison[121], and with that a Russet Lamprey Sauce[122].

27. To instruct the person who will be charged with preparing the lam-

---

[119] Chiquart uses the word *gentil* here, which has connotations of distinguished refinement. The color which will lend this quality to his dish is the *verd gay* produced typically by cooks by mixing parsley and saffron.

[120] Pomegranate seeds are naturally in general culinary use in the Iberian peninsula (for instance, in garnishing the *Ginestada* of Ruperto de Nola, ed. Dionisio Pérez, p. 68). However they were certainly not unknown in the noble kitchens of France, at least in the fifteenth century. The dish called a *Menjoire* in the Vatican copy of the *Viandier* (p. 188) is garnished with pomegranate seeds; and in the *Recueil* the author sprinkles them over the top of his *Broet blanc de poisson* (§21). According to Pérez, what is used by cooks is the seed from the unripe fruit, which adds a piquant flavor to the dish. On the Saracen origin of the pomegranate as a comestible, see Wilson, Vol. I, pp. 14–15.

[121] "In place of venison": the salted dolphin, served with rice, replaces the venison, with frumenty, in menus for lean days. Chiquart makes the same commentary at the end of Recipe 30a (folio 57v).

[122] *Roux de lamproyes*: this word *roux* written by Jehan de Dudens may very well be in error for the word *roust* which was copied in the Table (folio 4r) in the name of this very dish: *Lamproyes en roust*, Roast Lampreys. This latter certainly seems to be a good name for what is described in Recipe 27.

preys[123], he should put them into a two-handled pot or jug depending on the quantity he has of them, and they should be in good hot water; he should scrub the slime off them, scrape out the mouth with a good knife so that none of those little bones there are left[124], slit them under the throat and pull their tongue out—and be very careful that it /53v/ does not stay in; then cast the lampreys into good fresh water and wash them well and then set them on a good table to dry. Then see that you have your good clean spits, and when you put the lampreys on those spits, get the best claret wine that can be had, get good, very clean pans and set them underneath to collect the blood. When those lampreys are well and properly spitted, wash them well and properly with that good claret wine; keep it and put it with the blood and don't pour it out; when you lay them to the fire to roast, get good silver dishes or good clean pans and divide up the wine and blood among those silver dishes or pans, putting as much in one as in another, then set them /54r/ under the lampreys where they will receive the grease from which the sauce will be made. While the lampreys are roasting, get enough white bread for the quantity of lampreys you have and set it to toast well on the grill; when the lampreys are well roasted, put them into the dishes or pans which are under the lampreys; after that take those dishes or pans and put everything that is in them all together in a good clean bucket. If

---

[123] Probably the dish which is called Roast Lampreys in the Table (folio 4r). This "Russet Lamprey Sauce" can, however, be compared with the Lamprey Sauce for loin of beef which might be considered its meat counterpart and whose ingredients are almost identical to its own. See also the *Viandier* (pp. 95 and 190), the *Menagier* (§185), and the *Sent soví* (§139: *Lempresa en ast*, that is to say, "on a spit, roasted"). In the recipe for *Lamproyes et bourrees* (a sort of fish) *a la saulce chaude* which is found in the *Recueil* (§29), the spice list includes grains of paradise, cloves, nutmegs, ginger and mace. In the *LVII Ricette*'s *Lampreda arrosto* (§30), the lamprey is basted with orange juice while it is roasting, and then dressed with a *salsa fritta* consisting of fine spices, sugar, orange juice and wine.

[124] In the *Menagier de Paris* this operation of cleaning the mouth of a lamprey is described thus: "With a round-tipped knife peel the lamprey and scrape the inside of its mouth, and remove the scrapings" (§185).

it seems to you that there is not enough broth, add more of that claret wine until you have the amount you need. Then get your spices[125]: white ginger, a large amount of cinnamon, depending on the quantity of lampreys there are, grains of paradise, cloves, nutmegs, mace, galingale and pepper—and not too much—and strain all of this thoroughly; and add in enough vinegar /54v/ for the amount of the sauce—being careful that it is not excessive—and salt. When that is properly strained, get

---

[125] The State Archives in Turin contains, in its Archivio della Camera dei Conti, Conto Tes. Gen., for the year 1416, reg. 61, a document in which we can read a reference to Chiquart in respect of this Roast Lamprey Sauce and the spices which enter into it. A notation in the household accounts testifies that Chiquart received from the hand of the apothecary those spices necessary, and perhaps in the relative quantities necessary, to make this very sauce.

> Libravit Iohanni Belleni appothecario pro specibus suprascriptis ab eodem emptis pro dicta salsa lampree (sic) facienda et tradictis dicto magistri Chiquardo. Et primo pro una libra zinziberis albi, .I. flor, .VI. gross.; dimidia libra cinnamoni, .VI. den. gross.; uno quarterono grane paradisi, .III. den. obl. gross.; uno quarterono piperis, .II. den., .I. quart.; uno quarterono garioffilorum, .IIII. obl. gross; dimidio quarterono gallericorum, .IIII. den. obl. gross. (folio 604r)

The passage is reproduced in Castorina, *Farmaci* (p. 511, n. 32). Four years later, in the *On Cookery*, Chiquart lists the first five spices which we read in the account book as well as nutmeg, mace and galingale. The spice *gallericus* (which Castorina glosses in Italian as *galle*) is indeed probably the nutmeg. If in 1416 it did not simply happen that Chiquart had adequate supplies of mace and galingale already on hand, these other two ingredients may have been considered optional reinforcements, mace for the nutmeg, and galingale for the ginger. It may be also, of course, that Chiquart's recipes had changed over four years, so that a broader variety of spices became used. Or it may be that, as he writes the *On Cookery*, Chiquart is allowing himself the vicarious luxury of placing himself and his reader in an ideal kitchen which is totally unconstrained by those considerations of "finances" of which he speaks on folio 15v in his preamble.

a good clean pan to boil it in, and while you are boiling it make sure there is a helper always stirring it with a good spoon so that it will be in no danger from the fire. When that sauce has boiled, put it back into a bucket or a two-handled pot which will hold it, then dress it out wherever the lampreys are served up.

28. Again, Almond-Milk Flans[126]: depending on the number of flans you will be making, get that quantity of almonds, have them skinned neatly and have them well ground; get very good clean water and let him strain his almond milk into a bucket or a two-handled pot which is good and /55r/ clean in an amount appropriate for the flans he is to make. Then get good starch, wash it in good fresh water and put it in a fine bucket when it is washed; then take your almond milk and pour it in to soak the starch, and add in a little saffron to give it color; then strain that through a good bolting cloth into a good clean bucket, and put in a little salt and a great deal of sugar. When this is done, call your pastry cook for the pie shells to be made, and have him put them in the oven for a little while to become firm. Then the pastry cook should have a good spoon of either wood or iron attached to a good stout stick to fill the shells of the flans in the oven.

29. With that, Fish Pies[127]: /55v/ to instruct the person who will be doing this job—because not everyone is a master of it—he should get his fish, that is, good bellies of tuna, good big filets of carp, good big fresh eels—and of all that he should get the quantity that is needed for the number of pies which he is ordered to make; take all of it and cut it into good-sized pieces and set it to cook in a good clean cauldron appropriate

---

[126] This dish seems to have been furnished as a lean counterpart for the cream flans mentioned on folio 26v. Cf. Eberhard's Recipe §11, *Einen fladenn von fischenn*, whose name indicates that it is appropriate for serving on fish days. It contains no fish and uses almonds and rice as its base.

[127] These *Tartres de poyssons* are quite similar to the Tartes of Fysshe found in the Harleian ms. 279 (ed. Austin, p. 47), and to the Venetian recipe for *Torta de pesse* in the *Libro per cuoco* (ed. Faccioli, p. 91). An echo of this latter recipe appears in the *LVII Ricette* as *Torta di battuto di pesce* (§31) where the fish specified for use is tench. Cf. also the *Pasteden* of Meister Eberhard (§15).

in size for the amount you have; when it is cooked, take it out onto fine tables which are good and clean, and cull through all your fish to remove any scales or bones, then chop it up well. Get good candied figs, prunes and dates and slice these up small, to the size of small dice; get pinenuts and have them cleaned thoroughly /56r/ and get candied raisins and clean them well so there are no seeds left; of all this take an amount proper for the amount of the fish filling you are making, wash it well in white wine, then mix it in with your fish in a fine pan. Then get another pan which is good and clean in which you will clarify good fine oil; when it is clarified put enough of that oil into your filling for the amount of it, then set it on hot coals to heat up, and stir it continuously with a good spoon. Then get good spice powder and put in a reasonable amount of it, and a lot of sugar. Then order your pastry cook to make large or small pie shells for you, and they should be covered.

Sauces for the sea-fish[128]: /56v/ for turbot, Green Sauce should be provided; salmon is eaten with Camelin Sauce; ray fish, with Camelin Garlic Sauce which is made from almonds and its liver[129]; lobsters, with vinegar; sturgeons, with parsley, onions and vinegar; fried sardines, with mustard; fried sole, with sorrel verjuice and orange juice[130]; eel, roasted

---

[128] In this list of sauces specified for particular fishes, Chiquart adheres to traditional French practice. The *Viandier* recommends the same sauces as Chiquart for turbot (p. 106), salmon (p. 105), ray (p. 106), lobster (p. 108) and sturgeon (p. 107).

[129] For the preparation of this unusual sauce for ray fish, see the *Viandier*: "Camelin Garlic Sauce: grind cinnamon, bread [rather than Chiquart's almonds], and garlic; moisten this with vinegar and verjuice, and grind the liver of the ray fish in with it" (this recipe is copied in only the Mazarine Library manuscript, 3636, p. 141). The sauce is called Ray Garlic Sauce (*Aulx de la roye*: *Viandier*, p. 104), as well, either because of the inclusion of ray liver among its ingredients, or because of its principal use upon ray fish. For the method of preparation of ray fish for cooking, see the *Viandier*, p. 106.

[130] The serving sauce which Chiquart specifies for sole is closer to what is given in the Mazarine copy of the *Viandier* than to what appears in any other version of this work: "Roast sole on the grill and eat it with sorrel verjuice"

on the grill, with verjuice; anchovies, with parsley, onion and vinegar, and spice powder on top.

30. For fresh dolphin[131]: to instruct those who will be preparing it, they should take their dolphin and cut it up into good pieces, then wash these very well and put them to cook in good cauldrons big enough for the quantity you have, in equal parts of wine and water, with salt. Then get white bread and slice it into rounds, put them on the grill, then set them to soak in an amount of good claret wine and vinegar /57r/

(p. 141 of the manuscript). The Mazarine manuscript was copied in the fifteenth century. The two possible sauces which Chiquart mentions for fried sole are bitter, which might perhaps suggest some distant influence of Arabic cookery: see Wilson, Vol. I, pp. 15 and 20. In the fifteenth century orange trees were cultivated as far north as Lombardy in Italy. The commercial and cultural relations between this region and Savoy (whose boundaries included much of Piemonte) were of course well developed in Chiquart's day.

[131] This is the recipe which the *Viandier* indicates is for Porpoise, *Porc de mer* (p. 103). In Chiquart's work the dish constitutes the lean counterpart for the Venison which is served on meat days. Fresh dolphin is prepared in just the same way—as the *Viandier* says, "Porpoise is cut up into slices just like venison," p. 103)—and is presented in the same way in its own bouillon, with either a side-dish of frumenty (see above, folio 26v; and Furmenty with Purpaysse, Austin, pp. 17 and 105; *Forme of Cury*, §§69 and 116), or rice (used to accompany the salted dolphin in Recipe 30a, and further on, among the menus, on folio 110r). See also in the *Menagier*: "*Porc de mer, marsouin, pourpoiz* ... are served in a dish in their own water like venison" (§203). Chiquart's recipe for fresh dolphin is reproduced closely in the *Sent sovi*, §207. In his *Historia naturalis* Pliny considers that dolphin is the best sea-fish for the table, although Magninus Mediolanensis expresses some reservations on the question: "*Dicamus ... que pisces bestiales sicut porcus marinus, canis marinus, delphin et morua non multum competunt in santitatis regimine*" (*Regimen sanitatis*, Part 3, Ch. 18). Chiquart has already echoed Pliny's opinion about dolphin (see folios 16r v, above). The *Recueil* mentions a sauce called Vinegrette which is to go over Porpoise (*marsouin*) (§30), but without explaining its composition.

which will depend on the quantity of the sauce you will be making. Get your spices: a great deal of good cinnamon, ginger, grains of paradise, cloves, nutmegs, mace, galingale and a little pepper, and all this should be strained nicely into a good clean pot; and put in an amount of salt proper for the amount of the sauce you have; then set it to boil, and have the mixture stirred by someone with a good spoon so that it does not burn. When your dolphin is cooked, take it out onto a good wooden table, skin it properly, then cut it into good slices. When it goes to the dressing table, put it out in good dishes with that sauce over top as it should be.

30a. If your dolphin is salted, put it to cook in good chunks, and when it is almost cooked take it out and wash it in good fresh water, and put it on a good clean wooden table and cut it into good slices; then put it into a good broth of equal parts of wine /57v/ and water. When it is cooked, put it onto fine dishes. It is served, in place of venison, with rice.

31. Corresponding to the Camelin Broth for meat, a Camelin Broth for fish: to apprise you how to make this, take an amount of almonds for the quantity you are charged with making, and have them well cleaned and well washed in four or five changes of good warm water; have them well ground and moistened with pea puree. When they have been ground well, depending on the amount you have of them get pea puree, and wine according to the amount of the broth, and verjuice. Then get your spices: a great deal of cinnamon, so that it shows the color of cinnamon[132], white

---

[132] "The color of cinnamon" might be a popular translation of the adjective *camelin*. "*Camelinus:* '*Fercula et salsamenta ... alia cinereum fere colorem usurpant et vocantur celebrato nomine camelina, quia colorem pilorem cameli pretendunt.*' J. Godard, *Ep.* 223" (Latham). The term *camelin*, in part because of the color it represented and in part because that spice is always the major ingredient in Camelin Sauce or Camelin Broth, must have allowed some semantic confusion with the word *canelle*, "cinnamon". The classic cookery book of the sixteenth century, *Platine en françois tresutile et necessaire pour le corps humain* (Lyon, 1505, folio 76) spells the preparation as *Sausse canelline*. The *Recueil* directs that to make the *Broet hamelin* (sic) *de poisson* (§22), the

ginger, grains of paradise, nutmegs, mace and cloves—and of these minor spices put in only reasonable amounts. When it is strained, set it to boil in a good clean bright kettle or cauldron in which it has room to boil, and put /58r/ in a great deal of sugar according to the amount of what you have, and salt—and all of these things in reasonable amounts; then boil it. Once boiled, it is taken to your dresser; get your fish and set them out on your fine dishes, and the broth on top. And do not forget the candies which should be scattered over top.

32. Corresponding to the Pink Broth for meat, make a Pink Broth for fish: to explain it to the person who will be making it, let him get a great quantity of almonds, in the amount of what he has been charged with making, have them well skinned, washed and cleaned and ground up, and moisten them with white wine. When they are all ground up, get what pea puree you need for the quantity of broth you are wanting to make, and add into it white wine and verjuice, and spices and white ginger, grains of paradise and a little pepper—and not too much—and strain those. Get pea puree according to the quantity there is of the almonds, /58v/ then strain that into a good two-handled pot and set it to boil in a good clean kettle or cauldron depending on the quantity there is of it; add in a great deal of sugar and whatever amount of salt is appropriate—and check that there is neither too much nor too little of anything—then put it boil. When this is done, get a good big frying pan which is very good and clean, and put very good clear oil in it and heat it up; when it is very hot and boiling, throw in good cleaned alkanet and cook it and heat it, and strain it neatly through a layer of bolting cloth into fine dishes; then add it carefully into your broth so that the color of that broth is more pinkish than red. Then set out your fish in good dishes, with that broth on top; and also scatter the necessary candies over this.

33. Next, a Party White-Dish in four colors served all together[133], that

---

cook should add in "a great deal of cinnamon".

[133] Though this Party White-Dish contains no fish, it is clearly intended for meatless days as an alternative to the version described earlier in the *On Cookery* (§9)—which meat-day version makes use of beef or mutton broth for

is, /59r/ gold, blue, red and silver: to explain this preparation, the person who will be making it should get a large quantity of almonds and have them skinned neatly, washed and thoroughly ground, and moisten them with good warm water and strain them into a good clean two-handled pot; and do enough for the amount you want to make of that Party White-Dish. Put white ginger and grains of paradise into the broth you are making, then take your almonds out of the warm water and make milk out of them; then divide that milk among four good bright clean kettles, the same amount in each one, with a great deal of sugar in each one, too; and put in a reasonable amount of salt. Then put them to heat up on a sprightly fire.

Then get a great amount of starch, clean and wash it well and properly, and put some into a good clean dish for each /59v/ of those four kettles. Then take the milk of the kettle you want to bind and strain the starch through a good filter, then dump it into that kettle stirring hard continuously until you see that it is bound so stiffly that, when one is set out beside another on the same plate, they will not run together; and do the same with all four kettles.

To instruct the person who will be making these colors to do the Party Dish in four colors: in order to make the first color, gold, get beaten saffron in the amount you need, moisten it with milk from the kettle you have settled on for the gold Dish, then dump it into that kettle you want to have the gold color, stirring with a good spoon. /60r/

For the blue one, get your orchil lichen and let it soak in milk from the kettle you want to make a blue color, then strain it very thoroughly, into a good clean bucket, until there is no color left, then put it into the kettle you have set aside to contain the blue Dish. Moisten and strain your blue color, then put it into the kettle, pouring and stirring hard continuously with a good spoon until it is quite bound; then, when it is bound, move it back from the fire.

To make the red one, get well clarified oil and put it to heat up

---

its liquid. That the generic "white-dish" allowed a wide range of variations is evident in the *Blasmangiere di pesce* in the *LVII Ricette* (§24) which combines almonds, rice and sugar along with cloves, pinenuts and even several pieces of actual fish (pike and tench).

very hot in a good pan. Then get your alkanet and throw it in, stirring with a good holed spoon, then strain it through a bit /60v/ of bolting cloth into a good dish; and get your starch and strain it with the broth in which you are to make the red Dish, then pour it into your milk, stirring hard continuously, in the pot in which you are making your red Dish. When it is bound well, take your color and add this in carefully until it has a reddish color.

With the silver White-Dish, take your starch and steep it in the milk, strain it through the bolting cloth, and then bind it stiffly.

When the four Party Dishes are thus made, to serve them put some of each of the four Dishes out onto each plate, that is, some of the gold Dish, then /61r/ the red one along side, beneath, then the blue one, and finally the silver one. When it is all divided and set out on good plates like that, as has been outlined, get your candies and on each color of that Party Dish put the proper candy.

For the fish supper: first, roast pickerel and pollack, which are served with green sorrel verjuice; and White Almond Sops; with that, fish jelly[134], and white sea-fish and fresh-water fish; also, Brown Sorengue of eels; a good Larded-Boiled Dish of tench; and fried fish in good Saupiquet.

34. To inform the person who will be doing the Sorengue[135], he should get his eels and completely remove the slime from them /61v/ in good hot

---

[134] According to the *Kochbuch* of Eberhard, the jelly which is made "of pike is said to be good and pure, so that it becomes transparent" (§22). The *LVII Ricette* specifies the use of tench to make its *Gelatina di pesce* (§27). See the recipes for fish jelly added at the end of the *On Cookery* (§79 and §81).

[135] This is a very well known dish in the fourteenth and fifteenth centuries: cf. *Une soringue* in the *Viandier* (p. 97, and in the printed edition, p. 154), in the *Menagier* (§127), and among the Anglo-Norman *Recettes culinaires* published by Meyer (§19); and the English Sore sengle and Elys in sore (Austin, pp. 25 and 89; cf. the Soree in Hieatt and Butler, I, §19). For the person responsible for the earliest copy of the *Viandier*, now located in the Archives of the Valais in Sion, Switzerland, the word *soringue* seems to have a generic value: he has a recipe for a Soringne or Soringue of pork kebab (*Soringne de*

water, then throw them into good fresh water and wash them in three or four changes of water; then make your dresser good and clean, and put them on it and prepare them and clean them out, neatly removing their guts, and cut them up into good slices; as you cut them, put the slices into good fresh water and wash them well, then set them to drain on the good clean dresser. Depending on the quantity you have, get a good clean kettle or cauldron to boil them in. Then get onions to the amount of the eels you have, peel and wash them, and chop them up nicely; then get good clean oil and a good pan and sautee your onions a little; then throw your eels on top and fry all of that together on good hot coals. Get enough white bread for the amount /62r/ of pottage you have to make, cut it into good slices, and put them to toast on the grill until they are toasted to a dark brown[136]; put them to soak in pea puree and the strongest claret wine you have[137], and flavour it with a little vinegar.

---

haste menue de porc) (ed. Paul Aebischer, *Vallesia*, 8 (1953), p. 87); for the compilers of other copies of the *Viandier*, the name of the same dish is simply *Une vinaigrette* (e.g., on p. 82).

The term *soringue*, of Germanic origin according to Grewe (*Sent sovi*, p. 55, and §78, n. 1), refers to a dish whose meat has been fried (cf. the Provençal *saurengar* and Catalan *sosengar*). "If you wish to make a *sosengua* of rabbit or hare, or of whatever meat you want—mutton, veal, kid—it should be cut into small pieces and sauteed or otherwise fried with bacon grease, oil or lard" (§81). A preliminary parboiling or searing of the meat over a flame, depending upon the relative humidity of the meat, is optional. A final stage sees the meat dumped into a pot of spiced broth with onions (fried) and an ingredient which will ensure some degree of binding.

Concerning the nature of this dish, see Claudia Roden, "The Spread of Kebabs and Coffee: Two Islamic Movements?" in *Oxford Symposium 1983. Food in Motion: The Migration of Foodstuffs and Cookery Techniques*, London (Prospect Books), 1983; Vol. I, p. 74.

[136] Chiquart wrote: " ... *Roustir sur le gril tant qu'il soit bien rous comme brun.*" This color of dark toast is the color which is indicated in the name of the dish itself. *Sor* is a dark red or dark russet color (*rous*); the word exists in a verb, *sorir* which is used by the *Menagier*: *pain sory sur le greil* (§118).

[137] An eel is considered by some health handbooks to be of a dangerously

Then get your spices, in amounts proper for the amount of your broth[138]: cinnamon, ginger, grains of paradise, pepper and cloves, and strain all those very carefully, according to the amount of your broth, and throw it in over your eels; with salt and all other things in reasonable amounts.

35. A good Larded-Boiled Dish of tench[139]: to instruct the person who will be doing it, he should have, in the quantity he will be given, filets of tench which are good and big enough for him to be able to cut into three, and big salt eels, as well; when these eels are skinned, get big long strips of them to make lardoons for the pieces of tench. Then get white bread, toast it, and set it to soak in good claret wine; and get spices:

---

humid nature: "It bears a great similarity to mushrooms in taste, in viscous humidity and in evilness of nourishment" (*Régime*, folio 66v). Because this moistness was excessive, the eel had to be prepared in such a way as to counter it. Even before the measures which could be taken at both the cooking and saucing stages, the *Menagier* tells the cook, "Kill (the eel) in salt and leave it there, whole, for three full days" (§26). Eels are never boiled as the initial cooking method, but either fried, as is the case here, or, more usually, exposed to the full drying effect of a fire by roasting. Then the driest and warmest of the spices are combined in a final effort to ensure that none of the eel's potential harmfulness will remain by the time it is served for eating. Here, Chiquart specifies a mulled wine which is rich in spices, and these spices almost without exception are warm and dry in nature. Among the spices of the list which follows, it should be noticed that Chiquart uses pepper, an extremely warm and dry condiment to which he does not often have recourse.

[138] The addition of the bouillon has been implicit in this recipe.

[139] This is the dish which is called a Yellow Larded-Boiled Dish of Tench, With Sops, later on folios 110r and 113r. Chiquart does in fact direct his reader to add in "a little saffron to give it color". The *Viandier* offers only one *Boully lardé*, and that is to be made with any *chair ou veneison* at all, that is, any domestic or game meat (p. 79). For the *Menagier de Paris* (§80) the *Bouly lardé* is made only of veal, kid or stag. The Larded-Boiled Dish here in the *On Cookery* forms the lean counterpart to the Chyvrolee of Stag (Recipe §13), to which, at least in the way the two dishes are prepared, it bears considerable resemblance.

ginger, grains of paradise, pepper, cloves and a little /62v/ saffron to give it color, and strain this and flavour it with verjuice. When you have put your larded pieces of tench into good clean pans or kettles to cook, pour in your broth and flavour it nicely with salt and verjuice.

Besides that, sea-fish or fresh-water fish which are nicely fried, and make a good saupiquet to go over them.

36. To instruct the person who will be doing the Saupiquet, he should take onions and prepare them well, slice them and chop them up very small; then he should get well clarified oil and sautee his onions properly in it, /63 r/ then drain the oil off them so that none is left on them. Then get a good clean kettle and very good wine, and put in enough for the amount of fish he will have fried; then he should get his spices: ginger, grains of paradise, saffron and pepper—and, of all these, put in reasonable amounts depending on the quantity of fish that is to be eaten with that saupiquet. He should flavour it good and lightly with vinegar, and with salt, too.

For the following day, the dinner for those who do not eat meat: the salt dish is of big eels, big salt trout, pollacks and herrings; in a separate dish, eggs cooked on the coals[140], White Leeks, Puree with Sops, a Georgé Broth on fried fish, a Gravy of Fish Tripe garnishing fried fish, and turnips. /63v/

37. To instruct the person who will be making the Georgé Broth[141], he should get the amount of almonds necessary for the pottage he is to do, have them skinned well and neatly ground, with white pea puree to draw them out, and he should flavour them with good white wine and verjuice. He should get his spices: white ginger, grains of paradise, a

---

[140] In the *Menagier* we read: "Lost Eggs (*Oeufz perdus*): Break the shell and drop yolks and whites onto the coals, or onto good hot embers; and then clean them and eat them" (§226).

[141] The Georgé Broth on fried fish seems to be a lean version of the dish called simply *Brouet georgié*, for poultry, in the *Viandier* (p. 82) and in the *Menagier* (§103). However, Chiquart's broth does not resemble the others very closely. The sense of the qualification *georgé* may be a reddish yellow color.

little cinnamon, but not too much, nutmegs, cloves, a little pepper, and a little saffron to give it the color of that broth[142]—and there should not be too much—and a great deal of sugar, depending on the amount of broth there is; he should taste it for all ingredients, and salt. When it goes to the dressing table, pour it over the dishes /64r/ of fried fish; and don't forget the candies which should be scattered on top.

38. To make the Gravy[143], get bread, slice it into rounds and put it to toast on the grill until it is brownish; get a lot of your pea puree and good claret wine, get a jug or large pot or two-handled pot, depending on the amount you will be making, in which you set your toast to soak, with some vinegar to sharpen the taste—and be careful that it's not too much. Then get your spices: a great deal of cinnamon, white and Mecca ginger in the amount required by the quantity, grains of paradise, cloves, nutmegs, mace, galingale and a little /64v/ pepper—add this only in moderation—and salt, too. Get the tripe of fresh fish and split them open, clean and wash them fully, and put them to cook. When they are cooked, take them out and cut them up into little dice-sized pieces; get finely chopped onions and good clarified oil, and brown those onions and tripe nicely together, and drain the oil from them; put the tripe and onions into the gravy mentioned above. Then get your fish, both sea-fish and fresh-water fish, which you are furnished for this dish, set them out

---

[142] "The color of that broth" is to be influenced by saffron, and should probably therefore be of a reddish yellow. In its recipe for *Ris engoullé* the *Viandier* speaks of a russet color being imparted by saffron: ... *Du saffren pour le roussir* (p. 93). For the color of his *Broet georgé*, the *Menagier* says "this dish should be brown with lard" (§103); and, with a slightly different notion, the Vatican manuscript of the *Viandier* describes its proper color as *blanc brun*, while two of the other manuscripts say simply *blanc*.

[143] That is, the Gravy of Fish Tripe which was mentioned in the menu for this second day's dinner of the lean banquet (folio 63r). In the *Viandier* (pp. 10 and 97) and the *Menagier* (§128) this is the dish which is called, somewhat more specifically, Gravy of Loach and Gravy of Perch. The recipe is found in the *Libro della cocina* as well, under the even more descriptive name of *De l'interiori e budelli di pesci* (p. 47).

on fine dishes on your dresser, and put that gravy over top.

For the supper of those who do not eat /*65r*/ meat: white fish instead of roast, a Verjuice Broth on fried fish, Parmesan Pies, fried fish with Saupiquet sauce over, and a Larded-Boiled Dish of big tench.

39. To instruct the person who will be doing the Verjuice Broth[144], he should have good, well ground almonds, and good white bread which he prepares well and puts to soak in good white wine and verjuice in the amount of the pottage he will be making. Then he should take his fully ground almonds and his spices: good white ginger, grains of paradise and a little pepper—reasonable amounts of these things—and strain it all through a bolting cloth and put it to boil in a good pot. When it is time to set it out, take it /*65v*/ to the dresser, and check its saltiness carefully; then set out your fish on fish dishes, and pour that broth over top.

40. Now I, Chiquart, should like to instruct the person who is ordered to make the Parmesan Fish Pies[145] that he should get tuna bellies, if he is in a place where he can get sea-fish, otherwise he should get all the more fresh-water fish, that is, big filets of carp, big eels and filets of big pike, and of that fish he should get enough for the quantity of pies he is ordered to make. Get candied raisins, prunes, figs, dates and pinenuts, all of that in an amount appropriate for the quantity of those

---

[144] Both the *Viandier* (p. 84) and the *Menagier* (§111) offer preparations for poultry in which verjuice predominates: Verjuice Broth for Poultry; the *Viandier* adds "... or any other meat you may wish".

[145] This is one of the most complex preparations in the *On Cookery*; the opening words of the recipe indicate the author's awareness that he is presenting an exceptional dish whose elaboration will require the efforts of a particularly skillful master. Later in the book we learn that these same *Tortres parmeysines de poyssons* actually served as an *entremets* during the historical lean banquet offered to the Duke of Burgundy (folios 110r and 113r).

Chiquart's recipe is distantly echoed in the simply named Tartes of Fyssche edited by Austin (p. 47) and found also in the *Forme of Cury* (§170), as well as in the *Torta de passe* of the *Libro per cuoco* (p. 91).

/66r/ pies. Then, for those pies, this fish should be cut up, cleaned and washed, and set to cook properly; when it is fully cooked, take it out onto good clean tables or boards, and have all the bones carefully and completely removed so that not even the smallest bone is left[146], and cut it all up into tiny pieces. The raisins mentioned above should be carefully seeded, the pinenuts carefully cleaned, and the figs, prunes and dates chopped up to the size of small dice; when all this is done, everything but the fish should be fully washed in white wine, drained, and mixed in with the above fish. Besides this, you need, according to the quantity of the pies you have to make, parsley, marjoram and sage, and of each of these herbs an amount /66v/ depending on its strength, that is, more parsley and less of the others; they should be well cleaned, washed and throughly chopped up, then mixed in with the above fish. This done, get good clear, clean, well clarified oil, and a good big clean pan which is set over a good bright fire, and put all of that into it; you should have a good helper with a good big clean spoon to stir that pan energetically. Get your good thick almond milk and strain it through the cloth, and a lot of starch, depending on the quantity of pies you have, and put it all in to bind it. Then mix your spices in with your fish, stirring constantly and vigorously in every part of the pan: white ginger, grains of paradise, /67r/ a little pepper, enough saffron to give it color, whole cloves, a great deal of sugar which has been ground into powder, and a reasonable amount of salt. Have your pastry chef make the shells nicely for the pies; when they are done, take the abovementioned filling and put the right amount into each one. Then make sure you have a very great quantity of good fine slices of good eels which are perfectly

---

[146] Despite the vigilance urged here by Chiquart, these *ossellez* remained common in the dishes served even on genteel tables. In a conversation manual of the day we read that the young people who were serving at table should clear away such bones constantly during a meal: "Clean off the whole of the table of bits of bread, or fish bones, or any meat bones; when in front of a diner, take hold of the bones with your right hand, then put them into your left hand, and when your hands are full throw everything into a basket" (Jean Gessler, *Livre des mestiers de Bruges et ses dérivés*, Bruges, 1931; Vol. IV, p. 63).

cooked; when they have been cooked, put them to fry in good clean oil, and drain; when fried, remove their bones. Then on each pie put three or four pieces, one this way, the other that way, so they are not all together; then cover the pies and put them in the oven. When they are cooked, set them out in your dishes and go and serve them up. /67v/

If it should happen that this feast lasts longer than the two days mentioned, one should use the meats, dishes and entremets whose descriptions follow.

Firstly, a Coquart Pasty, the Pilgrim Capon, a Cold Sage, Calaminee, a Calunafree of Partridge, the Norse Pasty, Rissoles, a Party Hot-Dish, a Morteyruel[147], Green Shoulders of Mutton which are eaten with a sauce of the blood of those shoulders, Breast of Boar, Mortoexes, a Vinaigrette, a Jance, a Gruel Broth of capons, Glazed Kid Heads, Crow, a Gratunee, a Spanish Gratunee, and Shoulder of Mutton stuffed and glazed. /68r/

41. To explain what the Coquart Pasty[148] is, and of what ingredients it is made and should be made, and how, get beef and some of that fine grease from beef kidney[149], and this should be hashed up small; he should take care that, when the beef is cut up, he get all of its marrow and that he put it into his pasty. Then he should get the right spices, that is, ginger, grains of paradise, saffron and salt, and all of these things in moderation. The pastry chef should be advised to made the crust of the pasty so large, so good and decent, and in several compartments which are large enough that each one of them can contain what will

---

[147] The *Chaut mengier party* and the *Morteyruel* are listed separately in this menu, as if they were distinct dishes, yet according to the beginning of Recipe 52 they are alternate names for the same preparation: "... the Party Hot-Dish, which is also called *Morterieulx*" (folio 77r).

[148] The name of the *Pasté coquart* seems to designate some sort of fanciful creation. No similar name appears to exist in any other culinary manual of the time.

[149] That is, suet.

be outlined here: in the best one, the beef pasty should be located[150], in another compartment should be a lamprey, in another compartment should be set a young fat gosling, in another compartment /68v/ a dove, in another, pollacks, in another, small birds which are stuffed with fat cheese and beef marrow, in another, big chunks of good big fresh eel and partridge, in another, big chunks of fresh trout, and in another, the last compartment—provided you want nothing else in the pie—fat grain-fed capons.

42. Now it is necessary to know what sauces are appropriate for eating this pasty. These are: for the lamprey, Lamprey Sauce[151]; and to inform the saucer who will be making these sauces, he should get his white bread in the quantity of what he will be making, and toast it nicely; he should have the best vinegar in a reasonable quantity; then he should get his spices, cinnamon, white ginger, grains of paradise, cloves, and not too much of them, /69r/ nutmegs, mace and galingale, and he should put all of these spices with his bread and strain it all together, add in a little salt, and put it to boil; and put in a little sugar.

43. When the pasty is borne in, it is served with another saucing, the sauce for the gosling and the grain-fed capon, Jance[152]: to instruct the

---

[150] The different compartments alternate in their contents between meat and fish. The first of the supplementary dishes explained in this new section continues therefore to offer by itself a choice to those who may prefer lean foods to "meat" foods, or vice versa.

[151] This Lamprey Sauce is to be available on the dining table, along with the other sauces which will be mentioned below, ready to be used as soon as the Coquart Pasty is opened. In the *Viandier* this sauce is used in a dish called *Lamproye fresche a la saulce chaude* (p. 95).

[152] Jance was one of the most commonly used sauces in the fourteenth and fifteenth centuries. Although the basic ingredient was always the ginger which gave this sauce its essential character, there existed a number of sub-varieties of Jance depending on what other ingredients entered the mixture. The *Viandier* alone copies four distinct Jance sauces: Jance of Cow's Milk, Garlic Jance, and so forth. Chiquart's Jance resembles the *Viandier's Jance aux aulx* (p. 34), which is repeated in the *Menagier* (§§287 and 288); Chiquart adds grains of

person who will be making that Jance, he should get almonds in the quantity he wants to make of the sauce, he should skin them neatly and put them to be ground fully in the mortar. Depending on the quantity of that sauce, he should peel garlic in the necessary quantity, and he should not put in too much. He should get good white wine and verjuice, white ginger and grains of paradise, and strain it all together, and add in salt, though not too much, and then put it to boil in a good clean kettle; then dress it out to be served with the pasty. /69v/

44. For the salmon and for the trout, Camelin Sauce[153]: to instruct the saucer who will be making it, he should get his white bread in the quantity he will be making, and set it to toast on the grill. He should have good claret wine, the best he can get, along with a fair amount of vinegar, in which he should put his bread to soak. He should get the spices, that is, cinnamon, ginger, grains of paradise, cloves, a little pepper, mace, nutmegs and a little sugar, and mix all of that in with his bread and a little salt. Then you can serve it up when you wish.

The doves, with fine salt; the small birds produce their own sauce; the eel, with sorrel green sauce.

The chief cook making that pasty should watch very carefully /70r/

---

paradise to his version, though. In the *Recueil* we read "On large poultry, almond jance of white ginger and verjuice" (§36). S.a. the Gaunceli for gees in the *Forme of Cury*, Hieatt and Butler, IV, §146: this sauce is our Garlic Jance.

Other recipes for *jance* will be offered later in Recipes 46 and 58 of the *On Cookery*.

[153] Camelin is, like Jance, one of the classic, ubiquitous condiments in medieval gastronomy. Unlike Jance, Camelin is an unboiled sauce and has as its base the other "primary" spice of the period, cinnamon. (See Note 132, above, concerning the standard color of Camelin.) Recipes for Camelin are found in the *Viandier* (p. 109), and in the *Menagier* (§271) and even, as *Camellina*, in the *Opusculum de saporibus* of Magninus Mediolanensis (ed. Thorndike, p. 188). The *Salsa cammellina* in the *LVII Ricette* (§§46 and 47) is remarkably similar to Chiquart's, except for the omission of grains of paradise and the inclusion of hazel nuts in the earlier Italian recipe.

that his spices—white ginger, grains of paradise, a little pepper and saffron for color—are good, and to season all the meat of the above-mentioned pasty by rubbing it with salt.

And the chief cook should be sure to have a small piece of good pork which is good and clean, and which has been parboiled; this he should cut into long slices to place inside the pasty, putting two of them the length of the gosling, and also on the capon and on the doves.

45. To instruct the person who will be making the Pilgrim Capons[154], he should pluck his fat capons, prepare them carefully and clean them so as to mount them on the spit. If it is the time of the year in which /70v/ lampreys can be had, for every capon you are ordered to make see that you have a lamprey; and if they are not in season, see that you have big fresh eels to make the staffs for the Pilgrim Capons. When your capons are mounted on good clean spits, take your lampreys, scrub the slime from them, clean them out fully, remove their tongue and wash them good and thoroughly. Then, each capon should be girded and encircled with its lamprey; if you cannot get enough of them, do with big eels what you would have done with the lampreys, making sure that they are scrubbed of their slime, cleaned out and washed; fix them all around the capons by means of pretty good clean skewers or ties. When they are thus prepared, put them /71r/ against the fire to roast; and make the area beneath good and clean and put fine silver dishes to catch and collect the grease which will issue and fall from the capons and lampreys—if you do not have enough dishes, use good clean pans. While you are preparing your capons and lampreys or eels, set good pieces of beef to boil nicely, with marrow bones and mutton, and put some of that bouillon into the silver dishes or pans which are catching the lampreys' grease and blood, from which the Dodine[155] will be made.

---

[154] Chiquart's *Chappons pelerins* is found in the *Fleur de toute cuysine* (folios 11r–v) as well. The dish has a lean counterpart which Chiquart was accustomed to prepare, and which appears among the menus for the lean banquet at the end of the *On Cookery* (folio 109v): *Lucs dorés pelerins*, "Glazed Pilgrim Pike".

[155] *Daudine* is a sauce whose base is the drippings from the roast with

When your capons are well cooked, be sure to have a very clean pot, either a two-handled one or any other type, to make sure that, when your capons are well cooked and you are taking them off the spit, none of them will lose its /71v/ staff, that is to say, its lamprey. When your capons are off the spit, get a good pot which is very clean and get a good strainer and strain into that pot what you have collected in the silver dish or pan from the capons and lampreys; and if you see that there is not enough broth to make the Dodine, draw it out with your good beef bouillon. Get white ginger and a few grains of paradise, and flavour it with verjuice—though not too much—and with salt, too. Get good parsley, chop off its leaves; get your table bread and cut good slices for toasting; get very good Crampone cheese or Brie cheese, or the best cheese that can be had; of the slices of toast cut each into three strips, /72r/ then set them out on your dishes, with cheese over them, and then pour your broth over top of that. When they go to the dresser, those sops are served up; and in another dish put the Pilgrim Capons.

46. It now remains to be explained with what sauce the Pilgrim Capons should be eaten: the Pilgrim Capons should be eaten with Jance sauce, and to inform the saucer who is to make it, he should get good almonds and shell and clean them well, and grind them up thoroughly; he should get white bread without the crusts, in the quantity he will need, and he should have the best white wine he can obtain, and some verjuice, in which he should set his bread to soak. When his almonds are ground, add to them a little /72v/ ground garlic; get white ginger and grains of paradise in an amount needed for the sauce, and strain all of that together, drawing it out with white wine and a little verjuice; add in some salt too; and set it to boil in a good clean pot.

If the staffs are lampreys, make the Lamprey Sauce in the way outlined above for the Lamprey Pasty.[156]

---

which it will be served and which has the flavor of verjuice. The printed *Viandier* (p. 178) contains one of the possible versions of a Dodine. (See also the *Viandier*, pp. 88 and 91.)

[156] This Lamprey Pasty is the section of the Coquart Pasty which contains the lamprey, and the Lamprey Sauce has indeed been described in Recipe

If they are eels, Green Garlic Sauce made of sorrel and verjuice.

47. The Calunafree of Partridge[157]: the person who will be making this dish should get his partridge and clean them fully, plump them, lard them well, then mount them on the spit and /*73r*/ roast them nicely; when they are roasted, take them down onto good clean wooden tables, then take them one after the other and dismember them in the proper way, leaving the wings whole and cutting up the white meat just as small as if you were carving in front of your lord, and put all that into good silver dishes – and if you do not have enough silver dishes, put it into a good clean pan. Take a lot of camelin sauce and spread it on in such a way that everything is bathed in it, and put on only enough mustard to give a slight flavor of it, and only enough verjuice to wash over everything. According to the amount of meat you have, get kidneys[158], chop them up very small and add them in, with sugar, and season it with salt properly; then set it to boil. /*73v*/ Then, when it comes to the

---

42. A recipe for a separate Lamprey Pie is offered in the *LVII Ricette*, §28: *Lampreda in crosta*.

[157] In the *Menagier de Paris* (§285) a recipe called *Calimafree, ou Saulse paresseuse* is composed of mustard, ginger, vinegar and verjuice; it is served with a carp or with a capon. Neither Brereton and Ferrier in their edition of the *Menagier*, nor Pichon in his, indicate that the various manuscripts of the *Viandier* show any hesitation in the spelling of the name of this dish. For Jehan de Dudens, however, the name is never written with an *i*, even though on folio 67 v, the *i* in the name *calaminee*, which precedes *calunefree*, is clearly distinguished with a superscribed vertical stroke. The *Galimafree* of the printed *Viandier* (ed. Pichon and Vicaire, p. 168) and of the *Fleur de toute cuisine* (folio 25) is a dish of poultry similar to the *Menagier*'s preparation.

[158] In the manuscript the word is *rignions*, which means "kidneys". There is the possibility, however, that what was copied is a scribal error for *oignions*. The Tremollete of Partridge (§12) which this dish resembles in some ways does indeed make use of gizzard and liver of the fowl. But onion is normally fried before being used as a culinary ingredient. We have just seen that the Coquart Pasty requires *de la belle gresse du roignion du beuf, et cela soit haché bien menu* ... (folio 68r).

dresser, dole it out into fine dishes in a suitable manner.

48. To instruct the person who will be making the Calaminee and the Cold Sage[159], he should get his poultry in the quantity he is ordered to make of those sauces, and suckling piglets as well; take it, prepare it and clean it thoroughly; quarter the poultry and cut up the piglet into good little pieces, wash it all well and completely, then put it to cook in a good clean cauldron, with salt according to the amount he is ordered to make of it. Get a great number of eggs and boil them in a good cauldron, and cook them until they are hard; /74r/ then get white bread that is well trimmed of its crusts, sliced and put into the two two-handled pots in an amount proper for those sauces. Then get egg yolks, put them to steep with the bread in the two-handled pot in which you are making the Calaminee. The get your spices in the amount you will be making of that sauce: that is, white ginger, grains of paradise, pepper, saffron and sugar, and enough verjuice for the quantity of the sauce, and salt. Make the sauce very thick, and strain it very thick until it does not run together with the other.

49. To inform you how to make the Cold Sage[160], see that you have a

---

[159] *la calaminee et la froyde sauge.* These are two quite distinct sauces, the first being boiled and of a yellow color, and the second unboiled and green. They accompany two meats which are likewise different, though both white. Concerning the name *Calaminee* it should be observed that other sources offer recipes for a dish which is regularly spelled with an *s*: *Salamine* (for example, in the printed *Viandier*, p. 147; and even later in the work of Chiquart himself, on folio 110 r), *Salemine* (*Menagier*, p. 180, l. 5), *Salomono* (*Libro per cuoco*, p. 89) and *Salaminee* (made for carp and pike, in the *Menagier*, p. 181, l. 32). According to DuCange, the word *salsamentum* had a form *salamentum*: "condimentum, Gall. *sauce*".

[160] The *Froid sauge* is a widely used poultry sauce in the Middle Ages. In the *Enseignements* (l. 19) the *Savor verte* used on fresh pork is composed of "pepper and ginger and parsley and sage, moistened with verjuice or with vinegar or with straight wine". The *Sauce verte* of the *Viandier* (p. 33) and of the *Menagier de Paris* (§276) no longer calls for sage, but a recipe for *Une froide sauge* which is almost identical to what is in Chiquart appears in both

great deal of parsley, a great deal of sage, and that they are properly /74v/ culled, washed and drained, and well ground up, and grind an amount large enough that the sauce is quite green; when they are well ground, mix them in with your bread. Then get your spices, that is, white ginger, grains of paradise and pepper, and strain all that, season it with vinegar and salt, and strain it very thick. When your meat is well cooked, take it out onto good boards and good clean tables, then divide up the meat, that is, the poultry to one side and to the other the pieces of the piglet, so that when it comes to the dresser you can put in each dish four pieces of that meat, that is, a quarter of poultry and a little piece of the piglet in the upper half of each dish, and in the other half the same again; and in each dish in one part put some of the Calaminee, and in the other part some of the Cold Sage. /75r/ Then get some egg whites and chop them to the size of small dice, then scatter them over those dishes on top of the Cold Sage, and put candies on top of the Calunafree.[161]

50. Again, Norse Pasties[162]: to instruct the person who will be making them, he should get his good pork in the amount he is to make of them, then get a great quantity of poultry gizzards and livers, clean them well and set them to cook; get a good, very clean piece of bacon lard, a good cut of meat, and put it in to boil with the other; then when his meat is cooked, he should take it out onto good clean wooden tables and separate his pork and hack it up very small; he should take the gizzards and livers

---

works: *Viandier*, p. 94; *Menagier*, §244.

[161] Is this *calunafree* in error for *calaminee*? In the careful details of the garnishing of this composite dish, Chiquart's concern for colors and for the attractive appearance of the finished dish is particularly noticeable.

[162] The name of this dish, *Pastez nurriz* in Chiquart, is found in various forms in the French recipe collections of the time: *Pastez norreis* (of fish, in the *Enseignements*, l. 170), *Pastez nourroys* (of cooked meat, in the *Viandier*, p. 128), and *Pastez norroiz* (of cod liver, in the *Menagier*, §258). For Godefroy *norois* means "nordic", yet the form of the word used by Chiquart suggests the possibility of an etymon such as *nutritus*, or at least a confusion in his mind with the semantic field of which "nourishing" would be a part.

and his chopped meat and put them in and brown all of that together. He should get /75v/ his spices: white ginger, grains of paradise, saffron, a lot of sugar depending on the amount of the filling, and he should flavour it with salt and spices so that there is neither too little nor too much of anything; and eggs, too, according to the quantity of the filling. Then deliver it to the pastry chef, and your cook should advise his pastry chef to make his crusts quite small and tall for frying; and see that you have a lot of fresh pork fat filling your pots to the top in order to fry the pasties. Then see that you have a good pot quite full of the best and finest wine that can be obtained, and put it to boil on a good bright coal fire, and boil it until it is reduced to a half or a third; get a loaf of sugar and have it broken up, and put in an amount of it proper for the quantity of the job you are doing, and if there is not enough /76r/ in one loaf, put in more or less that amount. Get your spices: cinnamon, ginger and grains of paradise, and put in a moderate amount according to the quantity of the broth, and a little salt, and put in whole cloves, an ounce or two, more or less, depending on the quantity of wine syrup or conserve you've made. When it comes to the dresser, set out your pasties in fine dishes and pour that syrup over the top.

51. Again, Rissoles[163]: to instruct the person who will be making them depending on the quantity he will be making he should get a quantity o fresh pork and cut it up into good pieces which are good and clean anf

---

[163] Recipes for *Rissoles* can be read in most of the cookery books of the late Middle Ages, but there is very little uniformity between them. The version of this dish transmitted by the *Menagier de Paris* (§261) has certain features in common with the Raysols in the *Forme of Cury* (§152) and with the Rissheus in the *Liber cure cocorum* (p. 39), but all three are much less rich in ingredients than Chiquart's *Rosseolles*. In the *Libre de sent soví* (p. 150) there is an even simpler recipe named *Resoles de paste e d'ous e de fformatge*. The dish has many variations in English cookery: see, for example, Risschewes in Austin (pp. 43, 44, 45, 85, 93, 97, etc.). And in Italian cookery other names represent the same type of preparation: see, for example, *Rafioli* and *Pasteri* in Faccioli (pp. 78, 79, 83). DuCange gives the following gloss: "*Roisola, roissola: Placentae genus si dictae a colore subrubido*" (Vol. VII, p. 208 a).

On Cookery

put them to cook, with salt added; when his meat is cooked, he should take it out onto good clean tables and draw off the skin and remove all the bones, then hack it up very small. See that you have figs, prunes, dates, pinenuts and candied raisins; remove the seeds from the raisins and the shells from the pinenuts, and anything else /76v/ that is not clean; then wash all that thoroughly two or three times in good white wine and put it to drain on good clean wooden tables; then cut the figs, prunes and dates to the size of small dice and stir them into your filling. Then see that you have the best cheese that can be made, get a great amount of good parsley leaves, wash them and chop them up into your cheese; then stir that thoroughly into your filling, and eggs too. Get your spices: white ginger, grains of paradise, and not too much, saffron, and a great deal of sugar according to the quantity you will be making. Then deliver your filling to your pastry chef, and he should have been told to have a supply of good gold-colored puff pastry[164] prepared; when the pasties are made, he should bring them to you, /77r/ and you should have a supply of good white pork fat to fry them. When they are fried, you should have a supply of gold leaf: for each glazing there is, you need a gold leaf to put on top. And when it comes to the dresser, set them out in fine dishes and then throw suger over the top.

52. Again, a Hot-Dish: to instruct the person who will be doing the Party Hot-Dish[165], which is also called *Morterieulx*[166], he should get a lot of pork meat in the amount that he is ordered to make, he should

---

[164] The word which Chiquart uses here is *doreures* (*ses beaux folliés de paste pour faire les doreures*); the term normally means simply glazings. It is clear, though, here that what is meant is the pastry sheath or envelope which encloses the mixture of chopped meat and fruit, and that *doreure* may perhaps retain something of its etymological sense of "gilding". In certain English pasties (for instance in the Ryschewys close & fryez, ed. Austin, p. 45) the recipe calls for saffron to be added into the pastry mix; this would lend a golden color to the dough even before it is fried.

[165] This dish appears to have several possible names. The *Menagier* makes use of two of these alternative names: *Potage party* and *Faulx grenon* (§246).

[166] The dish to which Chiquart initially gives the name *Chaut mengier*, then *Chaut mengier parti*, is described in the *Menagier de Paris*, under the name

clean it, wash it thoroughly, and set it to cook, putting in salt; when it is cooked, take it out onto good clean wooden tables, remove the skin and the bones, and then hack it up very small. Then get good bread and let it /77v/ soak in your good beef bouillon; with that get spices and add in white ginger, grains of paradise, pepper—and not too much, and saffron to give it color, and strain it, adding verjuice and white wine, and strain all that together; then put it to boil in a good pot on good hot coals. Then put the meat to brown lightly in good white lard in a fine pan, fry it good and nicely, and when it has been fried add in a little of the bouillon; then get enough eggs for the amount there is of the pottage and strain the yolks into it through a bolting cloth in order to bind it. When the time comes to take this to the dresser to serve up, see that there is a big dish full of powdered cinnamon with a lot of beaten sugar /78r/ in it; at the dresser, put your *Faugrenon*[167] in your dish, and cover the

---

Mortereul, as a variety of *Faulx grenon* (§236). The name *Faugrenon* is also used by Chiquart towards the end of his recipe (on folio 78r) to designate this dish. The manuscripts of the *Viandier* make no mention of a *Morterel* although this name does appear in the printed editions of the work at the end of the fifteenth century (ed. Pichon and Vicaire, p. 159). The dish is the Latin *Martoriolum* (*Liber de coquina*, Part II, §22; cf. Part I, §31); the English Mortrewes (Austin, pp. 14, 28, 70, etc.; *Forme of Cury*, §45 and §46, Hieatt and Butler, IV, §46; *Liber cure cocorum*, pp. 9 and 13); and *Mortrellus* (in the English *Diuersa servicia*, ed. Hieatt and Butler, II, §5); the Anglo-Norman *Double mortrels* (Meyer, §8); and the Italian *Mortarolo* (Faccioli, p. 76). In the Catalan *Libre de sent soví* there are seven varieties of dish called *Morterol* (Nos. 104-108; and App. I, Nos. 37 and 71) for the preparation of other meats, which are chopped up but not ground. See *mortariolum* in DuCange: the word derives from *mortarium*, "mortar".

[167] Chiquart uses the word *faugrenon* as an alternate name for the Party Hot-Dish "which is also called *Morterieulx*". The recipes for *Faulx grenon* in the *Viandier* (p. 91) and in the *Menagier* do indeed resemble Chiquart's recipe here quite closely. The *Menagier* even offers a variation on his own *Faulx grenon* which he calls *Potage party* (p. 246). The commentary which the *Menagier* writes about this dish is not entirely applicable to Chiquart's dish: "*Mortereul* is made like *Faulx grenon*, except that the meat is ground up in

one half of that pottage with the powder and leave the other half bare, and in that way it will be "party".

53. Again, to serve up the Green Shoulders of Mutton in the blood from those shoulders[168]: to instruct the person who will be doing them, he should get the foreshoulders, wash them, and mount them on very clean spits. He should see to it that, in the morning when bulls are butchered, the marrow bones are set aside to be boiled in a good big clean pot. When the shoulders are laid on the fire and dried of the moisture on them, get fine silver dishes—or good clean pans if there are no such dishes—and set them underneath, and put some beef bouillon in them so that they can catch the blood of the shoulders; /78v/ then, when they are cooked, take your dishes and what is mixed in them, and strain it through a good bolting cloth. Then get your spices: cinnamon, for the amount that is being made, ginger, grains of paradise and cloves, and get wine and a little vinegar to flavour it, sugar and a reasonable amount of salt, and boil all of this together. Then set out your shoulders in good dishes with that sauce over top.

54. The Breast of Boar.[169] I can instruct the person who will be charged with making it: if it should happen that the boar is young, he should take his breast and let it boil fully on a hot fire, then wash it thoroughly and scrape it clean; then he should have a good spit and spit the breast skillfully between the hide and the flesh, so that /79r/ when it is half

---

the mortar with spices of (*sic*) cinnamon; and there is no bread (in it), but cinnamon powder (sprinkled) over top" (§236).

[168] On folio 67v the dish was called "Green Shoulders of Mutton which are eaten with a sauce of the blood of those shoulders." For the *Menagier de Paris* (§140), the distinctive color of these shoulders comes from the parsley sauce with which they are basted during their roasting.

[169] Other versions of this *entremets*-like preparation can be read in the *Menagier de Paris* (§146: *Bourbelier de sanglier*), in the *Viandier* (p. 89: *Boubier de sanglier frez*), and in the *Fleur de toute cuysine* (folio 15 r: *Boubellier de sanglier*) where the recipe seems more closely related to Chiquart's. Cf. as well the *Queue de sangler* which is described in the *Menagier* (§§42 and 293) and in the *Recueil* (§13).

roasted he can remove the hide. When this is off, lard the boar carefully and put it back to roast until it is almost done, then take it off the fire; see that he has good whole cloves and that he sticks the breast with them properly[170], then put it back to cook in a pretty bright fire until it is done. The breast of this sort of young boar should not be cut up but should be set whole between two gold dishes, and then borne in before the lord.

54a. Should it happen that the breast is large, that is to say, the boar, and that it is in the month of October or November when they are in season, the huntsmen should deliver the breast to the Chief Cook whole, without removing anything, and /79v/ the Chief Cook should split the breast into two halves lengthwise, then remove the skin carefully; when this is done, he should wash the halves fully in good clean water, then set them to plump in good beef or mutton bouillon—and if he has neither beef nor mutton bouillon, he should make his bouillon of equal quantities of wine and water, with sufficient salt—and leave the breast in there long enough. When it has boiled enough, take it out and rinse it in good fresh water, then set it to drain on good wooden tables; when it has dried, lard it carefully, then mount it on good clean spits and put it to roast. When it is close to done, take it down; see that you have good whole cloves and stick them into the meat properly; when they have been stuck in, return the half-breasts to the fire /80r/ until they are completely done. When they are done, take them off and put them whole into good dishes, and then present them to the lord.

55. To instruct the person who will be making the sauce which is appropriate for this[171], he should get his white bread and cut it into good slices and put it to toast on the grill until it is brown—and don't let it burn; then he should get the best claret wine available in which to set his

---

[170] Of the cookery books of the fourteenth century, only the *Menagier* (§146) speaks of sticking the breast of boar with whole cloves.

[171] In the fourteenth century this sauce was used to garnish the Breast of Boar in the *Viandier* (p. 89), and in the *Menagier* (§146) who writes: "And this sauce is called Boar's Tail (*Queue de sanglier*) . . . ." See the same recipe in the *Menagier* at §293.

toast to soak, and he should get a little lean beef or mutton bouillon and add this in moderately according to the quantity of sauce he wants to make, and vinegar, too, moderately. Then he should get his spices: white ginger, grains of paradise, cloves—and not too much, a little pepper, a lot of cinnamon[172], a little mace, and two or three nutmegs depending /80v/ on the quantity needed; he should put his bread into this, and a reasonable amount of salt, too; then he should pass all of this through a good clean bolting cloth. Then you put this sauce, made like that, to boil; and watch carefully that it does not burn; when it has boiled as much as it should, dish it out into good clean bowls. It is served up with the Breast of Boar.

56. To instruct the person who will be making the Mortoexes[173], he should get kid and calf crows and wash and clean them very well and put them to cook in good clean water; when they have cooked enough, take them out onto good clean work-tables and drain them well, then chop them up very small; when they are all chopped up, add in herbs, that is to say, sage and hyssop—both in moderation—and marjoram,

---

[172] This sauce for Breast of Boar is essentially a cinnamon sauce and resembles the Camelin sauce (of Recipe 44) specified for piglet (folio 26r). By its nature, the flesh of wild boar shares the qualities of pork, being cold and moist, but at the same time it is influenced by its habitat and to some extent takes after the nature of wild animals, which generally are warmer and dryer than their domestic counterparts. Boar meat can therefore be assimilated to that of the relatively temperate creatures, such as partridge, pheasant, veal, salmon and trout (folios 26r, 34r, 56v, 69v) for whom Camelin sauce is an appropriate condiment.

[173] The fourteenth-century Italian *Libro per cuoco* (ed. Faccioli, p. 77) contains a recipe similar to Chiquart's Mortoexes, called *Mortadelle bone e perfette*. Cf. also the *Mortadelle* of Maestro Martino, *Libro de arte coquinaria* (*idem*, p. 128). They are a sort of spiced sausage in the form of ravioli. For the word *mortadelli*, Faccioli offers the following gloss: "*Insaccati (dal latino myrtatum) salame condito con coccole di mirto)*" (*idem*, p. 22, n. 2). See Jacques André, *L'alimentation et la cuisine à Rome*, Paris (Klincksieck), 1961, p. 200.

too, and /*81r*/ a great deal of parsley which has been culled, cleaned and washed; chop them into the meat, and very good cheese as well, though not too much, and salt, too, and spices: white ginger, grains of paradise, pepper — not too much — and saffron to give it color; then get eggs and add them in. Mix all of that together, and then, when it is boiling, make the Mortoexes. See that he has kid and calf cauls —and if there are not enough, get sheep cauls—and make sure they are good and clean, then stretch them out on good clean wooden tables; when they are stretched, get eggs and rub them on them. When this is done, get the filling, put it on them, and make the Mortoexes in the same way as ravioli[174]: wrap them up in the cauls, and then put them /*81v*/ to cook on the grill. And if he should want to make them party-colored, that is, in green and yellow[175]: for the green he should get a lot of parsley, enough for the quantity he would like to make green, take the leaves, wash them well then put them in the mortar and grind them strongly; then he should add in some flour and some eggs in an amount for the quantity he wants to make, then strain that very carefully; when this is done, he should take the Mortoexes he wants to make green and drop them into that green mixture and move them around in it, then return them to dry on the grill. When they have dried and are ready, these Mortoexes are served up when it is time to serve them.

57. Again, a Vinaigrette[176]: to instruct the person who will be making

---

[174] On the making of ravioli see the *Forme of Cury*, ed. Hieatt and Butler, IV, §94; and the *Libro della cocina*, p. 35: *Dei guanti, cioè ravioli*.

[175] The process for creating a green color seems alone to be treated in what follows. The author has not overlooked the yellow, however, since those Mortoexes which are not made green remain, by default, yellow in color because of the eggs and saffron they contain. The "green" mortoexes will consequently in fact be of a *"verd gay"* hue.

[176] This is essentially the same recipe as is found in the *Viandier* (p. 82) and in the *Menagier* (§105); in these versions the meat is small cuts (*menue haste*, normally various viscera) of pork. In its recipe for *Une vinesgrete de menuz hastez de porc*, the *Recueil* (§2) explains the term *menuz hastez*: " ... That is, livers, spleens and tripe (*frasez*)."

the Vinaigrette, /*82r*/ he should get pork livers and wash them, then put them on the grill over fine glowing coals until they are cooked enough; when they are done, put them on good work-tables and slice them up to the size of small dice; then get a lot of onions, peel, wash and slice them very small, and brown all that together in good fine lard. To make the Vinaigrette, he should get very good claret wine, the best he can obtain, enough for the amount of the pottage, and add to it whatever beef or mutton bouillon is necessary; then he should get some good white bread and cut in into good slices and put it to toast on the grill until it is quite brownish, then set it to soak in that wine and bouillon. When it has soaked, get spices: white ginger, grains of paradise, pepper—and /*82v*/ not too much—a lot of cinnamon in the necessary amount, and salt, too[177]; then pass all of that neatly and properly through the strainer, and set it to boil; when it has boiled, dump the fried meat into it. Then serve it up when it is time to.

57a. If it should not be the time of year when pork livers are available[178],

---

[177] Chiquart has forgotten to mention the liquid in which these spices are to be moistened, vinegar, the essential ingredient from which the name of the dish itself derived. The authors of the *Viandier* and the *Menagier* macerate their spices in the vinegar at this point in their recipes.

[178] The availability of the various meats usually varied according to the season of the year. Louis Stouff shows the changing proportions, month by month, of each species of meat in the total of the carcasses passing through the butchery of the town of Carpentras during that very year in which Chiquart was writing his book, 1419-1420 (*Ravitaillement et alimentation en Provence*, Paris-The Hague (Mouton), 1970, p. 185). In his charts it can be seen that, between the months of March and September, pork constituted only a minor part of this butchery's product, whereas mutton, lamb and beef accounted for much the greater amount of its activity. On the other hand, during the period between October and February the movement of pork reached its maximum, claiming up to 15% of the total market in the month of November. See also the same sort of very detailed study by S. Frescura Nepoti, "Macellazione e consumo della carne a Bologna ... per gli inizi del secolo XV," *Archeologia Medievale*, Vol. VIII (1981), pp. 281-297.

get good loins of beef and legs of mutton, and wash them mount them on the spit and roast them thoroughly; when they have roasted, take them down onto good clean wooden tables, then cut them up to the size of small dice as was said above for the pork liver; and onions, too, as was said above, and brown everything together; when it is done enough, put it into the pottage which was outlined above. /83r/ **58.** A Jance[179]: to instruct the person who will be making this Jance, he should get good fine table bread in a quantity large enough for what he is wanting to make, and grate it carefully over a fine cloth. Then he should get a good bright clean kettle and strain some fat beef and mutton bouillon into it, and check that it is not too salty. Then he should get eggs and mix them with the bread and then put that into the bouillon slowly, stirring continuously with a good wooden spoon. He should put in his spices as well, that is, white ginger, grains of paradise, a little pepper, and saffron to give it color, and flavor it with verjuice. Have all of this boil together, then serve it up.

59. A Gruel Broth of Capons[180]: /83v/ to instruct the person who will be making that Gruel Broth of Capons, he should get his fat, castrated capons and pluck them neatly, wash them thoroughly and then put them to cook along with whatever meat is appropriate, that is, in wintertime good fresh pork loins and feet, and in summer good kids and veal[181] and salt pork, whichever will meet the need, which has been very well cleaned, washed and parboiled a little ahead of time. Those who will be doing them would be well advised, the day before the gruel broth is made, to see that he has good whole oats; he should cull through them and clean every grain of them so that nothing is left but the bare grain, then wash them thoroughly in three or four changes of warm water and set them to boil in good water in a good bright clean pot; and he should

---

[179] This is the third occurence of a recipe for Jance (see above, §§43 and 46). Ginger sauces were clearly favorites with Chiquart, and perhaps with his master as well.

[180] This combination of ground almonds and oats was a generally known preparation: in the *Forme of Cury* (§86) it is called Grewel of almondes.

[181] See Note 177, above.

prepare the quantity of it that he is /*84r*/ ordered to do. When it is half cooked, take it down and remove it from the kettle, from the water in which it has been boiling, then set it again to boil in water which is good and clear and clean, and put it back to boil for an hour or so. When it has boiled enough, let it sit until the next day. Depending on the quantity of the broth he is ordered to make, he should see that he has enough almonds, he should skin, clean and wash them very well, then grind them in the mortar moistening them with the capon bouillon, and draw them out; put in that bouillon in the quantity of the pottage he wants to make, and he should give it the flavour of verjuice and of white wine. According to the quantity of that broth, he should add in some spices, that is, white ginger and grains of paradise, and strain all that along with the almonds; when everything has been strained, he should see that he has a bright, good, very clean kettle large enough for the quantity of broth, and /*84v*/ put it all in it, then set it to boil on a good bright fire; put in a lot of sugar proportionate to the quantity of the broth, and a moderate amount of salt, and a little beaten[182] saffron to give it a little color. Then get that oat mixture which has been sitting, squeeze the water from it through a good bolting cloth, and be careful to check that there is nothing that should not be in it; when this is done, put it into the broth which was spoken of above. After this, take out the capons and meat onto good clean wooden tables, then arrange those capons and meat in good dishes, with the gruel broth poured over top.

60. Glazed Kid Heads[183] set alongside the crow: to instruct the person

---

[182] The word *batu* is added in the margin of the manuscript.

[183] The *Fleur de toute cuysine* (folio 35r) contains this recipe under the name *Testes de chevreaulx frites dorees*, but the preparation of the kid heads is not nearly as carefully done there as Chiquart directs. See as well the *Frazes de seing de chevreaux et de testes* in the *Recueil* (§15), in which the heads are "split on the grill, and they should be wrapped in the caul of the kid so that the brains do not fall into the coals." In the *Sent sovi* (§15 and §182), there is what might be termed a more utilitarian than ornamental treatment of sheep, kid and calf heads: they undergo a cooking intended solely to separate the flesh from the bones.

who will be preparing these Kid Heads, he should get the heads and clean the eyes and ears /85r/ thoroughly; under the throat he should make a little cut, and not too big so that it doesn't open up, and clean them out carefully by it, and wash them; then in each head he should insert a skewer crosswise so that they do not open up and the brains come out; then put them to cook properly in a kettle or cauldron in which they have room to cook, and add in some salt. When they are cooked, take them out onto good clean work-tables to drain and, when they are quite dry, pull out the skewers and put each head into two halves. Then he should see that he has the cauls of those kids—and if there are not enough of them from kids, he should see about getting calf cauls, and lacking those, sheep cauls—and check that they are very good and clean; /85v/ then stretch them out on good clean work-tables and, once they are stretched out, he should get fresh eggs to rub on each one of the cauls; when this is done, he should take each half-head and wrap it in the caul of the kid, calf or sheep, and then put them on the grill.

61. For Crow[184]: he who will be in charge of the Crow should get kid livers—and if there are not enough from kids, he should get them from calves—and clean and wash them well, then put them to cook nicely; once cooked, take them out onto good clean work-tables and, when they have dried, chop them up very small; /86r/ when they are chopped up well, he should see that he has good lard, properly melted in good clean pans, then put that chopped liver into them to fry and brown it nicely. Then see that there are a great number of eggs, break them into good dishes and scramble them all together; add in spices: that is, white ginger, grains of paradise, saffron, and salt in good measure; then put all of that slowly into the pans to fry along with the liver, stirring and stirring, continuously mixing with a good spoon around the pans until it is well cooked and dry and on the brownish side. Then, when it comes to the dresser, he should arrange the previously mentioned heads /86v/

---

[184] The same dish is found in the *Viandier* (p. 86), in the *Liber cure cocorum* ("For a froyse," p. 50) and in those recipe collections published by Austin ("Froyse," pp. 45 and 86). Chiquart's recipes here can be compared with those for *ffrexures* contained in the *Sent soví* (§§121 125).

in good dishes, and in each dish beside the heads he should set out this crow.

62. A Gratunee[185]: to instruct the person who will be making it, if it should happen that he is in the season when new peas are available, he should get fresh new peas in the quantity he is ordered to make, they should be neatly shelled and so thoroughly cleaned that there is nothing left but the pea itself; then they should be well washed and put to cook in good water in good clean kettles, and with them there should be a piece of salt pork which has previously been /87r/ thoroughly cleaned, washed and parboiled a little. When the peas are cooked nicely, without bursting and while still whole, take them out onto good clean work-tables for the water to drain from them; then take that piece of salt pork which was cooked with the peas and slice it up to the size of small dice. Then see that he has his poultry which is fully plucked, cleaned and washed, then cut into halves; and depending on the quantity of the poultry, see that he has kid meat which has been cut into little pieces roughly the size of those half chickens; all of that, that is, the chickens and the kid meat, should be put to cook together in a good clean kettle or cauldron in which it has room to cook, and with it a piece /87v/ of salt pork which, like the other piece of pork, has been well cleaned, washed and parboiled little; and put in a moderate amount of salt as well, and cook it well. For the quantity he is to make of that Gratunee, he should see that he has enough milk and strain it into a bright, good and clean kettle and boil it; then take a lot of egg yolks, put them through a strainer, and proper amounts of white ginger and grains of paradise, and a little saffron only to sustain the color of the egg yolks; all of that should be put into the milk when it comes to a full boil, pouring gradually, stirring continuously and mixing with a good clean spoon; and keep adding it in until the milk /88r/ is quite bound. Then take out the chickens and meat to dry on good clean wooden tables; then get a lot of good lard and melt

---

[185] A somewhat more simple version of this dish is described in the *Viandier* (p. 80) and in the *Menagier de Paris* (§95) under the name of *Cretonnee de poys nouveaulx*. In the *Libro della cocina* (ed. Faccioli, pp. 34, 38 and 47), the name *Gratonata* refers to a chicken dish which is quite different.

it good pans and, when it has melted and is clarified, put the chickens and meat into it to fry nicely; when they are thoroughly done, take them out onto good clean work-tables or into two-handled pots, that is, the chickens to one side and the meat by itself; then fully strain and clarify the lard, returning it to the pans. Then get good fresh eggs and cook them whole in good water until they are hard and can be shelled whole; when they are shelled, divide each egg in half and when they have all been divided put them into the lard to fry until they are brownish, then take them out. After that, /88v/ get the green peas and the piece of salt pork which was diced as was said above, and brown them together in the lard; when they are nicely fried, throw them into the bound milk, and check that as far as salt and anything else is concerned there is nothing in excess. When this is done, set out the chicken halves in good dishes with the meat, and the broth over top; and, besides that, halves of eggs as described above for fried fish[186], laid out on top of each dish, one this way, the other that way. Then they are served.

63. Again, a Spanish Gratunee[187]: to instruct the person who will be charged with doing it, because it is made /89r/ at the time of year when new peas, chicks or kids are not available[188], he should see that he has cockerels and have them plucked, eviscerated and cleaned thoroughly; and he should have fresh pork backs, and pigs ears and feet, too, which have been well skinned, cleaned and washed; then all of that should be put to cook in a good bright clean kettle or cauldron, with salt and a piece of salt pork, a good cut, which has been well cleaned, washed and parboiled a little. Then see that he has great lot of almonds which

---

[186] Jehan de Dudens wrote: ... *des moytiés des oefs ainsi comme dessus est dit frites poissons.* Chiquart may have meant that the eggs are to be prepared as in the recipe for fried fish (?), or that they are to be fried *as* fish (?).

[187] The *Menagier de Paris* mentions a *Cretonnee d'Espaigne* among the dishes of its menus (p. 177, l. 19). The *Gratonia spagnola* of the *Libro della cocina* (ed. Faccioli, p. 34) does not seem to be closely related to Chiquart's dish.

[188] This dish would seem to be offered as a sort of seasonal alternative to the preceding.

he should skin; clean and wash them thoroughly and grind them up in the mortar energetically, and moisten them with the bouillon of those cockerels and the other meat which is with them; then strain this over a good clean two-handled pot, together with the spices, that is to say, good white ginger, grains of paradise and a little cloves, and saffron to give it colour; and add to them /89v/ enough of that bouillon for the quantity he will be wanting to make. Flavour it with good white wine and verjuice, and set it to boil. Check the meat, mentioned above, that it does not overcook; when it is nicely done, take it down onto good clean work tables where it can drain and dry well, and when it is well drained he should take his cockerels and quarter them, and cut up the other meats mentioned above to the size of those quarters. Then see that he has very good, well made lard, and he should prepare and fry all of that meat perfectly; when they have fried enough, set the quarters of cockerel to one side and the meat by itself on good clean work-tables or in two handled pots. Then get that piece of salt pork mentioned above, slice it up into pretty slices, then set them to fry /90r/ in the lard in which he has fried the meat—which lard should previously be thoroughly filtered of any burnt particles of that meat; when they have been fried well, take them out into good dishes. Then check on the bouillon, that there is neither too much nor too little of anything, and add in a lot of sugar according to the quantity of broth there is. Then set out and place the cockerel quarters in fine dishes, and with them the meat mentioned above, and pour the broth over top; and as well, over top, set out the slices of fried salt pork spoken of before, in each dish two or three. Then, when it is time to serve it, serve it up happily.

64. Again, Shoulders of Mutton, stuffed and glazed[189]: to instruct the person who will be charged with making those Shoulders, he should see

---

[189] This same recipe for *Espalles de moustons farcies et dorees* can be read, with some variations, in the *Viandier* (p. 129), in the Latin *Liber de coquina* (Ch. II, §42: *De spatula implenda*, ed. Mulon, p. 407), in the *Libro per cuoco* (*Spalle de castron implite*, ed. Faccioli, p. 87), in the *LVII Ricette* (*Spalle di castrone ripiene*, §14) and in the *Recueil* (§12). Cf. also §5 (*Com se ffercex espatle de molto*) in the *Sent sovi*. Interestingly enough, for the bourgeois *Menagier* this preparation requires more effort than it is judged to be worth;

/*90v*/ that he has the number of good sheep shoulders he is supposed to make, and that he has, too, as many sheep legs; when he has his shoulders and legs, he should rinse and wash them carefully and put them to cook in good bright clean basins or cauldrons, and put in a lot of salt, though in good measure. When they are done, take them out onto good clean work tables, remove all the flesh and leave the bones of each shoulder connected all together, and watch carefully that they don't come apart or break up. Take that meat from the shoulders and legs, and chop it up very small; when it is well chopped up, put it into a good clean two handled pot or pan. See that he has Brie or /*91r*/ Crampone cheese, or the best that can be made; he should chop it up small and mix it in with the meat just mentioned. Then see that he has a lot of good parsley, marjoram and a little hyssop and sage; they should be culled carefully, cleaned, washed and drained of the water, chopped up fine and mixed into that mixture, along with the proper amount of spices, that is, good white ginger, grains of paradise, and whole cloves are put on top; and see that he has good fresh eggs, and add in enough of them for the mixture to be bound thickly, and put in saffron to give it colour. Then he should go to the butchers to get the same number of mutton cauls as he has shoulders to do; then he should set them to rinse a little in good fresh water and he should /*91v*/ rinse them thoroughly; when they have been well washed, he should take them out and stretch each caul on good clean work tables and, when they have dried well, rub two fresh eggs on each caul to glaze it. When this has been done, take the mixture outlined above and spread out a layer of it, then set up the bones from each of the shoulders so that they hold together, and do not remove the ligament: it should be left whole and should keep the three bones of each shoulder from falling apart. Then, on top, put more of that mixture and wrap it all up in the caul in the proper shape and way; and nothing else should be put in than just the mutton shoulders; and

---

according to him, it resembles in this the dish called "Stuffed hens, colored and glazed", concerning which he warns: "There is too much work in it, and it is not the sort of thing for the cook of a bourgeois, or even that of an ordinary knight. For that reason I leave it aside. *Item* for Shoulders of Mutton, *quia nichil est nisi pena et labor*" (§§364 and 365).

the caul should be held up in position like that /*92r*/ with little wooden skewers. When this is done, he should get his grills, which are good and clean, and set those shoulders on them very gently, then set them out over a pretty little fire until they have firmed up, turning them over gently on the grill. If he should be asked to do any that are glazed with a green colour, see that he has a great deal of parsley and green herbs which have been cleaned and washed, and ground up in the mortar; then draw it out and pass it carefully through a strainer; and enough flour and eggs for him to make that glazing in the necessary quantity. He should put it in a pot big and deep enough for those shoulders to wallow and turn freely in the green mixture. This done, /*92v*/ return the shoulders back onto the grill to dry, minding not to overdo them, so that the glazing is not spoiled but stays quite green. After this, when the shoulders get to the dressing table, put two or three of them in each dish, then go and serve them up.

Since at such a noble, great and notable feast as is outlined above, attended by such great companies of great, noble and worthy lords as are named above, it would be surprising if there were no sickly or delicate individuals, or none who were afflicted with infirmities or illness: therefore I, Chiquart—always making allowance for the prescriptions and orders of the noble, good and worthy lord doctors[190]—wish to instruct and advise, /*93r*/ to my limited knowledge, how to make and prepare some dishes which are good and refreshing for the sick.[191]

---

[190] Cf. the end of Recipes 65, 66, 69 and 69a, where Chiquart will remind his cook that it is solely the patient's physician who will determine whether each of these dishes is suitable for him. On the important role of medical doctors at the Court of Savoy, see the Introduction.

[191] A standard variety of medical text in the Middle Ages had for a long time been the handbook dealing with foods appropriate for the sick. A respected instance of such a treatise was the thirteenth-century *Summula Musandini*: "*Incipit summula de preparatione ciborum et potuum infirmorum, secundum Musandinum*," ed. Salvatore de Renzi in *Collectio Salernitana*, 5 vols., Naples (Filiatre-Sebezio), 1852–59; Vol. V, pp. 254–68. Arnald of Villanova himself wrote a *De modo preparandi cibos et potus infirmorum in aegritudine acuta*: see

Nota pro infirmis.

Firstly, a Restorative, a Precipitate, an Almond Butter, Stuffed Crayfish, a Green Spinach Puree prepared in two ways, Rabbits[192] in Pastry, also in two ways, a Cullis, Pears cooked without touching coals or water, an Applesauce, a White-Dish of Capons, another White-Dish, of Partridge, Oatmeal, a Pea Dish, a Semolina Dish, a Barley Dish.

65. To instruct /*93v*/ the person who will be doing the Restorative[193] he should see that he has a fine big flask of double glass[194] as strong as you can find, then he should wash it and rinse it fully; when it is washed, sit it on a wooden trencher or small wooden table, and bind it there tightly with cords and fastenings. Then he should get one or two good big grain-fed capons, depending on the amount of the Restorative he wants to make, pluck it, clean and wash it well, then drain the water from it fully; when it has drained, chop it up very finely, meat and bones too all together, then put it into the flask, with a small half-glass or so

---

this in his *Opera*, Lyon (Fradin), 1504. The *Viandier* and the *Menagier* each contain a relatively brief section of "Viandes pour malades" (at pp. 100–101 and §§297–311, respectively.

[192] The word *cuyns* was copied as *connins*. This dish is the Quince in Pastry which was announced in the Table (folio 5v) and for which the recipe is given in §70, below. The error appears to be the result of the scribe's inability to read Chiquart's writing.

[193] The influence exercised by the Court doctors, and medical theory in general, upon activities in the Duke's kitchen can be surmised in this recipe. In 1420 one of the doctors in service at the Court of Savoy was the learned Antonio Guainerio (Anthonius de Garneriis), sometime professor at the University of Paris and prolific author of, *inter alia*, works on pleurisy, fevers, diseases of the head and of the stomach, gynaecological maladies, plagues, and a certain *Practica medicinae* published in Pavia in 1488. See Castorina Battaglia, "Medici e chirurghi alla Corte di Savoia (1300–1440)," pp. 1389–93.

[194] ... *une belle et grand anmolle de voyre double*: this is a sort of glass double-boiler. Bruchet lists an *amola vitrea* in the inventory of equipment at Amadeus's residence at Ripaille (p. 593).

of good rosewater[195] and as much again of good fresh water and a /94r/ little grain of salt, an ounce or more of fine pearls put in a very small bag made of a pretty clean fabric of strong silk or linen; and, with these, very good, potent, efficacious and worthy precious stones[196], that is: diamonds, Margarite pearls, rubies, saphires, turquoises, emeralds, coral, amber, jasper, jacinth, chalcedony, onyx, crystal, chalcedony, emeralds, sardonyx, chrysolite, beryl, topaz, chrysoprase, and amethyst, and all other good and potent precious stones—though only those which the doctor orders; they should be put together in another little bag made likewise of clean white linen cloth, strong enough, though, not to break so that those stones cannot become mixed together with the capon meat; including, furthermore, /94v/ sixty or eighty or more pieces of pure gold[197], ducats and gems, and other pieces, which have previously been well washed in three or four changes of warm water and wiped and dried carefully on a bit of good clean white linen towelling; then each of those gold pieces is bent across so it can fit easily through the mouth or neck of the flask; put them in adroitly and gently, letting them fall onto the flesh of the capon so they will not break the flask, then stop it up tightly so that no vapor can escape.[198] When this is done, see that he has a

---

[195] Rose water is a distilled beverage of Arab origin which was highly valued in the MIddle Ages for its medicinal virtues. Arab medicine, which had a fundamental influence upon the medical schools of Montpellier and Padua, attributed extensive curative and prophylactic properties to rose water. See Wilson, Vol. II, pp. 21–23.

[196] For the use of these precious stones in medieval medicine, see Jean Gero, "Les pierres précieuses en thérapeutique," *Thèses en médecine*, University of Paris, 1933, §449.

[197] The medicinal properties of gold were highly esteemed by the physicians of the time, and this esteem naturally had an influence upon what cooks were required to prepare in their kitchens. See the *Liber de coquina*, Ch. 2, §31: "*De auro ponendo in pastillo; contra quasdam infirmitates, ponitur aurum pro divitibus in omnibus cibariis.*"

[198] This same cooking method, in a tightly closed container, is specified in the preparation of the Gravy of Small Birds in the *Enseignements*: the birds are put to cook "in a pot, completely dry", the author says, though with lard,

good bright clean kettle, large enough for that flask to fit in comfortably; the neck of the flask should be tied to two sticks, and the sticks should be tied to /*95r*/ the kettle, so that when the water in the kettle boils the waves and bubbles of the water cannot move or shake the flask, or bounce it out of the kettle; fill the kettle with good fresh water, then set it on a bright coal fire and keep it boiling. See also that alongside it there is another kettle full of good water and that it is always at a full boil so that while the kettle with the flask is boiling it can always be topped up with the boiling water, for if cool water were to be put in, the flask would break, and all the work of what had been done would be lost. When the Restorative is well cooked, he should get a good bit of board and warm it up thoroughly by the fire; when it is quite dry and warm, he should get a little cloth, too, and heat it up, then fold it several times and put it on the hot board; then he should very carefully remove the flask from its kettle /*95v*/ and sit it on that hot cloth and board, and let it cool there until he can hold it without burning himself. When it has cooked enough like that, he should get a good new clean bolting cloth which has not yet been used for anything; put it over a fine gold dish and into it empty his Restorative which is in the flask. If it is not to be emptied right away, he should get a neat little wooden hook and stick it into the flask and pull out what is inside; when everything is out, he should get the little bags of pearls, precious stones and gold pieces mentioned above, and then he should squeeze what is left into the strainer; when it has been all squeezed out and collected in the gold dish, pour it out again into a fine gold pan and take it to the sick person who will receive it and use it on the doctor's order. /*96r*/

66. Again, a Precipitate[199], which is very useful for easing the patient, for comforting his veins and restoring his health; to instruct the person

---

wine, water, pepper and ginger, and the reader is told, "Keep the pot tightly sealed so than no vapor can get out before everything is fully cooked" (p. 184, ll. 115–18). This method of cooking a food in a sealed pot, *à l'étouffée*, without additional moisture, may well be Arabic in origin: see Lucie Bolens, "L'Art culinaire médiéval andalou," p. 145.

[199] Chiquart's term is *Une ressise*: the word is etymologically and semantically related to the Latin *sedere* and the French *seoir*, "to sit". (Cf. *ressuir*,

who is to make this Precipitate, how it is made and of what, he should get a quart of the best fine wheat that can be had, from the best lands, which has been so carefully culled and cleaned that nothing is left but the grain of wheat itself, as if it were expressly for the making of host wafers, have it ground down in a finely regulated mill; and when it has been properly ground, he should set it aside in a good leather bag. When he wants to make some of that Precipitate, he should get a good sieve or filter, put the wheat flour in it and strain it, leaving the good fat bran; that bran which is left in the sieve should be put in a good clean basin, with good fresh water in it, and he should stir it strongly around the basin with his hand. Then he should have /*96v*/ another good clean basin along side the first, and take that bran and what has been strained out, and squeeze it in his hands over that other basin; when the bran has been squeezed out like that in his hands over the basin, let what is in the basin sit and settle a short time; when it has sat and settled enough, gently pour off the water which is on top, and there will be left pure wheaten flour in the bottom of the basin. When this is done, put in more good fresh water again, and stir it around a little with your hand or with a spoon until the flour is mixed with the water, then cover the basin with a bit of good clean cloth and let the flour sit and settle, settling out /*97r*/ at the bottom of the basin. While it is settling out on the bottom of the basin, get a great quantity of good almonds, in the amount of the Precipitate which is to be made, skin them, clean and wash them well and grind them up in the mortar – and watch very carefully, in any cookery for the sick, that the mortar have absolutely no odour or flavor of garlic[200]—and moisten those almonds with good fresh water

---

"to settle," in the *Viandier*, pp. 18 and 94, and *passim*.) The name of the dish refers to what has been allowed to settle out of a suspension.

[200] According to the humoral theories of the age, garlic possesses a nature whose properties are extremely warm and dry; as a foodstuff, therefore, garlic would be highly dangerous for any febrile invalid. See, for example, Arnald of Villanova, *Regime de santé en françois*, or Aldobrandino of Sienna, *Le Regime du corps*. Garlic would be useful in the treatment of phlegmatic types of disease, that is, those in which the cold and moist humors had become overwhelmingly predominant.

and make milk of them straining them through a good clean bolting cloth; then put that milk into a good clean pot and set it to boil on the fire, with a very little salt. Then gently take the basin the Precipitate is in and drain off the water down to the Precipitate; take some of the Precipitate and put it through the strainer with the almond milk into a fine silver dish. /*97v*/ When what seems to him like a useful amount has been strained, put it with the almond milk which is boiling until the milk is thickened, with whatever sugar is proper and necessary.[201] When it has boiled enough, let the doctor know that the Precipitate is ready for whenever he wishes, and take it to the sick person in a fine golden bowl or cup.

67. Again, an Almond Butter[202]: to instruct the person who is to make it, he should see that he has a great quantity of very good sweet almonds, and he should skin, clean and wash them well and put them to be ground in a mortar which does not at all smell of garlic; /*98r*/ they should be

---

[201] Since the nature of sugar tends toward the temperately warm and the temperately moist, it approximates the qualities of the healthy human being. For this reason sugar is a common ingredient in dishes prepared for the sick, that is, for those persons whose humoral balance has been temporarily disturbed. It is particularly useful in the treatment of melancholic types of maladies, in which cold and dry humors predominate.

[202] This dish occupies several lines in the chapter entitled "Pottages for the Sick" in the *Menagier de Paris* (§§ 302 and 305). Cf. also *De l'amandolato per li'nfermi* in the *Libro della cocina* (p. 55). A dish called Botyr of Amondes is copied in the manuscript Arundel 334 (ed. Austin, p. 355; s.a. Hieatt and Butler, III, §5, and IV, §87), *Beurre d'amendes* in the *Fleur de toute cuysine* (folio 38r); and, of perhaps a thicker consistency, *Einen kese von mandel* and *Einen mandel wecke*, both in the *Guter Spise* (§§72 and 73). This almond preparation is particularly useful for lean days, on which butter, an animal product like milk or lard, is not to be eaten. "If you wish to make butter of almond oil, to make dishes on a Friday or in Lent, take three pounds of almonds ... " (*Libro per cuoco*, p. 66): this is in fact precisely the name given to the dish in the copy of this recipe made by the *LVII Ricette*, §9. See also the *Butiro contrafacto in Quaresma* in Maestro Martino (p. 171).

ground up very strongly and moistened with good cool or warm water; when they have been ground up, he should take them out, strain them very hard through a good, very clean bolting cloth into a fine silver dish. Then see that he has a good bright clean pan and empty it all into it, then set it on a pretty good fire, stirring continuously with a good spoon until it has cooked enough; and put in a little salt. When it has cooked, see that he has a good clean strong straining cloth, spread it out over a fine silver dish and have him pour out his butter on it, wrap it up in that cloth, then twist it good and strongly until the water inside comes out; after this, have him empty it into a good clean silver dish, then he should get a lot of very good beaten sugar—what is needed, at least—and mix it into the almond butter. /98v/ Should it happen that he wants to make some which is particolored, he should put half of the butter into another silver dish and mix enough beaten saffron in with it to make it yellow; when it comes to the dressing table, he should get his gold or silver dishes and put in each dish some white butter in one part, and along side in the same plate some particoloured butter; then it is served up.

68. Again, Stuffed Crayfish[203]: to instruct the person who will have to do these stuffed crayfish, see that he has a great quantity of crayfish, that he washes them throughly, sets them to cook in good water with salt; when they have cooked, take them out onto good clean work-tables. Take the largest ones for stuffing and remove the big shells, clean them and set them aside in good dishes; then take the necks and /99r/ legs of those large crayfish and enough of the others to stuff the number of crayfish he intends to stuff, and remove the meat from inside them; in the necks take out the entrails that are there, then put them on a good

---

[203] The *Menagier de Paris* contains the recipe for a dish which seems similar to Chiquart's *Escrevisses farcies, Tuille* (or *Tuillé*) *d'escrevisses* (§77); the recipe consists of only one sentence, however (as Pichon showed in his edition, p. 152), and there is no need to supply a verb in it (such as the *broyez* in the Brereton and Ferrier reading (p. 208). The appearance of the finished dish here is as of the series of tiles on a roof. See also the *Tuille de char* in the *Menagier* (§118) which corresponds to the *Tuillé* in the *Viandier* (p. 126).

work-table and chop them up very fine and put it in a good dish. Then he should see that he has very good parsley which has been cleaned, washed and drained; he should chop it up very fine and mix it in with the crayfish meat, with a little good white ginger and saffron to give it colour. Then get the crayfish shells which were set aside above, and put some of that filling into one shell and place another one face down on it, and put each of them like that one against the other. Then see that he has good clarified oil and put them to fry in good clean pans; when they have fried, take them out into fine dishes and sprinkle sugar on top of them. Then they are served up when it is time. /99v/

69. Again, a Green Puree of spinach and parsley for the sick[204]: to instruct the person who will be doing it, he should have good fine spinach[205] and parsley in the amount that he is to be making of that puree, and he should clean them and wash them carefully, then set them

---

[204] This is the dish which is called Spynoches yfryed in the *Forme of Cury* (§180). In the *Libro della cocina* (p. 21) spinach is combined with parsley (and several other herbs) as in this *Puree verde pour malades* of Chiquart.

Recognition of the medicinal usefulness of spinach was general among physicians: in the *Summula* of Musandinus (ed. cit., p. 255) the puree called *Spinachia* is found under the general rubric "On the preparing of foods and drinks against constipation of the stomach and against the discomfort of a marked fever". In the middle of the thirteenth century Aldobrandino was disseminating the doctrine of spinach as a restorative: "Spinach is cold and moist at the end of the first degree, and its nature is to quench bitter bile and to cool a warm stomach; ... it is good for those whose chest is dry and whose lungs are warm" (ed. cit., p. 164). According to the Vienna *Tacuinum*, spinach is cold and moist in the first degree: "It is good for a cough and for the chest" (ed. Cogliati Arano, §*xl*). These properties would render spinach suitable for helping to restore the balance of humors in someone suffering with a choleric or bilious type of disease. Such maladies, being warm and dry, tended to manifest themselves in a fever.

[205] Spinach as a foodstuff was introduced into Europe by Arab cookery, though initially and primarily because of its therapeutic qualities; see Wilson, Vol. II, pp. 23–4.

to boil; when they have boiled, he should take them out onto good clean work-tables and chop them up very fine, and drain them; then he should get a good bright clean kettle and put them to sautee nicely in it, with a little salt and whatever boiled water[206] is necessary. If he does not have good almond oil made up, get a great quantity of good sweet almonds, clean them well and wash them in three or four changes of warm water, then let them drain and dry on a good clean work-table; when they have dried, take them to be broken up /100r/ on the good stones used for making nut oil, and have oil made from the almonds; after that, put it into a good jar which will hold it, and then sautee the spinach and parsley lightly. When they've been nicely prepared, let the doctor know, and they are served up to the lord.

69a. If it should happen that the doctor does not wish to give that Green Puree to the sick person, the spinach and parsley are prepared nicely as is said above up to the point where he puts them into the pot; then he should get a suitable quantity of good almonds, he should clean, skin and wash them carefully and put them to be ground in the mortar; and this should not smell of garlic—*Hoc est allia:* "*Allia, faba, vina, Venus, fumus, ventus et ignis, ista nocent oculis, sed vigilare magis*"[207] /100v/—and he should grind them up and moisten them with good fresh water, and put them through a good clean strainer, make milk of them and put it into a good pot. Then he should set it to boil quite gently on a good bright little fire, or on good coals, putting in a very little salt;

---

[206] Jehan de Dudens wrote ... *y mecte souffrire bien et appoint en ung pitit de sel et de bonne eaue boullie*: one wonders whether *eaue* should have been *oille (d'amendres)*.

[207] The lines of warning which Chiquart quotes come from the *Regimen sanitatis salernitanum*:

Balnea, vina, Venus, ventus, piper, allia, fumus,
    Porri cum caepis, lens, fletus, faba, synapis,
    Sol, coitus, ignis, labor, ictus, acumina, pulvis:
    Ista nocent oculis, sed vigilare magis.

Flos medicinae, ll. 1317–20, ed. Salvatore de Renzi, *Collectio Salernitana*, Vol. 1, p. 488.

when the milk boils, put in the spinach and parsley, along with a little almond oil, and cook them nicely. When they're well cooked, do as is said above and let the doctor know.

70. Again, Quince in Pastry[208]: to instruct the person who will have to prepare them, he should see that he has good fine quince, he should clean them thoroughly, then make a hole through the top of each and clean out the seeds and what they are held in; and he should be careful not to break them open on the bottom or anywhere else. /*101r*/ After this, he should set them to boil in a good clean cauldron or kettle in good water; when they are as good as done, take them out onto a good clean work-table and turn them upside down without breaking them apart. Then he should go off to the pastry makers and order the pie shells from them, to hold, in some, three or four quince, or in others even more. When the shells are made, fill the hollow centres of the quince with good sugar, then set them out in the shells, cover them over and put them to bake in the oven; when they are done, they are served up.

70a. If it should happen that any lords want to eat the Quince in Pastry as is described above[209], the person who is to make them should go to the butchers' for them to give him enough beef marrow for the quantity he is to make of those pasties, and he should put it /*101v*/ in a good dish and pour over it some lean beef bouillon, which is warmish, to wash out of the marrow any little bones or blood or anything else which might be there; then it should be put back into another dish with more of that bouillon again to clean it even more of any little bones; then he should put it out on a good work-table to dry and put it back into good dishes.

---

[208] See the Quyncis in Past edited by Austin (pp. 51 and 97). There is as well a dish called *Pastelli de poma cotogne* in the *Libro de arte coquinaria* of Maestro Martino (ed. Faccioli, p. 170), but this is somewhat different from the sickdish which Chiquart describes.

[209] The difference between this and the preceding preparation seems to be that the inclusion of beef marrow in the quince pasties is appropriate for only a noble invalid. Chiquart indicates the exclusive nature of the intended class of recipient of this dish at the end of his recipe: *si en service on ceulx que l'on devra servir.*

When this is done, sprinkle a sufficient amount of good white ginger and cinnamon over the top. Then he should get his quince, prepared exactly as was said above, full of sugar and set out in the same way in the pastry shells, and all around each quince in the shells he should put that beef marrow which has been prepared as was just described; then he should cover the pies properly and put them in a hot oven to bake. When they are done, they are served up to those who are to be served them. /102r/

71. Again, a Cullis[210]: to instruct the person who will be doing it, he should get capons or poultry or partridge, whichever the doctors order from him, he should take that fowl and pluck it, clean and wash it thoroughly, and put it to cook in a bright, very clean kettle with a little mutton and a very little salt; it should cook nicely over a bright little fire. While it is cooking, he should get a great quantity of very good almonds, in the amount needed, and clean, skin and wash them very well, and put them to be ground in a mortar which doesn't smell in the slightest of garlic, and grind them thoroughly, moistening them with the poultry or partridge bouillon mentioned above. When they are sufficiently ground, take the poultry out into good dishes, take all the white meat off them and chop it up fine and then put it into the mortar with almonds and grind everything strongly together; while grinding, moisten with the bouillon. When it is sufficiently ground, /102v/ draw it out with that bouillon and strain it through a good clean bolting cloth and make milk of it; and don't put in any spices unless it is by the order of the doctor.[211] Then set it to boil and, when it has boiled, put it into fine silver or gold bowl and have it borne to the sick person.

---

[210] The *Couleiz d'un poulet pour malades* which is included in both the *Viandier* (p. 100) and the *Menagier* (§306) contains no almonds. In the fifteenth-century printed version of the *Viandier*, however, a *Coulis pour malades* is found which is made with a chick. In the recipe for this dish we read, "On grinding it up, add in a dozen almonds so that it will be more substantial (*substancieulx*)" (ed. Pichon and Vicaire, p. 167). Among English recipes the dish is known as a Colys (Hieatt and Butler, II, §11), Coleys (Austin, p. 10) and a Kolys (*Liber cure cocorum*, p. 20).

[211] It should be recalled that throughout the Middle Ages those condiments which we would consider to be standard cooking herbs and spices remain fun-

72. Again, pears cooked without coals or water[212]: to instruct the person who will be cooking them, he should get a good new earthenware pot, then get the number of pears he will be wanting to cook and put them into that pot; when they are in it, stop it up with clean little sticks of wood in such a way that when the pot is upside down on the hot coals it does not touch them at all; then turn it upside down on the hot coals and keep it covered over with coals /*103r*/ and leave it to cook for an hour or more. Then uncover them and check whether they have cooked enough, and leave them there until they are cooked through. When they are cooked, put them out into fine silver dishes; then they are borne to the sick person.

73. Again, an Applesauce[213]: to instruct the person who will be making

---

damentally pharmaceutical elements, *materia medica*. In the case of the household of Savoy stocks of these substances are in fact maintained and dispensed by a pharmacist: see the fine study by Mara Castorina Battaglia, "Notizie sui farmaci usati alla corte di Savoia dal 1300 al 1440," *Minerva Medica*, Vol. LXIX (1978), pp. 501–25.

[212] Here, as in the Restorative (§65, above), the desire on the part of the physician is to retain the essence of the foodstuff without risking, by the admixture of additional ingredients, any complication in the net effect or virtue of the nutriment. Pears are universally considered to be cold in either the first or second degree and dry in the second degree (Aldobrandino, *Regime de santé*, *Nef de santé* and various *Tacuina*): these qualities would therefore make them a particularly valuable food for someone with a sanguine type of ailment in which the warm and moist humors predominate. The *Tacuinum* of Liège indicates as well that pears are therapeutically useful for those with a weak stomach.

[213] This dish is called *Emplumeus de pomes* here and in the Table (folio 6r), but *Ung plumeus de pomes* on folio 93 r. The name *emplumeus* appears to derive from the German *Apfelmus* (as in the *Guter Spise*, §69) and perhaps in turn to have influenced the English Appulmoy (*Forme of Cury*, §79; Hieatt and Butler, IV, §81), Appulmos and Apulmose (Hieatt and Butler, II, §§17 and 35), Apple Moys and Pomesmoille (in Austin, pp. 30 and 113), and Apulmos (*The Noble Boke of Cookry*, p. 121); cf. as well the Anglo-Norman *Poumes ammolee*

it, get good Barbarin apples[214] in the amount that are to be done, pare them properly and slice them up into fine gold or silver dishes. He should have a fine, good clean earthenware pot, put good clean water in it and set this to boil over good bright coals and set his apples to boil in it. He should see that he has a great quantity of good sweet almonds, depending on the amount of the apples /*103v*/ he has set to cook, he should skin them, clean and wash them thoroughly and put them to be ground in a mortar which doesn't smell at all of garlic; he should grind them well and moisten them with the bouillon in which the apples are cooking. When these apples are cooked through, take them out onto good clean work tables, and strain his almonds with that water and make milk which is good and thick of them, and put it back to boil again on bright, clean, smokeless coals, with a very little salt. In the meantime, while it is boiling, he should chop up the apples very finely with a clean little knife; then, after that, he should put them into his milk, and put in a great deal of sugar depending on how much applesauce there is. Then, when the doctor asks for it, put it into fine gold or silver bowls or pans. /*104r*/

74. Again, a White-Dish of Capons[215]: to instruct the person who will be making it, get two young, grain-fed capons, pluck and clean them

---

(Meyer, §9). The second element of the Germanic word means "mush".

[214] The identity of these cooking apples, which are written *pomes barberines* in the manuscript, remains uncertain. The *Menagier de Paris* refers to a plant by the name of *barbarin*: in his edition of the *Menagier* Pichon guesses that "*barbarin* might be a synonym for *berberie*, the barberry (*épine vinette*: *Berberis vulgaris*)" (Vol. II, p. 204, n. 5); on the other hand, Brereton and Ferrier gloss the word only as a "Kind of herb" (§221).

[215] This version of the *Blanc mengier de chappons* was regularly prepared as a dish suitable for a sick person: cf. the *Viandier*, p. 101, and the *Menagier*, §107. While the use of ginger in this White Dish is usual in other books, Chiquart makes its addition here conditional upon the physician's approval: those who are suffering from a fever should avoid any foodstuff whose natural qualities might exacerbate that unnatural warmth. Cf. also in the *Sent sovi* (§49) where the recipe for *Manjar blanch* calls as well for rice, as in the English versions of the dish (e.g. Austin, p. 85), and where the dish is garnished with sugar. The German *Blamensir* whose recipe is found in the *Guter Spise* (§3)

thoroughly, and put them to boil in a good pot. Get a little lard from a good cut, and clean and wash it properly and set it to parboil a little, then put it in with the other. While his capons are boiling, get a great quantity of good almonds, depending on the quantity of the White-Dish he is to make; pluck, clean and wash them, and put them in a mortar and grind them strongly, moistening them with the capons' bouillon. When the capons have cooked, take them out into good dishes, then take the tougher capon and set aside the more tender one; set the tougher capon on a good work table /*104v*/ and remove its bones, and chop up its flesh finely, then grind it well in the mortar; when it is well ground, moisten it with the capons' bouillon; draw it out, and the almonds as well, and pass all of that through a good clean bolting cloth, and set it to boil in a bright, good and clean kettle, and make it on the thick side; put in very little salt, and a great deal of sugar depending on the amount of the White-Dish, and ask the doctor whether he should put in any white ginger. When it has boiled, put some of it over the capon which was set aside above; then it is borne to the sick person.

74a. Again, a White-Dish of Partridge[216]: that White-Dish of Partridge should be made in a manner similar to what is said above for the White Dish of Capons; he should make sure /*105r*/ to make it out of the tougher partridge and to set aside the tender one; and he should be very careful about the salt, and not put any spice in it without the orders of the doctor.

75. Again, Oatmeal[217]: to instruct the person who will be doing it, he

---

is likewise a mixture of chicken, rice, almonds and sugar. See the comment on Blank Maunger in Hieatt and Butler, p. 172, and the note by C. Anne Wilson, *Petits Propos Culinaires*, 4 (1980), pp. 17–19.

[216] According to Aldobrandino, partridge (along with kid and veal) offers good, safe nourishment when a person is sick (*Régime du corps*, p. 61): "Above all birds' flesh it is the best and it produces the best quality of blood, and for that reason those who wish to have the best blood and maintain a healthy body should eat it" (*ibid.*, p. 130). See also the *Nef de santé*, Paris (Anthoine Verard), c. 1508, *s. v. becasse* and *perdrix*.

[217] Chiquart's recipe for *Avenast* is closely echoed in the *Avenat* of the *Sent*

should get his oats and rub them grain by grain so that there is nothing left but only the grain of oats; when it has all been cleaned like that, wash it in three or four changes of warm water and put it to boil in a bright, good and clean kettle; when it has boiled well, drain the water off it and, after that and after the kettle is rinsed again, put the oats back into that kettle with good water and set it to boil again. When it has boiled enough, let it sit in that same kettle for four or five hours or more, or until the next day. Then he should see that he has whatever he needs of good almonds; he should skin, clean and wash them, and grind them thoroughly in a mortar—making sure that it doesn't /105v/ smell of garlic. Then he should take the settled oats, pour the water from them and put them again to boil in a change of good water in that same kettle, which has been cleaned and rinsed, or in another good clean kettle; moisten the almonds with this oat bouillon and draw them out with it and strain them by passing them through a good bolting cloth, with a very little salt, and the necessary amount of sugar. When it has boiled enough, it is served up to the sick person when he asks for it.

76. Again, a Pea Dish[218]: to instruct the person who will be preparing

---

soví (§99), and in the *Gruyau* of the *Menagier* (§310) which is expressly a dish for the sick. Both of the English versions, Grewel of Almandes (*Forme of Cury*, §86) and Gruel of Almondes (*Liber cure cocorum*, p. 14), list saffron among the ingredients. The printed *Viandier* contains a dish called *Du grueu ou avenat* which is enriched (the English cookery books say "Gruelle aforsydde") with eggs and saffron. Cf. also in the French translation of Platina, the dish likewise called *Du grueu ou avenat* (Ch. lxxi). The Latin *Tractatus*, in its chapter on food for the sick (*De condimentis delicatis dominorum, ad naturam confortandem et appetitum provocandum*), combines several of these recipes of Chiquart in its §9, which begins, "Cook grains of wheat, or oats, or rice, or millet . . . ."

[218] A variety of Chiquart's *Syseros* which is not, however, designated for the consumption of sick persons and which contains onions, is known in England under the name of Chiches (*Forme of Cury*, §72). Cf. also the preparation called in Latin *Cicera* (which likewise contains *radices petrossillorum*) in the *Liber de coquina* (ed. Mulon, Ch. I, §22; p. 398). The *Tractatus* notes that,

the Pea Dish, he should get his chick peas and cull through them one by one so that there is nothing left but only the peas themselves, then he should wash them in three or four changes of warm water and put them to boil; /106r/ when they have boiled, he should remove them from that water and put on new, fresh water and put them back in it again to boil. When they have boiled, he should let them sit in that kettle until the next day, when he should drain off the water and again put in new fresh water and put them to boil, with a very little salt, some almond oil, whole parsley, its roots cleaned—those roots should be peeled and well washed—and a little sage. And don't put in anything else without the doctor's orders: if he should order that a little cinnamon be put in, and a little verjuice, to give it flavour, then put some in; otherwise no.

77. Again, a Semolina Dish[219]: to instruct the person who will be preparing the Semolina Dish, he should see that he has very good almonds, he should skin them, clean and wash them very well and properly, and grind them in the morter, /106v/ moistening them with good fresh water and drawing them out to make good proper milk, and set it to boil. He should get his semolina and wash well it in three or four changes of fresh water, drain the water fully from it and put as much of it as is necessary with the almond milk, with a little salt. Watch carefully that it doesn't burn.[220] Put in sugar according to the amount of semolina. When it is ready, it is served up to the sick person.

78. Again, a Barley Dish[221]: to instruct the person who will be getting

---

"*(Quedam cibaria ... apte sunt ...) infirmis et debilibus uelud gruelus de riso uel auena uel ordeo factus, et lacte amigdalarum conditus, ciceres et pullorum brodium ...*" (*ibid.*, p. 384).

[219] This particular preparation, a sort of almond cream of wheat, is called *Semolla* in the *Libre de sent soví* (§109).

[220] ... *Et advise tresbien qu'il n'y prenne de feu.* The author of the *Sent soví* is equally anxious that the delicate flavor of this porridge not be tainted by the wood smoke: "And he (the cook) should have it stirred constantly and protect it from any smoke" (§109).

[221] A barley porridge was long one of the most widely used foods in medical regimens in the Middle Ages. Even in the sixth century Anthimus wrote,

it ready, he should see that he has his pure barley and have it ground in such a way that the grains remain whole; and, when it has been ground, put it back into the winnowing-sieve and winnow it and remove all straw from it, then cull through it and /*107r*/ clean it so that only the grains remain, then wash it in three or four or more changes of warm water until it is thoroughly cleaned; then put it to boil in good water in a bright, good and clean kettle, skimming it carefully. When it has come to a boil, drain the water off it, then, when it is well drained, put in good fresh water again and put it back to boil until it is done; then take it down onto warm coals and let it sit there until the next day, covering it good and neatly. On the next day the person who will be preparing it should see that he has whatever almonds are needed to do that Barley Dish, skin, clean and wash them properly and put them to be ground in a mortar which does not smell of garlic, moistening them with good fresh water, and draw them out with it too and pass them through the strainer and /*107v*/ make good thick milk; set it to boil in a bright, good and clean kettle, with a very little salt. He should empty out his barley into good dishes, and the water it has been in should be thoroughly drained away; and he should check carefully that there is nothing there that shouldn't be there. Then pour in the almond milk and boil it until it is properly done; add in whatever sugar is needed. When it is ready, let him know so that when the sick person asks for it he may get it right

---

"*Tesinas que de ordeo fit qui scit facere bone sunt et sanis et febricitantibus*" (*De observatio ciborum*, ed. Weber, p. 41). In his *Liber de preservatione ab epydemia*, Magninus Mediolanensis continues to propose *aquam ordei* as a good medicine, especially against fevers (ed. R. Simonini, Modena (Orlandini), 1923, p. 25. For Chiquart's recipe, see the *Viandier: Ung gruyau d'orge mondé* (p. 101); and the *Menagier de Paris*: *Orge mondé ou Gruyau d'orge* (§304). The author of the *Sent sovi* offers an optional garnish according to the state of health of the person to receive his *Ordiat*: "If it is a person who has no fever, put white sugar on it an give it to him" (§97). According to Bartolomeo Sacchi (*alias* Platina), *Ordiat* is made in the same way as *Fromentee*; while the latter "is of slow digestion and great nourishment", the former "is more commendable to some people's way of thinking than Frumenty" (*Platine en françoys*, folio lxxi).

away.

---

1. For every good man who is sensible
   it is but right to give thanks
   to those from whom he benefits:
   else he would be an ingrate. 4

2. Therefore, to the lofty Trinity,
   full of all great goodness—
   that is, God the Father, the Son
   and the blessed Holy Spirit— /108r/ 8

3. I, Chiquart, render praise and thanks
   for the benefits I receive from Him,
   and for the singular grace
   He granted me to finish this. 12

4. There remains to render praise and honor
   to the most high and mighty lord
   at whose insistance and order
   this work I've humbly done. 16

5. And to my most respected lady
   and to their children, our lords,
   and to all of their forebears
   may God grant endless life. 20

6. May the Holy Ghost hold in his love
   all noble advisors of theirs,
   and may He grant them to give counsel
   which be useful to all people. 24

7. The Master, He, above all masters, /108v/
   so is He over those earthly servants;
   may they so serve in this household
   that each of them derive honour from it. 28

8. May they by the Creator's grace
receive their county's love,
and may the good people of the land
receive *their* love alone.   32

9. So that with rank ingratitude
toward my scribe I not be charged,
I wish here now to render praise
for the labor he has shared with me;   36

10. and so may God, together with
our mighty and most worthy lord,
in his goodness and great majesty
reward him for that labor.   40

11. Should anyone's opinion be
that I have erred in my treatise,
may they me pardon and excuse
for I lack high learning and wit.   44

12. May Paradise be granted us
and for us gained by the Virgin:
"Amen!" I pray you all to say
in a loud voice everyone.   48

    Amen /109r/

[The menus copied between folios 109r–111v have been omitted in this translation.[222]]

---

[222] In several instances there are signs that this first listing of the dishes for a two-day banquet was copied from an initial draft. Apart from the preamble which begins the repeated listing at the foot of folio 111r, however, there are a number of other variants, though relatively minor ones, between this listing and the later one. All such variants will be noted. At the top of folio 109r the text of the menus begins: "For the first setting of the dinner, firstly get big salt fish such as salt mullets ... ."

In the year of grace 1400,[223] Amadeus, First Duke of Savoy, /112r/ my most mighty lord, received my lord of Burgundy, and because I, Chiquart, who was his cook at that time, fulfilling my duty, prepared and ordered the preparation of several notable dishes for the dinners and suppers for that banquet, I ordered, made, or had made by order of my aforesaid most mighty lord, at the first serving of the dinner of the first day, and commanded to be written down, what follows here, to wit:[224]

Get big salt fish such as salt mullets with big pieces of filet of salt pike with several other salt fish, and set this out in fine dishes; then, with this, get herrings and set them out in another fine dish by themselves; for all that has just been mentioned there is no other sauce needed but mustard. /112v/ And peas and the puree, and a puree of greens will be the pottage for that serving, with a White Almond Broth[225], a Brown Sorengue of eels, and the pasties, and fish tripe carefully cleaned and prepared to make an Arbaleste. For the *entremets* of the first serving, pike cooked in three ways, that is, fried in the middle, the third at the head boiled, and the tail third roasted; other ones boiled in the middle, roasted at the head and fried at the tail; and because the above fish are called Glazed Pilgrim Pike[226], they should have over them a good roast lamprey which will be the staffs of those pilgrims—and anyone who does not have any lamprey can use eel; the staff, that is, the lamprey, should be eaten with /113r/ lamprey sauce, and the eel with garlic green verjuice sauce; of the pike the boiled part should be eaten with green sauce, the fried and the roasted parts with green verjuice or with oranges.[227]

---

[223] Jehan de Dudens wrote this date as *mil iiii^c*, leaving a centimeter of space before the end of the line.

[224] In the manuscript there is no paragraph division here, but the word *primo* is written in the margin.

[225] On folio 109r: ... a White Almond Broth on fried fish, a German Broth, a Brown Sorengue ... .

[226] This *entremets* of *Lucs dorés pelerins* is the lean counterpart, on fish days, to the *Chappons pelerins* already seen in Recipe §45.

[227] On folio 109 v at this point there follow these comments, which were not written in previously: "And fish tripe, well cleaned and properly prepared, to make an Arbaleste, and these tripe should be served before the *entremets*, and

At the second serving[228], first get all sorts of sea-fish set out by themselves in great gold dishes; fresh-water fish — big pike filets, big carp filets, big trout, fresh pollacks, dace[229], big char filets, big perch and other fish; lamprey in lamprey sauce, a Salamine[230], a yellow Larded-Boiled Dish of tench, with sops, rice with the Venison of Dolphin[231], and crayfish in vinegar. Of the sauces appropriate for the abovementioned fish, no mention is made. For the *entremets*, Parmesan Pies /113v/ each one glazed and embanded with the arms of the lord before whom it is set.[232]

For the supper.

First, roasts of pickerel and pollack and all sorts of suitable roast fish; they are served with sorrel green verjuice; and White Sops of almonds, with fish jelly, white sea-fish and white fresh-water fish, Norse Pasties, fried onions, and fried fish in Saupiquet.

---

eel, in garlic green verjuice sauce, which will substitute for the lamprey of that *entremets*."

[228] On folio 110r a single line announces "The second setting"; then the text takes up, "At the second setting, first get all sorts of sea-fish ... ."

[229] On folio 110r, dace (*ferees*) are not mentioned.

[230] A Salamine is a prepared dish of fried fish covered with a sauce composed of ground almonds, pea puree, verjuice and spices: see the fifteenth-century printed *Viandier*, p. 147. The *Menagier* inserts *Une Salemine* into menus for lean dinners (p. 180, l. 5, and elsewhere). See the Anglo-Norman *Browet salmenee* (Meyer, §18), and the English Bruet salmene (Hieatt and Butler, I, §17); Austin publishes (p. 21) an English recipe for Salomene which resembles the *Viandier*'s.

[231] The Venison of Dolphin is a dish made simply by preparing this fish according to the standard recipe for large game meat. Chiquart has already provided this recipe for Fresh Dolphin in §30. Cf. the *Viandier*, p. 103.

[232] Recipe 40, above. The manner in which each pie is flatteringly decorated with the personal arms of the guests is described at the end of the "meat" version of the Parmesan Pies (§21, folio 48r).

Following this passage as it appears on folio 110r, Chiquart adds, "And if you want to make a third serving, I can find enough material to do it, although I advise /110v/ that that would make it all very long."

For the next day.

For the first serving of the dinner, /114r/ strained peas[233] and turnips, a Georgé Broth, a salt-dish of herrings by themselves in a fine dish, eels, trout and salt pollack, a Violet Broth on fried fish,[234] a Genista Broth[235] on fried fish.

The second serving: all sorts of white fish, either sea-fish or fresh-water fish, a Party White-Dish in four colours, gold, blue, silver and red, together with a Yellow Verjuice on fish, rice, small Almond Flans[236],

---

[233] These *Poys coulés* are prepared in quantity in Recipe 22.

[234] In the other version (on folio 111r) of the menu for this first serving at the dinner of the second day, there is an additional dish listed at this point: A Vinaigrette of Fish Tripe on fried fish.

[235] "*Genesté* is so called because it is yellow like a genista flower. And it is made yellow with egg yolks and saffron, and is made in the summer instead of civet; and it is made (ms. 'fried') in the same way as is described below (in the following recipe, for Veal Civet) except that there are no onions" (*Menagier de Paris*, §114). The generic term used by Chiquart for the sauce is *Une fleur de genete*, "A genista flower".

[236] A dish called "Small Flans" (*Flanciaux*) appears among the *Menagier*'s menus (p. 175, l. 31; p. 180, l. 30). What Chiquart is probably referring to here by *les Flannelles d'amendres* is the dish called *Flons de lait d'amendres* which he dealt with in Recipe 28 (above).

Galantine of lamprey[237], crayfish, and a Savoy Broth.[238]

For the supper. /114v/

First, white fish, pasties, Green Sops[239], a King's Broth, fish-tripe sausages[240], glazed Rissoles, a Chaudumel[241], and a Camelin Broth.

---

[237] *la Galatina des lamproyes*. This is probably the *Lamproye en galantine*, or *Galentine a la lampree*, found in the *Viandier* (pp. 96 and 221). S.a. similar English dishes in Hieatt and Butler, I, §17; II, §68; IV, §§130 and 131. Magninus Mediolanensis provides a general recipe for *Gelatina* in his *Opusculum de saporibus* (p. 188): "If you wish to preserve (fish) for several days, a *gelatina* should be made in the following way: Take cinnamon, galangale and cloves, mix them with toast soaked in vinegar and wine, and boiled; the *gelatina* is made with the water and wine in which the fish has been boiled, and is enough for ten people."

Among the expenses recorded at the Château de Ripaille for food for the Savoyard Court: "*10 mars 1416. Pro pluribus et diversis speciebus habitis pro lamprea, per ipsum apportata de Avignione, augmentanda et conservanda, 4 fl. 1 d. ob gr.* (Compte du trésorier général 61, fol. 613)" (Bruchet, p. 317).

[238] On folio 111v a sentence follows the mention of this last dish. "And if jousts, tournaments or other recreational activities should be held on that day, the cooks would be well advised to prepare all the lighter a dinner, and to make the supper that much more worthy and generous." This first listing of the menus is clearly just a series of practical suggestions for several grand formal meals, though undoubtedly these suggestions were inspired by this historical banquet offered to the Duke of Burgundy.

[239] The *Menagier* prepares what he calls a *Souppe despourvue* (§57), which we might translate as Quick Sops, for which the base is parsley fried in butter; it would be the color of Chiquart's Green Sops.

[240] These fish-tripe sausages may be the dish described in the recipe called *Tortelli e salsicce a brodetto di pesce*, §32 in the *LVII Ricette*.

[241] What Chiquart calls here *Un chau de mes*, and on folio 111v *Ung chaut de mes*, is probably the relatively common dish known as *Chaudumel* or *Chaudumet*. The *Viandier* (p. 97) contains a recipe for *Chaudumel au bescuit* (*i.e. beschet*, pike), which the Mazarine Library manuscript classifies as a *civel* rather than a *chaudumel*; and the *Menagier* (§277) describes a *Chaudumé*

Against the Plague.[242]

pour poisson d'eaue doulce.

[242] A somewhat different version of this ballade was published in a book entitled *Regime contre la pestilence faict et composé par messieurs les medecins de la cité de Balle (i.e.* Basel) *en Allemaigne, en laquelle depuis dix ans en ce a regné en ladicte cité,* Lyon (Claude Nourry), after 1519. Apart from the substantial variants apparent here, this version offers as well an envoy. A. Klebs and E. Droz reprint this version of the poem in their *Remèdes contre la peste,* Paris (Droz), 1925, p. 50.

1. Qui veult son corps en santé maintenir
 et resister contre l'epydimie,
 doit joye avoir et tristesse fouyr
 en frequentant joyeuse compaignie 4
 d'infection totalement bannie,
 boyre bon vin, nettes viandes user;
 ay bon odeur contre la punaisie;
 n'aille point hors si ne fait bel ou cler. 8

2. De grosses chairs se doit on abstenir,
 aussy de fruictz pour la plus grant partie,
 mengier bon pain, sa poullaile rostir
 et aultres chairs; pour toutes espisseries, 12
 canelle et clou, sans point de poyvrerie—
 tout de vinaigre ou d'esgrez destrempez;
 dormir matin: tout ce n'oublie mye;
 n'aille point hors si ne fait bel ou cler. 16

3. Jeun estomach ne se doit point partir
 sans manger, boire ou prendre droguerie;
 face feu cler en sa chambre tenir;
 de femme avoir ne luy souviengne mye; 20
 bains et estuves en son povoir de fouye (*sic*)
 car les humeurs font mouvoir et troubler;
 sans bozaard ne soit heure ne demye;

On Cookery   121

1. He who would keep his body in health
   and withstand the plague
   should be full of happiness and flee sadness,
   should avoid any place the illness is   4
   and keep happy company,
   drink good wine, eat clean meat;
   he uses a good odour against the stench,   7
   and he should not go out unless it is fine and clear./*115r*/

2. No stomach should take part in fasting,
   drink early in the day, lead a soft life[243]
   he should keep a bright fire in his room;
   he should not even think of having a woman;   12
   he should avoid baths and tubs as much as possible
   because they agitate and increase the humors;
   he should dress well and always have a happy face,
   and not go out unless it is fine and clear.   16

3. He should abstain from gross meats

---

   n'aille point hors si ne fait bel ou cler.   24

   Prince, ta haulte seignourie,
   que qu'il se veult de la peste garder,
   ne fain ne soif n'endure, quoy que on die;
   n'aille point hors si ne fait bel ou cler.   28

A third version of this poem is printed as number 1572 of the *Oeuvres complètes d'Eustache Deschamps*, as edited by Queux de Saint-Hilaire and Gaston Raynaud, 11 vols., Paris (Firmin-Didot), 1878–1904; Vol. 4, p. 100. And finally, a fourth version, quite similar to Chiquart's, was copied in the manuscript Paris, Bibliothèque Nationale, lat. 17730, on folio 12v.; it was published with a commentary by Ernest Hoepffner in *Romania*, 50 (1924), pp. 413–21.

[243] It might be difficult to determine whether Chiquart's version of the poem considers these last activities to be advisable or to be avoided, were it not for similar doctrine which can be read in other plague tractates of the time: *Dubitantes epydimiam non debent jejunare, nec famem, nec sitim sustinere, nec comestionem tardare, sed minus solito comedere et bibere* Simonini, *Maino de Maineri ed il suo Libellus de preservatione ab epydimia*, Ch. 9, p. 23).

and from most fruits;
he should eat rabbit, he should roast his poultry
and venison; any spices   20
cinnamon, cloves, ginger, the peppers —
should be distempered with vinegar and verjuice;[244]
he should sleep late in the morning: he should remember
                                                    all this
and not go out unless it is fine and clear.   24

Cheese, eels: deadly foods, the one and the other.[245]

A note by Virgil concerning his book *On Bucolic and Agricultural Lands*:[246]

---

[244] Because spices by their nature are warm in degrees which vary between high and (for pepper) extreme, any person exposed to the risk of a fever should always be careful to temper this warmth by mixing the spices with a relatively cool liquid such as vinegar: *In omni ... cibo utendum est aceto* (*ibid.*) Physicians further advised that, if a person had to leave his house in times of plague, he ought to hold a protective cloth soaked in vinegar over his mouth and nose: see l. 7 of the poem, above.

[245] *Caseus, anguilla, mortis cibus ille vel illa: Flos medicinae*, l. 365, ed. De Renzi in *Collectio Salernitana*, Vol. I, p. 456. From this point on in the manuscript, up to the end of folio 116r, everything is in Latin.

[246] A not entirely accurate rendition of Virgil's *Georgics*, Book I, ll. 187–192:

> *Contemplator item, cum se nux plurima silvis*
> *induet in florem et ramos curvabit olentis*
> *si superant fetus, pariter frumentis sequentur,*
> *magnaque cum magno veniet tritura colore;*
> *at si luxuria foliorum exuberat umbra,*
> *nequiquam pinguis palea teret area culmos.*

(In the edition of Henri Goelzer, Paris, 1935, p. 25.) John Dryden translated this passage as follows:

*Contemplacio item, et se nux plurima silvis
induet in florem, ramos que culuabit olentes:
vi superant fetus, pariter frumenta sequentur,
magna que cum magno veniet tritura colore;
ac si luxura foliorem exuberat umbra,
ne quitquam pyngues palea teret area culmos.*

See on the next page our gloss on the preceding lines: /115v/

Note that when the nut tree—*arbor nucis*—has many seeds, then the kernels will be abundant; and when there are not many, and its leaves are abundant, then there will be little fruit and only barenness.[247]

The Apostle Paul said: "But if any provide not for his own, and specially for those of his own house, he hath denied the faith, and is worse than an infidel."[248]

Helemosina is made up from *heloys*, that is, "to be merciful", and *moys*, which is "water", as of mercy: that is, "the water of indulgence".[249]

Note that there is a difference between *jus* and *fas*, for *jus* is human

---

        Mark well the flowering almonds (*sic*) in the wood;
        If odorous blooms the bearing branches load,
        The glebe will answer to the sylvan reign,
        Great heats will follow, and large crops of grain,
        But, if a wood of leaves o'ershade the tree,
        Such and so barren will thy harvest be ... .

(*The Works of Virgil*, Oxford (Oxford University Press), 1961, p. 52.) The *nux* (or *arbor nucis*, as someone, perhaps Chiquart, glosses) is probably a walnut (tree); it would be understood as such by any reader in the late Middle Ages.)

[247] What is written in the manuscript is the following: *Nota que quando nux* (and, inserted above the line, *arbor nucis*) *habebit multos grannos tunc debebit esse fertilitas frumenti et quando non habebit multos et erit habundantiam foliorem tunc erit granum carum et sterilitas.*

[248] I Tim. 5:8.

[249] Cf. Balbi, *Catholicon, s.v. Elemon.*

and *fas* is divine.²⁵⁰

Canon is from the Greek, *regula* from the Latin: hence *canonicus* comes from *canon* and from *icos* which is "keeper", and so this is "the keeper of the rule".²⁵¹ /116r/

79. A note on the making of jelly—in French, *de la jelee*—from both meat and fish.²⁵²

First put the fish into a pan in which you have already put some water or wine, then put in a mixture of half water and half wine, and let it cook there until it is done, skimming well; grind sugar and all other spices, draw them out with vinegar, and put them to cook with the fish; then you should strain this through a bolting cloth if you wish.

It should be made with meat in the same way, except that you should put in more wine and water for meat than for fish.

Do not condemn a man as a fornicator if you are chaste, for you will be breaking the word of the law—in the same way as that very man: for He who said, "Thou shalt not commit adultery" also said, "Judge not and ye shall not be judged."

Sufficient unto the day is the evil thereof.²⁵³ /116v/117r/

---

²⁵⁰ Isidore of Seville, *Originum seu etymologiarum libri*. Book V, Ch. 2: *Fas lex divina est, ius lex humana*. Balbi, s.v. *Ius*: *Est ius lex humana, fas lex divina*.

²⁵¹ Isidore of Seville, *Originum*, Book VI, Ch. 16: *Canon autem Graece, Latine regula nuncupatur*. See also Balbi, s.v. *Canon*.

²⁵² See the *Gelatina* which Magninus Mediolanensis included in his *Opusculum de saporibus* (ed. cit., p. 188); and, as well, the recipes for *Gelee de poisson a limon et de chair* in the *Viandier* (p. 94), for *Geladia a carn ho a pex* in the *Sent sovi* (§146), and for *Une gelee de cher de poulailhe, lappereaux et de cochons* in the *Recueil* (§9). The *Gelatina di pesce* in the *LVII Ricette* (§27) is made with three large tench, spices, saffron, and water and vinegar in a ratio of six to one.

²⁵³ Matt. 6:34.

80. To make meat jelly[254], get sheep's feet and skin them thoroughly and set them to cook in good clean water; then, when they are half cooked, get whatever quantity of pork or baby pork you need for the amount of jelly you want to make, and put it to cook with your sheep's feet, and poultry too. Then get white wine and vinegar and put it in, with a reasonable amount of salt, and cook it vigorously. When it is well cooked, taste it to see that it has a good flavour with the vinegar or the salt; get saffron and mix it in to give it colour, then remove your meat onto a good clean work table. Then get white ginger and pepper, moisten it and add it into your bouillon, bringing it to a boil; then get a cloth strainer and pour your bouillon through it two or three times so that it is good and clear. Then take your meat, pork and poultry, and make up your dishes, with the jelly over top. */117v/*

81. To make fish jelly, get your fish—pike or perch or carp whichever you want[255]—and chop it up into good chunks depending on what you want, then wash it thoroughly and put it into a good clean pan; then get white wine and water, as much of the one as of the other, put them into your pan with the fish in the quantity there is of the fish, with a reasonable amount of vinegar, too, and some salt; then put it to boil and skim it well. Then, when it is well cooked, get saffron, moisten it and add it in; then remove your fish onto a good clean work table and peel it carefully; then get white ginger, pepper and a little nutmeg, moisten them and mix them into your bouillon; taste it to see that it has a good flavour with the vinegar or salt or spices. Then get your strainer and pass it through it carefully until it is clear. Then take your fish and make up a proper dish with the broth over top. */118r/*

---

[254] The writing on these two pages is no longer that of Jehan de Dudens. Though more recent in time, the script is still of the fifteenth century.

[255] "Carp and barbels are slimy" (Deschamps, Vol. 8, p. 339; l. 116). It is the slime with which certain fish are covered which is rich in protein; when heated, this latter coagulates and jells. The *Viandier* was well aware that it is the unwashed skins of fish, and only of certain fish, which will effect this sort of gelification (pp. 94–5).

In the name of the Lord. /118v/[256]

---

[256] On the *verso* of folio 118 is, in Latin and in a very fine fifteenth-century hand, what appears to be a draft of a recommendation, addressed by Michael (Bernardi d'Allinges), Abbot of Saint Maurice (1438-1458), to the Bishop of Lausanne, Georges de Saluces or de Saluzzo (1440-1461), that a certain Girard Oddeti replace the deceased Jean Brayer as rector of the parish of *Sancti Albini supra lacum*.

Reverendo in Christo patri et domino domino Georgio de Saluciis episcopo Lausanensi vel eius in spiritualibus vicariis generalibus Michael permissione divina abbas indignus monasterii Sancti Mauricii Agaunensis ordine Sancti Augustini Sedunensis diocesis salutem et honoris augmentum.

Cum sicut audivimus parochialis ecclesia Sancti Albini supra lacum, Lausanensis diocesis, de praesenti vacet per mortem seu obitum venerabilis viri domini Johannis Brayer ultimi rectoris eiusdem, jusque prioratus (?) seu praesentacio eiusdem parochialis ecclesiae ad nos et in dicto monasterio nostro successores pertinere dignoscatur, nos igitur vobis reverendo in Christo patri et domino domino Lausanensi episcopo supradicto, ad quem jus instituendi seu institucio ipsius parochialis ecclesiae pertinere dignoscitur, venerabilem virum dominum Girardum Oddeti presbyterum sufficientem et ydoneum in dicta parochiali ecclesia Sancti Albini supra lacum unacum omnibus iuribus et pertinentiis eiusdem per reverendum patrem vestrum seu vicarios eiusdem instituendum praesentamus. In quorum omnium et singulorum fidem et testimonium praemissorum praesentes vestras praesentationes literes exinde fieri et per notarium scribamque nostrum subscriptum signare sigillique maioris nostri appensione fecimus et jussimus communiri.

Datas die ... mensis ... anno domini 14...

I am indebted to M. Bernard Truffer, Archiviste adjoint in the Archives du Valais, for the transcription of this barely legible text.

Index

This Index is intended to help the reader understand the use which Chiquart makes of particular ingredients, hardware and recipes. The names of prepared dishes, whether treated extensively by Chiquart or not, are printed with a capital.

alcohol (Chiquart—*eaue ardant*): 25v

alkanet (Chiquart—*or cannete, or-canite*): 14r, 28r, 29v, 58v, 60r, *Alkanna tinctoria* or *Anchusa officinalis*, plants whose roots yield a red dye, alkanet, dyers' bugloss (see Clair, p. 110)

almonds: 14r, 19v, *passim*; sweet almonds, 97v, 99v, 103r; almond oil, 99v, 100v, 106r; Almond Butter, §67, 93r, 97v; Almond Milk Flans, §28, 4r, 54v; Little Almond Flans, 111r, 114r

amber: 94r, a precious stone, fossil resin

amethyst: 94r, a precious stone

anchovies: 16v, 56v, a sea-fish, *Engraulis encrasicholus*

apples, see barberine apples

Applesauce (Chiquart—*Emplumeus de pomes*): §73, 6r, 93r, 103r, sickdish

Arbaleste: §24, 50v, 109v, 112v, a prepared dish of fish tripe

aune: 14r, 17r, measure of length for fabrics, of a little more than a meter (see Zupko, p. 11)

bacon: 38r, 75r, pork meat, which could be fat (20v) or lean (21v)

barberine apples (Chiquart—*pomes barberines*): 103r, a tart cooking apple, *Pyrus malus sativa* (see Eugène Rolland, *Flore populaire*, Paris, 1904)

barley: 106v; Barley Dish: §78, 6r, 93r, 106v, 107v, a sickdish

barral: 22v, keg or cask of about 45 liters (see the *Bulletin DuCange*, Vol. 25-26 (1956), pp. 109 and 113)

baskets (Chiquart—*vans*): 17v (s.a. *cabas*)

beans: 32v

beef: fat beef, 22v, 23r; loin of beef, 22v, 23r and v, 82v; leg of beef, 23v

beet leaves: 47v

beryl: 94r, a precious stone

birds: 13r; little birds: 40r, 69v; river birds: 13r; game birds: 13r

boar: 5r, 24r and v, 67v, 78v, 79r and v, 80v; Boar's Heads: §5, 23v, 24v, 30v, an *entremets*; Breast of Boar: §54 and §54a, 5r, 67v, 78v, 79r

boces: 15v, casks (for vinegar) containing eight *sommes* (see Dubler, p. 42 *and* Zupko, p. 29)

bogue (Chiquart—*boz marins*): 16v, Mediterranean fish, bogue, *Sparus boops* L. or *Boops vulgaris* Cuv.

bouquet garni of herbs: 21v, 35v, 39v, 42v, sage, parsley, hyssop, marjoram

brachet hound (Chiquart—*brachés*): 32r

brains: kid brains, 85r

Breast of Boar (Chiquart—*Bourbulleys de cenglier*): §54 and §54a, 5r, 67v, 78v, 79r and v, 80v; *see also* Sauce

Index

Brie cheese: 46r, 71v

broths: 19r, 20v, *passim*, a sauce or pottage made from the bouillon of some foodstuff; German Broth (for meat), §2, 20r; German Broth for fish, §25, 4r, 51r, 109r; White Broth on capons, §1, 19v; White Almond Broth (on fried fish), §23, 49v, 109r, 112v; Camelin Broth (for meat), §7, 26v; Camelin Broth for fish, §31, 4r, 57v, 111v, 114v; Georgé Broth (on fried fish), §37, 4v, 63r and v, 114r; Gruel Broth of capons, §59, 5v, 67v, 83r and v; Leek Broth, §16, 37r; King's Broth, 11v, 114v; Pink Broth (for meat), §8, 26v, 27v; Pink Broth for fish, §32, 58r; Savoy Broth (for meat), §3, 21v; Savoy Broth (for fish), §26, 4r, 52r, 111r, 114r; Tile-Colored Broth, §15, 36r and v; Verjuice Broth (on fried fish), §39, 4v, 65r; Violet Broth (on fried fish), 111r, 114r.

Buchat of rabbits: §20, 41v, a prepared dish

burbots (Chiquart — *moteilles*): 16v, fresh-water fish, *Gadus lota*, loach

butter: 5v, 98r and v; Almond Butter, §67, 93r, 97v, 98r, a sick dish, combining ground sweet almonds and sugar

cabas: 14r, a woven wicker basket, of uncertain capacity (*see* DuCange, II, p. 114c: *capax*; *FEW*, III, p. 241b

calamary: 16v, 110v, 113v, sea-fish,

Sepia Calaminee: §48, 5r, 67v, 73v, 74r and v, a thick sauce with an egg base

Calaminee: *see Calunafree*

calf: *see* veal; calf crow: 80v; calf caul: 81r

Calunafree of partridge: §47, 5r, 67v, 72v, a prepared dish whose sauce is made of camelin sauce, mustard and verjuice; at 75r, a synonym for *Calaminee*

camelin: adj., a light-brown color, the color of camel hair; Camelin Broth, §7, 26v; §31, 57v, 111v; Camelin Sauce, §44, 26r, 34r, 56v, 69v, 73r; Camelin Garlic Sauce, 56v (*see* Zängger, p. 36)

camphor: 14r, 25v

candle (Chiquart — *bougie*): 17v

capons: 19v, *passim*; grain-fed capons, 26r, 68v, 69r, 93v, 104r; Pilgrim Capons, §45, 5r, 67v, 70r, 72r, a prepared dish, perhaps an *entremets*

carp: 16v, 55v, 65v, 110r, 117v

cauls (kid, calf, sheep): 81r

chalcedony: 94r, a precious stone

char (Chiquart— *umblos*): 16v, 110r, 113r, a fresh-water fish, *Salmo salvelinus*

charge (Chiquart— *charge*): 13v, 14r, a measure of weight (here for spices, almonds and rice), of varying amount but in the fifteenth century about 146 kg (*see* Zupko, p. 41)

chau de mes: 111v, 114v, a prepared

dish of fish

cheese: 76v, 81r; fine cheese: 17r, 39r, 46r; cream cheese (Chiquart — *fromage de guein*): 68v; *see also* Brie cheese, Crampone cheese

chick-peas (Chiquart — *syses*): 93r, 105v; *see also* Pea Dish

chicks: 44r, 89r

chitterlings: 19r

chrysolite: 94r, a precious stone

chrysoprase: 94r, a precious stone

Chyvrolee of stag: §13, 35r, a prepared dish

cinnamon: 13v, *passim*, one of the common or gross spices (*see* Pegolotti, pp. 361 and 374; Heyd, Vol. 2, p. 595)

civet of hare: 26v

claret, claret wine: 15v, 31r, 33v, 38r, *passim*, a moderately red or grey wine; 64r, a spiced wine, *see* Note 69.

cloth, napkin (Chiquart — *mantil*): 45r, 83r; (Chiquart — *mappe*): 94v, 95r, 96v; (Chiquart — *telle*, *toylles*): 2v, 17r; (Chiquart — *estamine*): 14r, *passim*, bolting cloth, filter, sieve

cloves: 13v, 20r, 46v, 64r, 115r, one of the minor spices; whole cloves, 79r and v (*see* Pegolotti, p. 373; Clair, p. 50)

coal: 15v; coal fire, 29r

cockerels: 35r, 44r, 89r and v

Cold Sage (a sauce): §49, 5r, 67v, 73v, 74r and v, 75r

conger: 16v, a sea-fish, variety of eel, *Conger conger*

Coquart Pasty: §41, 67v, 68r, a large pie comprising eight distinct compartments and a variety of meats in each

coral: 94r, a precious stone

Crow (Chiquart — *Fraise*): §61, 5v, 67v, 84v, 85v; kid and calf crows: 80v

Crampone cheese: 39r, 46r, 71v, 90v, made at Craponne in Auvergne (*see* Régis Pontvianne, *La ville et le canton de Craponne*, Le Puy, 1908, pp. 529-536)

cranes: 13r

crayfish (Chiquart — *escrevisses*): 16v, 110r, 111r, fresh-water crustacean; Stuffed Crayfish: §68, 5v, 93r, 98v, a sickdish

cream: flans of milk cream, 26v

crow (kid, calf): 80v

crystal: 94r, a precious stone

Cullis: §71, 5v, 93r, 102r, a strained sickdish

dace (Chiquart — *ferees*): 16v, 113r, *Coregonus fera*, fish caught in Lake Geneva (*see* J. Jud, *Bulletin du Glossaire des patois de la Suisse romande*, 2, p. 24; *FEW*, 3, p. 469a)

dates: 14r, 44v, 65v, 76r (*see* Pegolotti, p. 378)

deer (Chiquart — *chevrieu*): 13r, 35r

diamonds: 94r

doctor, physician (Chiquart — *medicin*,

Index

mege: 92v, 94r, 95v, 97v, 100r and v, 102r and v, 103v, 104v, 105r, 106r

dodine: 71r and v, a sauce

dolphin: 16v, 57r, a sea-fish, *Coryphaena hippurus*; Fresh Dolphin, §30, 4r, 56v; Salt Dolphin, §30a, 4r, 57r; Venison of Dolphin, 110r, 113v

doves: 31r; s.a. pigeons

dragee: 14r, 50r, 52r, 58r, 61r, 64r, pastilles of spiced candied sugar

ducat: 94r, a gold coin

eels: fresh-water fish, 16v, *passim*; sea-fish, 16v, *passim*; salt eels, 62r, 63r; Brown Sorengue of Eels, §34, 4v, 61r, 109r, 112v

eggs: 13v, 24r, *passim*; egg yolks: 24r and v, 77v, *passim*; egg whites: 24r, 75r; Eggs on the Coals: 63r

emeralds (Chiquart—*maragdos*): 94r, precious stones

entremets: 18v, 23v, 26v, 67v, an exceptional prepared dish, intended to delight the person to whom it is presented; a raised *entremets* (Chiquart—*ung entremets eslevé*): 30v, such a preparation constructed on a framework: a Castle, §10, 30v

Faugrenon: 78r; see also *Morterieulx* and Party Hot-Dish

figs (candied): 14r, 44v, 65v, 76r

firewood: 15v

fish, white fish: 65r, 111v, 114v; either salt- or fresh-water white fish: 61r, 110v, 111r, 113v, 114r

flans: 18r; Almond Milk Flans, §28, 4r, 54v; Cream Flans, 26v

flour: 81v, 92r; fine flour: 18r, 24r, 96v

frumenty: 26v

gall (of rabbits): 41v

Galantine of Lamprey: 111r, 114r

galingale: 13v, 23r, 54r, 57r, 64r, a minor spice, *Alpinia officinarum* and *Alpinia galanga* (see Pegolotti, pp. 295 and 374)

garlic: 69r, 72v, 107r; Camelin Garlic sauce, 56v; Green Garlic sauce, 72 Green Garlic verjuice 109v, 113r

geese: 36r

gems: 94v

Genista Flower (a sauce): 111r, 114r

Georgé Broth: §37, 4v, 63r and v, 114r

German Broth: 4r, 27r, 109r; for meat days, §2, 20r; for fish days, §25, 51r

ginger: 37r, 38v, *passim*; white ginger: 13v, 20r, 21r, 27r, 27r, 29r, 33v, 34v, 59r, 64r; Mecca ginger: 13v, 14r, 64r, one of the gross spices (see Pegolotti, pp. 360 and 419; Clair, p. 60)

gizzards (poultry): 34r and v, 75r

glass: 93v, a measure of capacity, about six ounces (Zupko, p. 181)

goat: 36v

gold leaf: 14r, 25r, 47v, 77r

goslings: 26r, 68r, 69r, 70r

grains of paradise: 13v, 20r, *passim*, *Amomum melegueta*, melegueta pepper, Guinea pepper, one of the gross spices (see Clair, p. 67; Landry, p. 196; Pegolotti, p. 295)

graters (Chiquart—*gratuises*): 15r; s.a. rasps

Gratunee (of Hens or Chicken): §62, 5v, 67v, 86v; Spanish Gratunee: §63, 5v, 88v

Gravy of Small Birds and Poultry: §19, 36v, 40r, a prepared dish; Gravy of Fish Tripe: §38, 4v, 63r, 64r, a prepared dish

grey mullets: 16v, a sea-fish, *Mugil cephalus*; salted: 48v, 109r, 112r

greylings (Chiquart—*umbres*): 16v, a fresh-water fish, *Thymallus thymallus*

Gruel Broth of Capons: §59, 5v, 67v, 83r and v

hake: 16v, a sea-fish, *Gadus merluccius*

hares: 13r, 26v, 32r; Hare Civet: 26v; Hare Sops: §17, 36r, 38r

Hedgehogs, Glazed: 32r, a dish of ground meat formed into the shape of hedgehogs, stuck with sliced almonds

hens: 5v; Gratunee of Hens: §62, 5v, 67v, 86v

herons: 13r, 26r

herrings: 49r, a sea-fish, *Clupea harengus*; salt herrings, 63r, 109r

hippocras: 17r, a spiced wine, a digestive

Hot-Dish, Party Hot-Dish: §52, 5r, 67v, 77r, a prepared dish, an alternate name for *Morterieulx* and for *Faugrenon*

household service (Chiquart—*le ordinayre, le commun*): 12v, 23v, provisions for feeding the personnel of the house

humors: 115r

hyssop: 35v, 39v, 80v, 91 an herb, *Hyssopus officinalis* (see Clair, p. 184)

jacinth: 94r, a precious stone

Jacobin Sops: §18, 36v, 38v, 39r and v, a rich blend of capons, marrow, cheese and herbs

Jance: 26r; §43, 67r, 69r; §46, 72r; §58, 5v, 83r, a ginger sauce

jasper: 94r, a precious stone

jelly: 17r, 34r; Meat Jelly: §80, 117r; Fish Jelly: §81, 117v; 61r, 110v, 113v; *Gelicidium de piscibus, de carnibus*: §79, 116r

John Dory (Chiquart—*dorades*): 16v, a sea fish, *Chrysophrys aurata* Cuv.

kid: 13r, 19v, 20r, 34r, 87r; kid crows: 80v; kid cauls: 81r; Glazed Kid Heads: §60, 5v, 67v, 84v; kid brains: 85r

kidney (beef): 68r, 73r; the fine grease from beef kidney (*i.e.* suet): 68r

kitchen squires (Chiquart—*escuiers de cuisine*): 14v, 36v, 49r; (Chiquart *maistres de cuysine*): 15v, the intendants responsible for kitchen expenses and efficiency

lamb: 13r, 20r, 26v, 36v; see also mut-

Index

ton

lamprey: 4r, 16v, 53r and v, 68r, 70v, 109v, 110r, fresh-water fish, *Lampetra fluviatilis*; Roast Lampreys: §27, 4r, 53r; Lamprey Pie: 72v; Lamprey Sauce—on loin of beef: §4, 22r;—on meat: 50r;—on roast lamprey: 72v, 109v, 113r

lard: 20v, 75r, 88r, *passim*, pieces of bacon; (Chiquart—*saing*): 44r and v, 75v, pork fat

Larded-Boiled Dish of Tench: §35, 4r, 61r, 62r, 65r, a prepared dish for fish days; Yellow Boiled-Larded Dish of Tench, with sops, 110r, 113r

lardoons: 62r, made of pieces of eel

leeks: 36r, 37v; White Leek Sauce: §16, 37r and v

linen: 94r

livers: 36v, 38r, 41v, 43r, 56v, 75r, 82r and v, 85v, 86r; (of capons) 33v; (of poultry) 34r and v; (of rabbits) 42v

lobsters: 16v, 56v, sea crustacean

loin of beef (Chiquart—*lomblos de beuf*): 22v, 23r, 82v

mace: 13v, 21r, 22v, 64r, a minor spice, *Myristica fragrans*, the finely ground husk of nutmeg (*see* Pegolotti, p. 375)

marjoram: 21v, 35v, 39v, 45r, 66r, 80v, 91r, a *Labiaceae* herb, *Origanum vulgare* or *Origanum majorana* (*see* Clair, p. 198; Freeman, p. 10; Landry, p. 153)

marmots: 36r, either the animals themselves or a dish of ground meat-paste shaped like them

marrow: 23r, 39v, 68r and v, 101r and v, beef and mutton marrow; marrow bones: 38v, 71r, 78r

Mecca ginger: 13v, 14r, 64r, type of ginger shipped via Mecca; *see* ginger

milk: 87v; Milk Cream Flans (Chiquart—*Flaons de creme de lait*): 26v; almond milk: 4r, 5v, *passim*

Morterieulx: §52, 67v, 77r, a prepared dish of ground meat, called also *Faugrenon* and Party Hot-Dish

Mortoexes: §56, 5r, 67v, 80v, 81r and v

mullets: *see* grey mullets *or* red mullets

mussels: 16v, a sea mollusk, *Mytilus edulis*

mustard (a sauce): 19r, 49r, 73r, 109r (*see* Clair, p. 208)

mutton: 12v, 18v; Shoulder of Mutton: §64, 78r, 90r; leg of mutton: 82v, 90v; mutton cauls: 81r; *see also* lamb

Norse Pies: §50, 5r, 67v, 75r, 76r, 110v, 113v

nutmeg: 13v, 21r, 64r, 117v, a minor spice, *Myristica fragrans*; *see also* mace (*see* Pegolotti, p. 374; Clair, p. 64)

Oatmeal (Chiquart—*Avenast*): §75, 6r, 83v, 84v, 93r, 105r and v

oil: 15v, *passim*; almond oil: 99v, 100v, 106r

onions: 20v, 50v, 51v, 82r

onyx: 94r, precious stone

oranges (orange juice ?): 31r, 109v, 113r; verjuice of oranges: 56v

orchil lichen (Chiquart—*tornesaut*): 14r, 30r, 60r, as a colorant (*see* A.L. Smith, *Lichens*, Cambridge, 1921, pp. 412-415)

Parmesan Pies (meat version): §21, 43v, 44r, 45v, 46r and v, 47v, 48r; Parmesan Fish Pies: §40, 4v, 65r and v, 67r, 110r, 113r

parsley: 21v, *passim*, an herb, *Petroselinum sativa* (*see* Clair, p. 211; Freeman, p. 11)

partridge: 13r, 26r, 32r, 34r, 68v, 105r; Calunafree of Partridge: §47, 5r, 67v, 72v; White-Dish of Partridge: §74a, 6r, 93r, 104v

Party White-Dish: *see* White-Dish

Party Hot-Dish: *see* Hot-Dish

pastry, puff pastry: 76v

pasty: 18r, 53r, *passim*; Coquart Pasty: §41, 5r, 67v, 68r; Lamprey Pasty: 72v; pasties of meat and fish: 18r, 53r; Quince in a Pasty: §70 and 70 a), 5v, 100v, 101r; Pasties of Fat Beef: 23r

peacock: 31v, 33r

Pea Dish (Chiquart—*Syseros*): §76, 6r, 105v, a sickdish of chick peas

pearls: 94r, 995v; Margarite pearls: 94r (*see* Pegolotti, p. 302)

Pears Cooked without Coals or Water: §72, 6r, 93r, 102v, a sickdish

peas: 32r; white peas: 49r, 63r; new green peas: 86v, 89r; White Pea Puree: §22, 49r and v, 63v, also called Strained Peas (Chiquart— *Pois coulés*): 111r, 114r; s.a. chick peas; *see also* Pea Dish

pepper: 13v, 21r, *passim*, a gross spice, probably *Piper nigrum*, black pepper (*see* Pegolotti, pp. 360 and 427; Clair, p. 67; Landry, p. 194)

perch: 16v, 110r, 113r, 117v, a freshwater fish, *perca fluviatilis*

pewter (Chiquart—*estain*, tin): 16r, 39r

pheasants: 13r, 26r, 34r

pickerel (Chiquart—*brocheriaux*): 61r, 110v, 113v, the young of the *Esox lucius*, pike

pies (Chiquart—*tartres*): 18r, 26v; Fish Pies: §29, 4r, 55r; (Chiquart— *tortes*, *tortres*): 48r, 66r, 67r; *see also* Parmesan Pies

pigeons: 13r, 26r, 47r, 68v, 69v, 70r; *see also* doves

piglet: 12v, 13r, 26r, 73v, 74v; suckling piglet: 73v; *see also* pork

pigs' trotters: 83v, 89r; pigs' ears: 89r

pike (Chiquart—*lucs*): 16v, 31r, 65v, 110r, 113r, a fresh-water fish, *Esox lucius*; salt pike: 48v, 109r, 112r; Pike Cooked in Three Ways: 30v, 109r, 112v, an *entremets* called Glazed Pilgrim Pike

Pilgrim Capons: §45, 5r, 67v, 70r, 72r; Glazed Pilgrim Pike: 109v,

112v (*see* Recipe §10, 30v)

pine nuts: 14r, 44v, 45r and v, 46r, 55v, 65v, 66r, 76r, pinenut kernels

plague (Chiquart— *ympydimie*): 114v

plaice (Chiquart— *pleybs*): 16v, a seafish, *Pleuronectes platessa*

pollacks (Chiquart—*pallés*): 16v, 61r, 110v, 113r, a fresh-water fish, *Coregonus hiemalis*; fresh pollacks: 110r; salted pollacks: 11r. 63r, 68v, 113v, 114r

pomegranate seeds: 52v

pork: 19v; salt pork: 86v; loin of pork: 19r, 83v; pork liver: 82r; *see also* pigs' trotters, ears; piglet; lard

Pots, Spanish Pots: 32r

pottage: 14r, 19v, *passim*, a liquid preparation of varying stiffness boiled in a pot (*see* Françoise Sabban, "Le savoir-cuire ou l'art des potages," p. 166 f.

poultry: 13r, 20r and v, *passim*; poultry gizzards and livers: 34r, 75r

powder, fine spice powder: 46v, 56r and v; *see also* sandalwood

Precipitate: §66, 5v, 93r, 96r, 97r and v, a sickdish

prunes: 55v; candied prunes: 14r, 44v, 76r (Castorina, *Farmaci*, §129)

psaltery: 32v, a stringed musical instrument

puree: 99v, 109r, 112v; puree of greens: 19r, 100r, 109r, 112v, a mash of green vegetables; Green Puree of Spinach and Parsley: §69, 5v, 93r, 99v, a sickdish; Puree of Almond Milk: §69a, 5v, 100r; Puree with Sops: 63r; White Pea Puree: §22, 49r and v, 63v

purveyors of game (Chiquart— *poullaylliez*): 13r

quart: 96r, measure of capacity for grains (Schüle, p. 373a; Bruchet, p. 611; Zupko, p. 148; cf. DuCange, Vol. II, p. 192b and Vol. VI, p. 596a)

quince: 100v; Quince in Pastry, §70, §70a, 7v, 100v, 101r, a sick dish

quintal: 14r, 17r, 39r, 46r, measure of weight, about 50 kg (Gonon, pp. 141 and 238; Stouff, p. 474)

rabbit: 13r, 26r, 34r; *saupiquet* for rabbit, 36r

raisins: 44v; candied raisins: 14r, 65v, 76r

rasps: 17v; *see also* graters

ratons: 18r, a sort of round pasty made of eggs and cheese; *see* Note 29

ravioli: 81r

ray, rayfish: 16v, 56v, a sea-fish of the *Rajidae* family

rebec: 32v, a stringed musical instrument

red mullet (Chiquart— *rogés*): 16v, a sea-fish, *Mullus surmuletus*

Restorative: §65, 5v, 93r and v, a sickdish

rice: 14r, 53r, 57v, 110r, 111r, 114r

Rissoles: §51, 5r, 67v, 76v; Glazed

Rissoles: 111v, 114v
rose water (Chiquart—*eaue rose*): 31r, 93v, a distillate from roses
rubies: 94r
saffron: 14r, 67r, *passim*, stigmas of the *Crocus sativus*; beaten (powdered) saffron: 59v, 98v (*see* Castorina, *Farmaci*, Nos. 45-47 and 140; Pegolotti, p. 376; Clair, p. 224; Freeman, p. 13)
sage: 21v, 35v, *passim*, an herb, *Salvia officinalis*; Cold Sage (a sauce): §49, 5r, 67v, 73v, 74r and v, 75r
Salamine: 110r, 113r, a prepared dish of fish
salmon: 16v, 56v, 68r, 69v, a sea-fish, *Salmo salar*
salt: 21r, 23v, *passim*; fine salt: 26r
salt dish (Chiquart—*la saleure*): 19r, 36r, 63r, 111r, 114r, a serving of salted meat or fish
sandalwood (Chiquart—*poudre sandre*): 37r, powdered wood of the *Pterocarpus santalinus*, used as a colorant (*see* Castorina, *Farmaci*, §143; Pegolotti, pp. 377 and 429)
saphires: 94r
sardines: 16v, a sea-fish, *Sardina pilchardus*
sardonyx (Chiquart—*sardios*): 94r, a precious stone
sauce: 4r, 19r, *passim*; Sauce for Breast of Boar: §55, 5r, 80r; Sauce for Peacock: §11, 33r; Green Sauce: 31r, 56v, 109v, 113r; *see also* Camelin, Camelin Garlic, Green Garlic, Lamprey, oranges, Mustard, Saupiquet, tripe, verjuice, Vinaigrette
Saupiquet: 26r, a sharp vinegar sauce; for rabbit: §14, 34r, 36r; for fried fish: §36, 4v, 61r, 62v, 65r, 110v, 113v
sea-urchin (Chiquart—*chatagnies*): 16v, echinus, of the family *Echinoidea*
semolina: 106v, hard granules left after flour is bolted
Semolina Dish (Chiquart—*Simolee*): §77, 6r, 93r, 106r, a sickdish
Shoulder of Mutton, Green: §53, 5r, 67v, 78r; Stuffed and Glazed Shoulder of Mutton: §64, 5v, 90r
shovels (oven): 15r
silk: 94r
sole: 16v, 56v, a sea-fish, *Solea solea*
sommes: 15v, 18r, a measure of capacity, about 52 liters in Paris (Zupko, p. 171)
sop, sops (Chiquart—*soupe*): 110r, 113r, a dish of bread or toast in a sauce; White Almond Sops (*Soupe blanche d'amendres*): 61r, 110v, 113v; Jacobin Sops: §18, 36v, 38v, 39r and v; Hare Sops: §17, 36r, 38r and v; Green Sops: 111v, 114v
Sorengue, Brown Sorengue of Eels: §34, 4v, 61r, 109r, 112v, a prepared dish
sorrel (juice): 72v, (juice of the leaves

of the) *Rumex acetosa*; Green Sorrel Verjuice: 31r, 56v, 61r, 69v, 110v, 113v

Spanish Gratunee: *see* Gratunee; Spanish Pots: 32r, a preparation made from ground meat

spices, gross spices: 13v; minor spices: 13v, 21r, 40v, 43r, categories of spices determined by the commonness of their use; for Chiquart minor spices included nutmeg, cloves, mace and galingale (folio 40r)

spinach (Chiquart—*espinars*): 47v, 99v, 100r, leaves of the *Spinacea oleracea*

spoon, long-handled, holed stirring spoon (Chiquart—*poche perciee*): 15r, 41r, 46r

spotted weever (Chiquart—*arany marine*): a sea-fish, *Trachinus araneus*, 16v

sprats (Chiquart—*melletes*): 16v, a sea-fish, related to the herring, *Clupea sprattus*

starch: 14r, 29r, 55r, 59r, 60r and v, 66v, flour which has been moistened, dried, powdered

sturgeon: 16v, a sea-fish, *Acipenser sturio*

suet (Chiquart—*supp*): 17v, used in candles

sugar: 14r, 20r, *passim*; loaves of sugar: 14r, 75v, 76r; beaten, powdered, sugar: 46v, 67r, 77v, 98r; *socrum* (Latin): 116r (*see* Pegolotti, pp. 362–365)

swan, skinned and redressed: 31r

Talmoses: 18r, 26v, a cheese and egg tart, custard pie

tench: 62r, a fresh-water fish, *Tinca tinca*; Larded-Boiled Dish of Tench: §35, 4v, 61r, 62r, 65r; Yellow Larded-Boiled Dish of Tench, with sops: 110r, 113r

topaz: 94r, a precious stone

torches: 17v

tuna: 16v, a sea-fish, *Thunnus thynnus*

tournaments: 111v, *see* Note 238

Tremollette of Partridge: §12, 34r, 35r, sauce of poultry gizzards, livers, served with roast partridge

trencher: 93v, cutting board

tripe, fish tripe: 50r, 51r, 64v, 109v, 112v; Gravy of Fish Tripe: §38, 4v, 63r; Fish-Tripe Sausages: 111v, 114v; Fish-Tripe Vinaigrette: 111r

trout: 16v, 69v, 110r, 113r, a fresh-water fish, *Salmo trutta*; fresh trout: 68v; salted trout: 63r, 111r

turbot: 16v, 56v, a sea-fish, *Scophthalmus maximus*

turnips (Chiquart—*naviaux*): 36v, 63r, 111r, 114r

turquoises: 94r, a precious stone

veal: 13r, 19v, *passim*; veal (calf) crow: 80v; veal (calf) caul: 81r; veal (calf) liver: 85v

venison: 13v, 26v, game meat or wild fowl; venison of dolphin: 110r, 113r

verjuice: 4v, 15v, 19v, *passim*, juice

and mash of verjuice grapes; green verjuice: 26r, new, sharp juice and mash of verjuice grapes; white verjuice, verjuice of white wine: 63v, 84r, 89v; green sorrel verjuice: 61r

Vinaigrette: §57 and §57a, 5r, 67v, 81v, sauce for fried meats; Vinaigrette of Fish Tripe on fried fish: 111r

vinegar: 31r, 33v, *passim*; white and claret vinegar: 15v; red vinegar: 22v

wafers: 47r and v

weever: *see* spotted weever

wine: claret wine, 15v, 31r, *passim*; red claret wine, 50v; white wine, 19v, 20v, *passim*; wine syrup (Chiquart—*julliet*): 76r

winnowing-sieve (Chiquart—*van*): 106v

White-Dish: of capons, §74, 6r, 93r, 104r; of partridge, §74a, 6r, 93r, 104v; Party White-Dish in four colors all together (for meat days), §9, 26v, 28v, 111r, 114r; Party White-Dish (of fish), §33, 4r, 58v

White Leek Sauce: §16, 37r and v; *see also* leeks

yolks: *see* eggs